STUDIO ALBUM DISCOGRAPHIES*
(1970–2022)

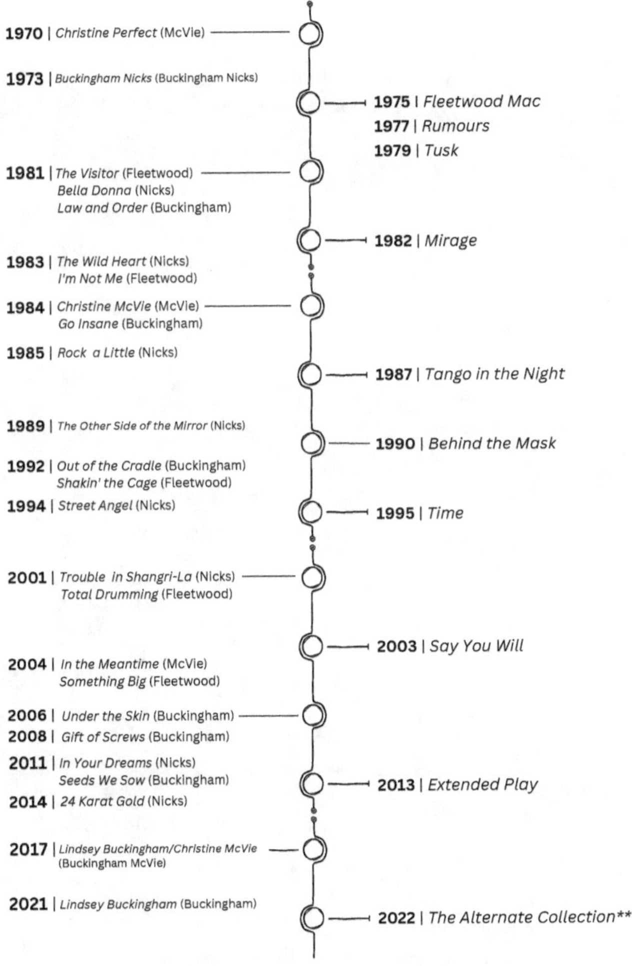

*Discographies for the band's "Rumours 5" line-up
**Contents originally released between 2016-2021

PLAYING IN THE RAIN

LINDSEY BUCKINGHAM & FLEETWOOD MAC

TYLER MARTIN SEHNAL

This book is dedicated to my family—particularly to my wife and my mother—who've tolerated me spouting Fleetwood Mac "fun facts" for years now (and for so much more that I could never fully list here).

P R E F A C E
2018–2023

———— **DECEMBER 15, 2022** ————

I initially wrote *Playing in the Rain* during my sophomore and junior years of college. In between homework, classes, and my job, I managed to find a little time to sit in the cubicles of my college's tiny library and put together this book. I was, and still am, obsessed with Fleetwood Mac and their music. I've been a fan of the band since high school—I can still remember the first time I heard my 11th grade English teacher play "Rhiannon" on CD. This book is a culmination and celebration of my love for Fleetwood Mac and all the memories in my life that have since been soundtracked by songs like Nicks's classic about "an old Welsh Witch."

I'd like to thank everyone who bought and read this book when it initially came out in 2019—everyone who bought the hurried, rushed, roughly edited product of several late, sugar-fueled nights spent writing on a tiny college campus in North Carolina. With deadlines for major assignments always looming and 8am shifts at work usually following my late-night writing sessions, *Playing in the Rain* debuted with a few (but critical) typographic errors. Additionally, the first version of this book excluded several interesting facts about Buckingham, the band, and their music—facts responsible for sparking my fascination with the band in the first place so many years ago. As such, in lieu of a formal "acknowledgements" section, I would like to extend a heartfelt thank you to everyone who supported this project in its early and (very) rough stages, including all my readers and reviewers, my aunt (for being my first-ever editor), my wife (for putting up with me spending long hours in our home's office editing and reworking this book), and Hippo Records, a record store in Greensboro, North Carolina that graciously agreed to sell early copies of my book to their customers.

I was encouraged to return to this project after the band released their "Alternate Collection" for Record Store Day's 2022 Black Friday event: an assemblage of 8 LPs featuring "alternate" recordings and outtakes from the band's *Fleetwood Mac, Rumours, Tusk, Live, Mirage,* and *Tango in the Night* sessions. Getting my hands on this hefty collection of "alternate" recordings reignited my love for the band and each of their most popular albums (and even for their later, less popular, and sometimes willfully forgotten works, like 1990's *Behind the Mask* and 1995's *Time*). While the release of the band's 8LP "Alternate Collection" showed the continued contemporary resurgence of vinyl's popularity among music lovers, the collection's release and popularity also demonstrated the timelessness of Fleetwood Mac. As such, this book features significant revisions: generally, there is a greater attention to detail throughout as well as more information about Buckingham's solo projects, including new chapters that discuss Buckingham's 2018 *Solo Anthology* and his 2021 self-titled solo effort, *Lindsey Buckingham.*

The process of editing and revising *Playing in the Rain* was a remarkably fun one (as much fun as one can have with forty-or-so tabs spread across a laptop and monitor screen). Reading up on articles and books written about the band since the original edition of this book was published led me down several fascinating rabbit holes, which is to say that I learned a lot more about the band, its members, and the Rolling Stones—among other things—while working on this edited and expanded edition of *Playing in the Rain.* Did you know, for instance, that Billy Burnette, who had a brief stint with Fleetwood Mac in the late 80s and early 90s, met Charles Manson several times in the 1960s and was even given a ride home by the head of the notorious Manson Family?

In addition to several added pages of information about the Mac's biggest albums and Buckingham's solo work, this edition of the book also includes extensive endnotes that provide additional trivia and facts concerning more recent updates and more "behind the scenes" information concerning the Mac's biggest albums, singles, and sensational live performances. I hope that this edition of the book is a welcome upgrade from the original: it is my goal that readers will ultimately find the book easily navigable and digestible.

I had plenty of help in making *Playing in the Rain* a reality. In writing this book, I utilized several viable, first-hand accounts to gather my information and to make sense of often-hazy timelines, including comprehensive accounts by Mick Fleetwood, like his 1990 and 2015 autobiographies, as well as Carol Ann Harris's 2009 autobiography *Storms: My Life with Lindsey Buckingham and Fleetwood Mac.*

I also used Stephen Davis's acclaimed biography of Stevie Nicks, *Gold Dust Woman,* as well as Zoë Howe and Simon Morrison's accounts of Nicks's life and career. Also useful were Rikky Rooksby's *Fleetwood Mac: The Complete Guide to Their Music,* Donald Brackett's *Fleetwood Mac:*

40 Years of Creative Chaos, and Bob Brunning's *The Fleetwood Mac Story: Rumours and Lies*. Additionally, I relied on numerous interviews and reviews from *Rolling Stone* and other digitally archived articles and interview excerpts as sources of valuable information so that *Playing in the Rain* could be told as accurately as possible and exist as an account largely grounded in Buckingham's own words.

Only a week after I started working on this revised and updated edition of *Playing in the Rain* in November 2022, it was announced via Christine McVie's official Instagram account that the brilliant talent behind hits like "Say You Love Me" and "Little Lies" had passed away at the age of 79. McVie was remembered fondly in a statement issued by the band shortly after her passing and by Stevie Nicks, who penned and released a heartfelt, handwritten letter to her "best friend" later that same day. Though this book's emphasis is meant to be on Lindsey Buckingham, there are several sections in which I couldn't help but gush over McVie's remarkable singing and songwriting skills. Not only were her early and late 80s tracks "Hold Me," "Everywhere," and "Little Lies" the band's biggest hits during the decade, but other soulful works, including her cover of Etta James's "I'd Rather Go Blind," "Don't Stop," "Songbird," and her 1984 solo hit, "Got a Hold on Me"—among many others—also undoubtedly left their mark on millions of listeners since she first arrived on the music scene in the late 1960s. She will be sorely missed.

Ultimately, though plenty of print resources exist that detail Fleetwood Mac's history and the illustrious life and career of Stevie Nicks, very few attempt to discern the impact Lindsey Buckingham has had on the band and the music industry as a whole since joining the folk-band Fritz in the mid-1960s and the soon-to-be global sensation Fleetwood Mac a few years later in 1974. Never before has any work attempted to thoroughly map Buckingham's journey from aspiring rock and roller to solo star, legendary producer, and chief architect of Fleetwood Mac's timeless sound, style, and superstardom.

I hope that this book is able to accomplish this.

TABLE OF CONTENTS

Fleetwood Mac is live at the Record Plant in Sausalito, a small, sunny city on the American west coast known for its idyllic views of the iconic Golden Gate Bridge. The performance, conducted against a solid black backdrop, is being recorded for KSAN-FM, a radio station serving the San Francisco Bay Area of California. KSAN's Tom Donohue introduces Fleetwood Mac as a band that's undergone "a few line-up changes" since its initial founding in late 1967—a huge understatement given the turmoil that's led up to this moment.

On the far-right-hand side of the stage stands Bob Welch, a man resembling the essence of the 1970s. Wearing thick-rimmed glasses and a tight, patterned, and partially fastened button-up shirt, Welch takes the lead on a stellar rendition of one of the band's earliest hits, "The Green Manalishi (With the Two-Pronged Crown)." Welch's vocals and searing guitar work are driven by Fleetwood Mac's iconic rhythm section of Mick Fleetwood and John McVie, the former of which is a tall, lanky man donning a red-banded top hat. He's hammering away at an expansive drum set while the mild-mannered McVie offers a more subdued performance, measuredly strumming his bass guitar a few feet to Fleetwood's right.

A few tracks later, McVie's wife Christine, a woman with an extensive resumé as a blues musician and an unmistakable, saccharine voice, assumes the lead on 1972's "Spare Me a Little of Your Love." Unbeknownst to Welch, Fleetwood, and the McVies, they've been keeping the band afloat during a huge transitional period in Fleetwood Mac's history—one preceding a period of unprecedented and astronomical success for the band. Ultimately, the four end their set with a performance of 1973's "Hypnotized," drawing to a close what would prove to be Fleetwood Mac's last performance as a quartet until 2003.

Though to most casual fans Fleetwood Mac might be best known for their work from the mid-

1970s onward, this doesn't mean that the band hadn't been making waves in the music industry prior to 1975.

Fleetwood Mac was originally founded in 1967 in London by guitarist and vocalist Peter Green and drummer Mick Fleetwood, along with slide guitarist Jeremy Spencer and bassist Bob Brunning. After recording a few instrumental demos as a quartet, the band engaged in its first official outing at the Windsor Jazz and Blues Festival on August 13, 1967. The band made its live debut alongside acts like Cream, Jeff Beck, and Donovan.[1] A few weeks after the festival, Brunning was replaced by John McVie, who, like Green and Fleetwood, was a former member of another famous British blues band, John Mayall & the Bluesbreakers.[2]

The band released their self-titled debut album[3] under the Blue Horizon label on February 24, 1968, only a few months after making their live debut. The album featured 12 songs and spawned one single, a cover of Elmore James's 1961 single "Shake Your Moneymaker." The debut of *Fleetwood Mac* was followed up by the release of the band's first two non-album singles of 1968: Green's "Black Magic Woman"[4] and a cover of Little Willie John's 1955 hit single "Need Your Love So Bad." Though none of the singles released in the immediate aftermath of *Fleetwood Mac*'s debut were able to attain anything more than mild success, the album itself nonetheless managed to peak at #4 on the UK Albums Chart and at #198 on the US *Billboard* Hot 200. The album was also widely praised by critics, including *Rolling Stone*'s Barry Gifford, who wrote in early August 1968 that:

> The English continue to prove how well into the blues they really are, and know how to lay it down and shove it back across the Atlantic. Fleetwood Mac are representative of how far the blues has penetrated — far enough for a group of London East-Enders to have cut a record potent enough to make the South Side of Chicago take notice.[5]

In the years following the successful release of the band's eponymous debut album in 1968, Fleetwood Mac released eight studio albums, including 1968's *Mr. Wonderful*, 1969's *Then Play On*, and 1970's *Kiln House*, albums which managed to peak at #10, #6, and #39 on the UK Albums Chart, respectively. These albums, with the exception of 1969's *Then Play On*, featured early (albeit uncredited) contributions by vocalist and keyboardist Christine Perfect to Fleetwood Mac's style and sound. In addition to vocal, piano, and keyboard work, Perfect also created the album art for *Kiln House*.[6]

By the time the band would release their follow-up to *Kiln House*, 1971's *Future Games*, Christine Perfect had become Christine McVie, having married Fleetwood Mac bassist John McVie in August 1968.[7] McVie had also become a full-fledged member of the band by then, along with 18-year-old guitarist Danny Kirwan.

The production, release, and promotion of these early albums by the band preceded the release of *Bare Trees*, which would be certified platinum by the RIAA more than ten years after its initial release in March 1972. Meanwhile, other albums by the band, like *Future Games* and 1973's *Mystery to Me*, would be certified gold in the years following their release.

In addition to several successful LPs, Fleetwood Mac also released several non-album singles in the late 60s and early 70s that debuted to greater success than previous singles, including "Albatross," "Man of the World," "Oh Well," and the euphemistic "Rattlesnake Shake";[8] of these, "Albatross" would manage to chart highest, reaching #1 on the UK Singles Chart in late 1968.

Despite the band's successes at home and abroad, however, the last album that the band released prior to 1975, 1974's *Heroes Are Hard to Find*, had been recorded with only half of the band's original lineup still intact. Founding members and guitarists Peter Green and Jeremy Spencer had departed the band several years prior, after Green had succumbed to serious mental health issues and Spencer had jumped ship to join the "Children of God"—a "Christian commune"—in February 1971.[9] Meanwhile, guitarists, singers, and songwriters Danny Kirwan and Bob Welch—the latter of whom joined the band in 1971 and had a brief tenure as Fleetwood Mac's lead guitarist in early 1974—had also either been forced out of the band[10] or would resign from Fleetwood Mac shortly after the release of *Heroes* in the mid-1970s.[11]

Though Green, Mick Fleetwood, and Spencer had formed the band with the intention to have as much fun making music as audiences would have hearing it, members' creative differences and substance abuse had inevitably torn the band apart several times since its inception by Green in the late 1960s. When Welch would break things off with the band in December 1974, Christine McVie, along with her husband John McVie and Mick Fleetwood—both of the band's namesakes— would be all that was left of Fleetwood Mac. Therefore, when Fleetwood traveled to Sound City Studios in Los Angeles in search of a new recording studio for the band, his encounter with Keith Olsen couldn't have come at a better time for him, his bandmates, or a young duo from California who had just missed the mark in their efforts to become the "next big thing."

1967–1974

——— FEBRUARY 14, 1974 ———

Lindsey Buckingham and Stevie Nicks, two aspiring rockstars living in Southern California, sit in their small, dimly lit apartment. The walls are largely bare. Buckingham, a man in his mid-20s with thick, dark curly hair, has his head down as he sits on the edge of the mattress he shares with Nicks. He holds a guitar with both hands, keeping the instrument propped up against his thighs and clutched tightly to his chest. His girlfriend, Nicks, sports a middle part dividing a sea of wavy blonde hair. She's a little over a year older than Buckingham and stands across the room, a phone in her hand. Tethered to a wall adjacent to their makeshift sleeping space, Nicks lets out a deep sigh, gently nuzzles the phone's receiver against her chest, and quietly calls for Buckingham.

"What is it?" Buckingham asks, looking up from his seat. Nicks says nothing and waves him over again. Buckingham slowly clambers up out of bed, leaving his guitar behind and allowing it to become enveloped by loose bedsheets. Nicks hands the receiver over to Buckingham, whose grip on the phone grows tighter the longer he listens to the voice on the other end of the line.[1] Nicks, standing alongside her boyfriend of almost five years, closes her eyes and holds her breath as the muffled voice explains to Buckingham that his father, Morris Hamilton Buckingham, a 55-year-old California native and one of Lindsey's greatest supporters, has died.

Morris Buckingham's death, which followed a heart condition diagnosis a little under a year earlier, dealt a huge blow to his youngest son Lindsey and his pursuit of musical superstardom: a pursuit which had already hit several roadblocks in the years leading up to Morris' untimely passing. While Buckingham and Nicks had managed to endure the failure of their debut album a year earlier and the continual worsening of their financial status into the mid-1970s, the death of Lindsey's father on Valentine's Day 1974 succeeded in grounding the duo's musical idyll to a screeching halt.

Lindsey Adams Buckingham was born on October 3, 1949, in Palo Alto, a city in the northwestern corner of Santa Clara County, California. The youngest of Rutheda and Morris Buckingham's three sons, Buckingham grew up under the guidance of both his parents and older brothers Jeff and Gregory. As the three matured, Buckingham's siblings took up interests elsewhere—Gregory, for example, was a swimmer and silver medalist in the 1968 Summer Olympics.[2] Lindsey, meanwhile, had shown an aptitude for music at an incredibly young age,[3] honing his skills throughout the early 1950s by playing a Mickey Mouse guitar to the tune of singles sampled from his brother Jeff's collection of 45s.[4]

An early supporter of his youngest son's budding interest in music, Morris Buckingham purchased Lindsey his first "true" guitar for Christmas in 1957—a three-quarter size acoustic Harmony brand six-string—a move that would get Lindsey kickstarted on his path to becoming a self-taught guitarist.[5] In fact, even without any formal training or the ability to read music, Buckingham would manage to develop an erratic, energetic playing style similar to that of the Kingston Trio by his mid-teens.[6] This encouragement and support from his father ultimately helped him to land his role in the post-high-school rock band Fritz by the time he was in his late teens.

Fritz, a folk-rock band originally called the "Fritz Rabyne Memorial Band," was initially formed in 1966 by Lindsey Buckingham and a group of friends at Menlo-Atherton High School. That same year, Buckingham met a young woman named Stephanie Lynn Nicks at a Young Life meeting on a Wednesday evening in late fall, just prior to the start of Menlo-Atherton's winter break.[7] After that, Buckingham and Nicks didn't reconnect until nearly two years later, when Buckingham invited Nicks to join his up-and-coming rock and roll band Fritz. Ultimately, by the time Nicks joined the band—named after a student at Buckingham and Nicks's alma mater as "a kind of joke"[8]—the band had undergone some significant line-up changes. Nicks, at the time, was a student at San Jose State College, studying speech communication. While Nicks would eventually drop out of college to pursue her dreams of becoming a legend of rock and roll full-time, she spent several years balancing school and her budding music career, often commuting back and forth between school and rehearsals several days a week.[9]

From 1968 until the early 1970s, Nicks was the only thing keeping Fritz from being just another all-male assembly trying to make it in the music industry while Buckingham—yet to fully master the guitar—served as the band's bassist and apparently, their chief talent scout. The band gave Buckingham and Nicks their first experiences in the world of rock and roll by allowing them to open for acts like Jimi Hendrix, Jefferson Airplane, and Janis Joplin in the years leading up to the pair's move to Southern California. Though Buckingham and Nicks would inevitably leave their bandmates behind in pursuit of their own fame, the pair would establish themselves as standouts long before they decided to leave the band.[10]

When Nicks joined the band in 1968, it was understood that no one in the band would be allowed to pursue her romantically—Buckingham included. Having this ordinance in place didn't stop the band's newest recruit from drawing attention from outside of Fritz, however. Fans of the band went wild over Nicks, so much so that when booking the band, venues would often ask for "the band with the "blondy brown-haired girl',"[11] effectively making Nicks one of Fritz's greatest selling points only a few months after she had earned the band's seal of approval. Shortly after joining the band in the late 60s, for the first time in their lives, the two 20-somethings were living like minor-league rock stars.

Despite the band's successes, however, by late 1969, Buckingham had broken the band's biggest rule—he and Nicks had become romantically involved only a little over a year after Nicks had joined Fritz. Worse yet for the band, come the early 1970s, its two biggest talents were considering pursuing their dreams of becoming rock and roll legends as a duo, rather than a quintet.

The duo's decision to split with Fritz was difficult, given the band's elevated status come the early 1970s. However, it wouldn't take long for the two musicians to find success following their move to Los Angeles—a reality that would undoubtedly make the duo's decision to dump their bandmates a bit easier to swallow: after only a few months spent recording demos on a four-track Ampex tape recorder in Buckingham's father's coffee roasting plant[12] and "shopping around" for a record company willing to sign two no-name artists from the US Southwest, the duo encountered engineer and producer Keith Olsen,[13] who agreed to assist them in scoring their first record deal. Suddenly, after nearly four years with Fritz, Buckingham and Nicks were left with no choice but to break the news to the other members of the band that they wouldn't be invited to join the duo down in Southern California. Said Nicks in 1994:

> We had some great demos. We shopped around. Over a period of time we got a deal with Polydor and made our first album, *Buckingham Nicks*. We had a taste of the big time. We had great musicians in a big, grand studio. We were happening. Things were going our way. But up until that point I had been thinking of quitting it all and going back to school because I was sick of being miserable and I hate being poor.[14]

And with that, Buckingham and Nicks made a break for the big time.

Free from the constraints of having to write, perform, and work with *four* other creative-minded musicians, Buckingham's obsessive nature would be put on display shortly after his and Nicks's departure from Fritz in the early 1970s.

Though both Nicks and Buckingham spent countless hours recording demos and writing music in their early twenties, it was Nicks who worked to financially support the couple following their move to Los Angeles to pursue a record deal as a duo. While Nicks took waitressing jobs and worked as a housekeeper for her record producer Keith Olsen, the obsessive Buckingham—based on a decision agreed upon by the pair—decided to remain unemployed (aside from an occasional job as a phone salesman) throughout the early 1970s, choosing instead to work on perfecting his guitar technique.[15]

During this time, Buckingham also came down with mononucleosis, leaving him bedridden for months.[16] Unsurprisingly, Buckingham used this time to continue working on his guitar technique. Finding that he "couldn't sit up and play his guitar in the standard fashion," Buckingham ultimately developed a unique finger-picking style. In 2012, Ken Caillat wrote:

> Instead of using a pick to play his guitar, [Buckingham] primarily uses his fingernails. Now this isn't unusual. Many folk guitarists use their fingernails when they're picking guitar

> strings, but they do it by plucking the strings in an upward direction, one string at a time.
>
> Lindsey, however, developed... a hybrid downward-picking style... play[ing] more than one string at a time by using the backs of his fingernails in a down strike, as well as up strokes. The result is that he can play multiple notes at nearly the same time.[17]

The time Buckingham spent perfecting the guitar would soon prove useful—only a short while after leaving Fritz behind[18] to pursue a record deal as a duo, Olsen secured Buckingham and Nicks a deal with Polydor, the label with which they would record their debut album, *Buckingham Nicks*.

Buckingham was obsessive, yes, but he was also—and remains—a devout perfectionist. Though he only had a short stint in the music industry to his credit come early 1973, there was already little difference between Buckingham and a post-*Dark Side*-era Roger Waters or a drug-addled Phil Spector by the time he and Nicks had taken to the studio to record their debut album. Buckingham's perfectionist attitude was evident both in and out of the studio: while preparing promotional materials for *Buckingham Nicks's* release, Buckingham instilled huge effort into creating the cover art for the album, which would need to grab the attention of potential listeners or consumers browsing his new label's extensive sound catalog. Unfortunately, at the time, Buckingham was just as convinced as other big names in the American entertainment industry that sex—or more plainly the casual exploitation of women and their sexuality—sells.

In preparation for the photo shoot, Nicks purchased a gown for $111—a mammoth amount of money given the couple's prior financial struggles—while Buckingham was content to strike a pose completely naked, sporting nothing more than a curly precursor to the full-on afro he would rock until the late seventies.[19] Equipped with the argument that they were trying to keep things "cohesive," Buckingham and photographer Jimmy Wachtel (the older brother of Waddy Wachtel) attempted to coerce Nicks into being photographed naked as well, a request which she initially refused. Buckingham argued back, claiming that Nicks was being a "child" and that the concept he had created was "art." Nicks eventually relented, and, as a result, the cover art for *Buckingham Nicks* would end up featuring a bare-chested Buckingham and a teary-eyed Stevie Nicks.[20]

The LP itself contained 10 songs—all but one of which were either written by Nicks, Buckingham, or by the pair of singer-songwriters.[21] The album's tracklist, for example, included songs like Nicks's "Crying in the Night" and "Crystal," songs stylistically similar to tracks like 1975's "Landslide" and 1977's "Dreams"—the latter of which would become Fleetwood Mac's only song to ever top the US *Billboard* Hot 100.

Buckingham, meanwhile, contributed tracks like "Without a Leg to Stand On" and the soft rocking "Don't Let Me Down Again," which would later be featured on the 1980 Fleetwood Mac album *Live*. Buckingham also contributed two songs named after women: the instrumental "Stephanie" and track #9 on the album, "Lola (My Love)," the latter of which was initially considered by critics to be one of the album's highlights.[22] Perhaps unsurprisingly then, "Lola" was often performed as the duo's set-opener on their subsequent Buckingham Nicks tour, which primarily made stops in and around the American south, including in Birmingham, Jacksonville, and Tuscaloosa, Alabama. This tour, which featured bassist Tom Moncrieff and drummer Gary Hodges, also starred American guitarist and record producer Waddy Wachtel, who assisted in the original production of *Buckingham Nicks*.

Even with its exploitative cover art and the inclusion of several tracks that would later become beloved by fans of Buckingham, Nicks, and Fleetwood Mac, the album performed poorly,[23] and despite the duo's efforts, critics including *Rolling Stone*'s John Milward subsequently dismissed *Buckingham Nicks* as "pleasant, albeit middleweight Los Angeles folk-rock."[24] Suddenly, less than a year after the release of their debut album, Nicks and Buckingham were back to square one, forced to weigh their options with no choice but to take jobs outside of the music industry to survive. The two artists became very domestic with one another in the years following the failure of their debut album, with Nicks cooking, cleaning, and working to take care of Buckingham, so much so that the two were living like a married couple come late 1974—all that was missing was a ring.

Despite their hardships and even after being dropped by Polydor, Nicks was still positive that she and Buckingham would be able to "make it big." In fact, Nicks was so confident in her boyfriend's brilliance that she was still happy to shoulder the workload for the pair—this time working jobs as a waitress, maid, cleaner, and dental assistant—so that Buckingham could remain unemployed and spend more time honing his guitar skills. Nicks would later remark:

> I loved being a waitress ... I did lunches, I was only gone from 11 to 4, I made good money I came home with good money it was enough to pay our rent and it was enough to pay our food and it was enough to pay for our Toyota that had no reverse. It was enough for us to call Triple A to get us out of the parking places we couldn't get out of because we had no reverse. We could never go backward, that's how we looked at it.[25]

Despite Nicks's optimism, Buckingham himself wasn't so sure that he and Nicks would ever be able to make it in the music industry. By late 1974, Buckingham had hit several roadblocks on his journey to achieve his dream of becoming a rock and roll legend, including his constant financial struggles, the failure of his and Nicks's debut album, and the untimely death of his father shortly after he and Nicks moved to Los Angeles in pursuit of stardom.

In spite of the circumstances, things would finally begin to look up for Buckingham and Nicks by the fall of 1974. By then, the two had been romantically involved for three years and were still less than a year removed from the release of their first album. While in the months following the debut of *Buckingham Nicks* the duo was released from their management contract with Martin Pichinson, the pair continued to work with *Buckingham Nicks* producer Keith Olsen, who would be instrumental in turning the two's fortunes around in the closing stages of the mid-1970s.

Fleetwood Mac drummer and namesake Mick Fleetwood bumped into Olsen while out shopping for a studio that his band could use as the setting for their next album, a planned follow-up to 1974's *Heroes Are Hard to Find*. Olsen suggested his workplace—Sound City Studios—and played Fleetwood the track "Frozen Love" in order to test the studio's sound and acoustics. "Frozen Love" just so happened to be on an album that Olsen had recently produced, *Buckingham Nicks*, and the finger-picking style of the band's guitarist immediately captured Fleetwood's attention. Thanks to a bit of self-promotion on Olsen's part, Fleetwood insisted on being introduced to Buckingham, who he felt shared a "similar soul" with the Mac's original founder, Peter Green. Olsen brought the two together and Fleetwood was even more impressed with Buckingham upon meeting him face-to-face.

With lead vocalist and guitarist Bob Welch's departure in mid-December imminent, it didn't take long for Fleetwood to decide what would come next. Later that same month, Buckingham received the call to join Fleetwood Mac. Though he and Nicks had been struggling to even make rent following the release of *Buckingham Nicks*, Buckingham wasn't initially convinced that joining Fleetwood Mac would be in his or Nicks's best interest.[26] After all, it was pretty well-known that the band had been in a bit of a slump following Peter Green's departure from Fleetwood Mac in the early seventies.

When Fleetwood's call came through to the couple, Buckingham was still unemployed, insistent on the idea that his getting a job similar to Nicks's would've equated to him having "sold out" in his pursuit of stardom. Nicks, meanwhile, among other odd jobs, was working as a waitress at Clementine's in Beverly Hills for a little over a dollar an hour by the mid-seventies. For the beleaguered Nicks, the choice was crystal clear, and she was instrumental in convincing Buckingham to take Fleetwood up on his offer, arguing that at the very least joining the band would help the two of them tackle a few overdue bills. As a result, amidst some light rain, Nicks would join Buckingham, Fleetwood, and the other members of the Mac at El Carmen, a Los Angeles-based Mexican restaurant on New Year's Eve 1974, immediately following her shift at Clementine's.

Though Fleetwood was originally only interested in Buckingham as a replacement for the band's outgoing guitarist Welch, Buckingham made it clear that he and Nicks were a package deal.[27] Desperate for a guitarist and having already been sold on Buckingham's skills, Fleetwood agreed to take in Nicks as well, despite the band already having a strong female vocalist in Christine McVie. The two were hired on the spot without so much as an audition, and suddenly, Buckingham and Nicks were one step closer to achieving their dreams of becoming rock and roll royalty. Whether or not Fleetwood Mac would actually be able to help them achieve this dream was yet to be seen, but Buckingham and Nicks were satisfied for the time being with the mere promise of a paycheck.

1975–1976

— **JUNE 11, 1976** —

Fleetwood Mac takes center stage as the stars of NBC's *The Midnight Special* to promote their newest album, a self-titled effort that includes the song, "Rhiannon," an eerie tune "about an old Welsh witch." Though the band was formed nearly 10 years ago in 1967, this is the first time many listeners will be exposed to the spectacle that is Fleetwood Mac. Better yet, this is the first time most will witness the magic of "Rhiannon" being performed live, years before the song would become one of the band's biggest hits. The track was originally released in 1975 as part of the band's "White Album" (so nicknamed because of the album's colorless cover art). Because their most recent studio effort was practically a debut album for what was still a newly collected Fleetwood Mac, most viewers tuning into *The Midnight Special* won't realize that the two band members bagging the most screen-time are newcomers to the world of rock and roll, having only joined the band a little over a year ago.

One of them is a young woman with layers of wavy hair and a voice and stage presence nearly akin to the late great Janis Joplin's. Unlike Joplin or any of the big-name stars who've preceded her as guest stars on *The Midnight Special,* however, this young woman isn't rock and roll royalty just yet, and hardly a soul knows her name. Regardless, though she's only a couple of years into what will become an illustrious career on stage and in the studio, Stevie Nicks is already managing to command the attention of audiences on set and at home with her hypnotic moves and searing vocals as she sashays her way through the third single from what would become one of Fleetwood Mac's best-selling albums.

Meanwhile, as Nicks lets out a lingering howl, a man sporting a white kimono, unkempt beard, and giant afro to match moves to take center stage, plucking away at a Les Paul guitar he picked up just after joining Fleetwood Mac around a year and a half ago. For about 45 seconds, he's the star attraction, keen to step back into the shadows following an impressive solo that no one expected from such an unknown up-and-comer. Longtime

Mac aficionado Christine McVie then takes over, setting the stage for Nicks to make an impressive return to the spotlight seconds later. Nicks gives a performance that seems to warrant an immediate exorcism as she becomes completely possessed by the Welsh Witch herself. The audience erupts into applause.

Buckingham and Nicks joined Fleetwood Mac having already performed songs like "Rhiannon," "I'm So Afraid," and "Monday Morning" as early as 1973, during live performances meant to promote *Buckingham Nicks*. The duo would also rerecord the song "Crystal"—which was actually included on their debut album's tracklist—for inclusion on the album *Fleetwood Mac*.[1] Despite just having joined the band in late December of 1974, production and recording of the album had begun in early January of the following year and was completed in only three months. *Fleetwood Mac* was a fresh start for the band, and the album's production and sound were heavily influenced by the band's newest members—namely Lindsey Buckingham, who would soon become the architect of Fleetwood Mac's new style and sound going forward.

Both Buckingham and Nicks were surprised with the amount of creative input they were allowed while recording *Fleetwood Mac*, despite their status as newcomers to the group. However, it wasn't long before Buckingham's perfectionist nature would inspire him to take several creative liberties with the band's arrangements and sound, a decision which would inevitably lead to him stepping on a few of his bandmates' toes in the process. In fact, Buckingham's attitude even managed to rile up the usually mild-mannered John McVie, who didn't take kindly to Buckingham's brash style or controlling nature. Only a few weeks into recording their first album together, McVie was keen to remind the new kid on the block that the band Buckingham was now a part of was "Fleetwood Mac"—of which McVie "was the 'Mac'."[2]

McVie's warnings did little to deter him, and Buckingham, regardless, managed to play a big part in shaping the album into a major success. Though he and McVie would never truly get along while recording *Fleetwood Mac* or any of the band's subsequent albums, McVie was eventually content to part with the band's original blues sound, allowing Buckingham to take creative control of the band after *Fleetwood Mac* producer Keith Olsen intervened. Olsen argued that though Fleetwood Mac was indeed moving in a less blues-oriented bearing, the new direction that Buckingham was taking the band would inevitably be better for McVie's bank account.[3] Though McVie still wouldn't take kindly to Buckingham's creative suggestions going forward, Olsen's words had at least convinced him to ride out the storm—a decision which would pay off for McVie only months after coming to terms with such drastic changes in Fleetwood Mac's style and management.[4]

Despite the rocky start between Buckingham and a few of his bandmates, things began to work much more smoothly once Buckingham had taken charge of manufacturing the band's sound and once McVie and Fleetwood had agreed to provide him with a rhythm section that would still be all their own. Using material that he and Nicks had written before joining the band along with new material that he had written specifically for *Fleetwood Mac*, Buckingham began testing the waters of production almost as soon as the band had taken to the studio in early 1975. First, Buckingham's brash "Monday Morning"—a track which was originally meant to serve as the opener on the planned follow-up to his and Nicks's ill-fated *Buckingham Nicks*—was selected to open the album. Immediately, listeners would be treated to a bold new sound from the former blues band.

"Monday Morning" was followed up by—among other tracks—a re-recording of Nicks's "Crystal" as well as Christine McVie's "Say You Love Me" and the "unpredictable" hit "Over My Head," the latter two of which Buckingham would overdub additional guitar work on in order to give them a more contemporary sound prior to their release as singles.[5] Additionally, despite the compromise Lindsey had made with Christine's husband John and drummer Mick Fleetwood, Buckingham was still able to make himself the star of tracks like "World Turning"—a track which he co-wrote—by using both an electric and resonator guitar during recording in order to give the track a distinct "metallic" sound. Buckingham also emerged as the very clear star of "I'm So Afraid"— an extended form of which would quickly become one of the band's most popular set-closers.

Though he wouldn't actually be credited as one of *Fleetwood Mac*'s producers, Buckingham also picked up the habit of working directly with Nicks during the production of the project in order to help her songs achieve a sound that they both deemed suitable for inclusion on the album. Though joining the band had put a big strain on the two's relationship by thrusting them head-first into full-time careers as recording artists, Buckingham remained steadfast in helping shape the sound and style of some of the works that Nicks and Fleetwood Mac would become best known for, including tracks like "Landslide" and "Rhiannon"[6]—the latter of which was released as the album's third single and would peak at #11 in the US and at #46 on the UK Singles Chart two years after its original release.

Though Buckingham would play a much larger role in shaping Nicks's sound during and following the production of *Rumours,* the band's 1977 follow-up to *Fleetwood Mac,* the pair's basic collaborative formula was established during the sessions leading up to the release of Fleetwood Mac's second self-titled effort in 1975. Nicks was a talented songwriter and Buckingham had recognized her exquisite sense of rhythm years ago during the production of *Buckingham Nicks*. Though she was a capable musician on her own, once handed off to Buckingham, Nicks's work would become something extraordinary, thanks to Buckingham's ability to create departures from the rhythms Nicks produced and his ability to flesh out her work to its full potential. Though his role as a producer wouldn't be formally recognized until 1979's *Tusk*—production on the album is still technically credited to "Fleetwood Mac"—Buckingham's contributions to prior albums' pristine production values are unmistakably evident.

If adding Christine McVie to the band's lineup in August 1970 had begun to move Fleetwood Mac in a bubblier, more pop-oriented direction, then Lindsey Buckingham's influence had pushed the band over the edge. Inspired by the painstaking arrangements produced by bands like the Beatles or by Brian Wilson of the Beach Boys, Buckingham was determined to make it so that not one of the album's eleven tracks would seem out of place on FM radio, should any one of them be lifted from the album for the sake of airplay. In his tireless pursuit of soft-rock and pop perfection, it became clear that Buckingham's approach to songwriting, composition, and production was vastly different not only from John McVie's, but also Christine McVie's as well. In a 1980 interview, McVie remarked:

I've never written with the intention of writing hits... I guess I'm a commercial writer, though. My songs do tend to come out two verses, bridge, guitar solo, last verse, and tag. When I've finished a piece I do have my opinion about whether it will sell, of course, but I'm not always right.[7]

Ultimately, Buckingham and his new bandmates' efforts would result in the July 1975 release of the band's first studio album produced with him and Nicks aboard and the last album that Fleetwood Mac would release under the Reprise label until 1997. And, as history would have it, even if she didn't intend them to be, Christine McVie's inadvertent knack for writing pop-rock smashes meant that many of *Fleetwood Mac*'s biggest hits would ultimately be attributed to the former Chicken Shack singer.[8]

Fleetwood Mac's next move was obvious: by late 1975, Buckingham and the band were embroiled in a North American tour that included stops in Phoenix, Cincinnati, and Columbus in an effort to promote their new album, which had only seen modest success in the months following its initial release. Early sales numbers were disappointing, but that didn't deter Buckingham or his bandmates, who were positive that they had created something special in *Fleetwood Mac*. After touring tirelessly across several different states, the band would be able to see its hard work come to fruition; sixteen months after *Fleetwood Mac* was released, the album managed to crack the top 10 of the US *Billboard* Hot 200, where it remained for 37 consecutive weeks in the company of albums like Queen's *A Night at the Opera* and Peter Frampton's *Frampton Comes Alive!*

It was no surprise that touring in support of the band's first album as a newly formed quintet boosted sales. After all, the band had always possessed a commanding stage presence. Peter Green and Danny Kirwan, for example, were meticulous on stage—never missing a note no matter how feverish their bandmates would become—while Bob Welch and Fleetwood himself would sometimes erupt into frenzied jam sessions, never knowing what was coming next or how exactly to end what they had started. To honor their predecessors, Buckingham and Nicks studied Fleetwood Mac's older material extensively long before ever taking to the stage.[9] Though they were a part of a "new" era in the Mac's history, it wouldn't have been right to alienate any of the band's longtime fans.

Buckingham often lent his vocals and finger-picking skills to—among his own original material—performances of Peter Green's "Oh Well" as well as to performances of Jeremy Spencer and Danny Kirwan's "Station Man" and "Spare Me a Little of Your Love." All of the band's rejuvenated renditions were a hit to new and old fans alike, who were impressed with Buckingham's skills behind the microphone and his ability to play old favorites while simultaneously making his own melodies. Meanwhile, Nicks's intense, fringe-doused performances were giving audiences something they'd never seen from Fleetwood Mac before. At the same time, Mick Fleetwood's wild child antics during performances of "World Turning" would cause the track to become an instant concert staple for years to come. Particularly popular too was the energetic set-closer "Blue Letter," another track originally slated for inclusion on a second *Buckingham Nicks* LP.[10] Nicks would later remark in a 2003 interview that, throughout the mid-70s, she and her bandmates were "playing everywhere" and kicking *Fleetwood Mac* "in the ass."[11]

Not only did the band's efforts on stage pay off, but along the way to becoming what was at the time Warner Bros.' best-selling album, in late September 1975, *Fleetwood Mac* was described by *Rolling Stone* as the band's "most consistent album since *Bare Trees*," while the article noted that an evident rapport among bandmates Christine McVie and Lindsey Buckingham added up to "an impressively smooth transitional album." *Rolling Stone* also offered further praise for Buckingham by claiming that he had given *Fleetwood Mac* "a distinguished and fitting guitar and vocal presence"—something that reviewer Bud Scoppa felt that the band had been lacking following the departure of Danny Kirwan four years before the band added Buckingham and Nicks to its lineup.[12]

Though the band's tour in support of *Fleetwood Mac* following the album's release was crucial to heightening its initially disconcerting sales numbers, Mick Fleetwood had felt that touring was in the band's best interest even before the album had become a fully realized work of art. Early on, he recognized the importance of branding 1975's Fleetwood Mac as being an entirely different band than any of its previous iterations, and he wanted to expose the world to new hires Buckingham and Nicks as soon as possible. Therefore, even before "Warm Ways" was selected as the album's first UK single,[13] Fleetwood had lobbied Warner Bros. to advance the band touring money in an effort to quickly garner Buckingham and Nicks exposure "outside of Alabama"—beyond which they were virtual unknowns, according to Fleetwood.[14]

More than a decade earlier, Buckingham had been told by his swimming coach that he'd amount to nothing after quitting Menlo Atherton High School's water polo team in order to pursue an interest in music.[15] At the time, it seemed like Buckingham's intention was to put a stop to tradition. After all, he'd come from a family of swimming jocks. His brother Gregory, of course, had managed a silver medal in the 1968 Summer Games in Mexico City, which if nothing else proved that swimming was more than just a hobby for the Buckinghams. Regardless, this was never Lindsey's cup of tea. As history would have it, by 1986, *Fleetwood Mac*, an album which Buckingham had largely engineered the creation of, would sell over seven million units in the United States alone, garnering it a remarkable 7x platinum certification by the RIAA.[16]

What a way to silence his critics.

With a growing fanbase and reviewers' approval to their credit, Fleetwood Mac concluded their self-titled tour on December 5, 1976 in Indianapolis, Indiana. Though album sales were booming and money was pouring in from fans eager to see the "new" Fleetwood Mac in concert for the first time, all was not well among the band: John and Christine McVie's marriage, for example, had begun to fall apart almost before the tour had even kicked off in early 1975. Married in 1968, John had since developed a severe addiction to alcohol and had taken to acting abusively toward Christine during the band's North American tour in support of *Fleetwood Mac*. In fact, back in September 1975, only a few months into their year-long trek across the country, Christine had moved out and she and John had begun to sleep in separate hotel rooms while out on the road.[17]

Trouble was also brewing between Buckingham and Nicks, whose relationship was frayed at best when it had come time to release the couple's first album with Fleetwood Mac. Buckingham was uncomfortable with not being able to call himself the "leader" of Fleetwood Mac, and his obsession with spending hours on end taking apart and piecing back together songs from the band's "White Album" had quickly isolated him from Nicks. While his girlfriend took to drawing in sketchbooks and curling up with cups of tea to combat loneliness, Buckingham was keeping tape recorders close and his guitar closer. Observers of the couple's relationship, including Mick Fleetwood and Christine McVie, could sense that things were "changing" between the two.

There was nowhere that these "changes" were more obvious than on stage: while on tour to promote *Fleetwood Mac*, Buckingham would quickly become jealous over Nicks's "sexy" stage presence and was uncomfortable with all the attention that her "witchy" moves would attract from audiences.[18] This was a vulnerable time for Buckingham, who now had to deal with not only having to assimilate into the democracy that was Fleetwood Mac, but also the sense that he was inadequate as a significant other to Nicks. Regardless, those close to the band—including Fleetwood Mac's road manager John Courage[19]— couldn't help but notice how much happier and successful the band had become following the addition of Buckingham and Nicks. The two were bright, lively, and had a youthfulness about them—unlike the band's former guitarist Bob Welch, a moody guy who often had a get-down-to-business attitude about him.

Though the addition of the two lovebirds seemed to have changed the band's dynamic for the better in the mid-1970s, the true nature of Fleetwood Mac's internal chaos would come to light as the band's "White Album" tour drew closer to its conclusion. By the time the band had taken to a recording studio in Sausalito, California in February 1976 to lay the ground for their next album, the McVies had already divorced after eight years of marriage and Nicks was tired—not just of touring, but of Buckingham as well. The two had been in a rough patch for several months and fought often. Meanwhile, Mick Fleetwood had his own troubles brewing after discovering that his wife—the mother of his two children—had cheated on him. Adding further fuel to the fire was the falling out between Fleetwood and Keith Olsen, which had led to Olsen's firing and the band's withdrawal from Sound City Studios.[20]

Despite all the drama behind the scenes, by late February 1976, with the help of producers Ken Caillat and Richard Dashut, the band managed to begin working on their follow-up to *Fleetwood Mac*—a new album which was tentatively titled *Yesterday's Gone*.[21] The band also continued to tour in support of their last album while simultaneously participating in studio sessions in Sausalito, though without Olsen's watchful eye, little progress was actually made in the studio for months.[22] Luckily, the band's previous album continued to sell well thanks to the band's continuous touring—prompting Warner Bros. to grant the band an extension on their next album's originally scheduled release date of September 1976.[23]

Unfortunately, despite the immense success of the band's "White Album," the odds still seemed stacked against Fleetwood Mac.

By mid-1976, The band was exhausted from non-stop touring. Christine McVie had struck up a rapport with the band's lighting director, and her ex-husband was beginning to catch wind of it. Stevie Nicks had dumped Lindsey Buckingham two months into recordings, and in response, Buckingham made several efforts to spite Nicks, including diving headlong into relationships with other women less than a month after the two had separated. Mick Fleetwood had just wrapped up his divorce from Jenny Boyd, a model who he had become infatuated with back in the 1960s.[24] At the same time, the band was picking up a serious cocaine and drug addiction, which would continue to haunt each of its members well into the late eighties.

Regardless, four things were true:

1. The band had built a whole new fanbase with the release of *Fleetwood Mac*—a fanbase that would be expecting nothing but the best from their new favorite band from here on out.

2. Based on the success of *Fleetwood Mac*, Warner Bros. had given the band a huge raise in royalty payments and a large cash

advance to assist them in the creation of their next album[25]—something that the band's label never would've granted Mick Fleetwood two years earlier.[26]

3. Warner Bros. was counting on the band to produce an album even more successful than their wildly popular money-maker *Fleetwood Mac*, which had sold more units in one year than most artists manage to sell in their entire careers.

4. They did.

MARCH 21, 1977

Fleetwood Mac is performing live in concert at The Spectrum in Philadelphia, Pennsylvania—just one of many stops on their year-long *Rumours* tour. Their setlist includes the live staples "Rhiannon" and "Over My Head," as well as new material, like the tracks "Gold Dust Woman" and "The Chain." A little over halfway through their setlist, Buckingham is the band's main attraction while performing the lead single from the band's most recent album *Rumours*. The song is called "Go Your Own Way," and is a track that—like *Rumours'* "Second Hand News" or "You Make

Loving Fun"—takes no prisoners in its lyricism, viciously calling out Buckingham's former flame Nicks as a floozy whose hobbies include "packing up, shacking up" and "turning everything around."

They've only recently called it quits, and the words coming out of Buckingham's mouth sting more than ever now. Though Buckingham had at first been the one most scorned by the duo's breakup (Nicks had been the one to officially end things between the two) Buckingham, in the months following his split with Nicks, had begun to take on a "fuck it" attitude. He'd added the phrase about Nicks "packing and shacking up" late in the production of *Rumours* and had begun to experiment with dating again only a short while after he and Nicks had called it quits. Worse yet, Nicks is standing right alongside him, providing backup vocals to Buckingham as he slanders her name in front of thousands of cheering fans who've had just enough time since the release of *Rumours* to learn the song's lyrics for themselves.

"Go Your Own Way" concludes with thunderous applause. Lindsey Buckingham and John McVie have brought the house down, bringing Lindsey's emotional breakup anthem to a close with a furious performance that perhaps more so than anything else shows just how far Fleetwood Mac has come from their roots as a blues band. Meanwhile, Nicks is cast off in the shadows, her head down and her expression buried beneath layers of thick, curly hair. With

Buckingham's "Second Hand News" still left to round out the band's setlist, Nicks won't get her revenge tonight. In fact, Nicks's "Silver Springs," an angelic yet scathing response to Buckingham's "Go Your Own Way," wouldn't give Nicks the retribution she deserved until nearly 20 years after the release of *Rumours.*

Released one month prior, in early February 1977, Fleetwood Mac's follow-up to their sensational "White Album" takes on an obvious and decidedly different tone than its predecessor. Following the rapid deterioration of the band's interpersonal relationships in the aftermath of *Fleetwood Mac*'s initial 1975 release, the soft, comforting tones of tracks like McVie's "Warm Ways" or Buckingham's "Monday Morning" are notably absent from *Rumours,* the band's second Buckingham Nicks era-album.

Instead, the album opens with "Second Hand News," a loud, brash, and in-your-face breakup anthem by Lindsey Buckingham, who wails for just under three minutes about someone having "taken his place"—an obvious reference to his failed relationship with Stevie Nicks. Though the moody track quickly sets the tone for the album as a whole, it hadn't always been Buckingham's intention to slander Nicks right off the bat. In fact, Buckingham had initially conceived "Second Hand News" as an instrumental track titled "Strummer" in an effort to spare Nicks a lyrical lashing akin to the one he would later hammer home with the album's first single "Go Your Own Way."[1] However, while recording the song for inclusion on *Rumours*, taking jabs at Nicks had become much easier for Buckingham to stomach as their relationship had continued to deteriorate. As a result, 30 seconds into *Rumours*, it's obvious that Buckingham Nicks is officially no more.

Like many tracks on *Rumours*, "Second Hand News" was both written and fronted by Buckingham, whose presence on the album takes form via a handful of tracks meant to spite a former lover and fellow member of Fleetwood Mac. Like Nicks's "Dreams" or Christine McVie's "You Make Loving Fun," which also (intentionally or unintentionally) pours salt into former lovers' open wounds, Buckingham's "Second Hand News" doesn't hold back. His biting lyrics are eager to make it known that he isn't suffering without Nicks and that he's doing just fine without her, finding romantic redemption in women aplenty now that he's gone solo. The song's lyrics would become well-known to Nicks, who not only would have to hear it performed every night in concert for years to come but had also lent the song her backup vocals.

Inspired by the upbeat sound of the Bee Gees' hit "Jive Talkin'," Buckingham had sought to give the song a "disco-like" effect, which he achieved by slamming the top of a Naugahyde chair with the palm of his hand.[2] Not wanting the track to debut with any stone left unturned in his pursuit of perfection, Buckingham also created his own bassline for "Second Hand News," which was re-recorded by John McVie prior to the song's release. Buckingham's efforts proved to be worthwhile, and the album's opener was a huge success. Though it was never released as one of the album's singles, "Second Hand News" was well received by critics and was retrospectively deemed by *Pitchfork*'s Jessica Hopper in 2013 as "perhaps the most euphoric ode to rebound chicks ever written."[3]

His work would garner the band great praise one track into what would become Fleetwood Mac's best-selling album and one of the best-selling albums of all time. In recording "Second Hand News," however, Buckingham's possessive nature had reared its head—it was the start of an uncompromising attitude that would guide Buckingham and the band through the creation of 1979's *Tusk*.

A skilled songwriter though not interested in the technical end of music, Nicks spent much of her time in the studio during the recording of *Rumours* without much to do and "bored out of her mind." As a result, she chose to spend a lot of time in Sly Stone's Pit, a "weird space" down the hall from the band's recording studio where she wrote the next song on *Rumours*' tracklist: "Dreams"—a song about her breakup with Buckingham as explained from her own point of view.[4] The song is a drastic transition from

Buckingham's "Second Hand News" in that Nicks nearly whispers her way through the song's lyrics, using her delicate voice to shed light on the "stillness" of remembrance and the feeling of being "washed clean." The track features some of the band's greatest lyricism and is a testament to the power of Nicks's voice. Though "Dreams" is an ode to heartbreak, Nicks tackles the track's subject matter without a hint of resentment in her voice. This comes in stark contrast to several other tracks included on *Rumours*, including Buckingham's "Go Your Own Way" or the band's collaborative effort "The Chain."

Buckingham reciprocates Nicks's vocal efforts on "Second Hand News" by providing backup vocals to "Dreams," which would go on to become Fleetwood Mac's only #1 single in the US. While it was Nicks's songwriting skills that initially set the stage for "Dreams'" success, Buckingham's influence and budding production skills were what ultimately helped bring the song to its full potential. As he had during the production of *Fleetwood Mac*, Buckingham took Nicks's "Dreams" and morphed it from a song that the rest of the band had initially deemed boring into one that would become one of Fleetwood Mac's greatest hits by adding three distinguishing sections of chords throughout the song to give structure to Nicks's lyrics.[5] *Rumours* co-producer Ken Caillat later wrote in 2012 that after Nicks emerged from "the pit" and began playing "Dreams" for the band:

Lindsey grabbed his acoustic guitar and started playing along. The acoustic guitar really added a nice color to the song. That's how songs are; you hear it one way with one instrument, and then you add another, and the whole vibe of the song changes. That's a major reason it took us so long to make *Rumours*. We kept looking for the perfect part to complement each instrument in our songs.[6]

Regardless of the band's initial reaction to Nicks's first, unpolished draft of "Dreams," her lyrics—which she had conceived of in only ten minutes[7]—are some of the Mac's best. They are also one of the main reasons the track has received extensive airplay and coverage by such a wide array of contemporary bands and solo artists. In fact, since 1977, outfits and individuals like Wild Colour, The Corrs, and Richie Havens have recorded cover versions of the song,[8] while Nicks's original alone has since sold over a million copies worldwide. The song was the first of many that would be considered a highlight of Nicks's career and in the history of Fleetwood Mac. It also marked the beginning of Lindsey Buckingham earning well-deserved recognition for his production and arrangement efforts.

The next song on the album, "Never Going Back Again," owes much of the same credit to

Buckingham. An acoustic ballad about heartbreak, "Never Going Back Again" is a relatively tame piece when compared to other songs on *Rumours*' tracklist like Christine McVie's optimistic anthem "Don't Stop" or Buckingham and Nicks's peppy "I Don't Want to Know." Here, Buckingham gets down to the nitty-gritty vocally and instrumentally, crooning about "being down" over and over again for just under two-and-a-half minutes. His finger-picking prowess is on full display as he fills the gaps in between the song's pessimistic lyrics with gorgeous guitar work. In an April 1977 review of *Rumours*, *Rolling Stone* critic John Swenson would describe "Never Going Back Again" as "the prettiest thing" on the album.[9]

The song's subject matter is similar to the rest of *Rumours* and serves as a warning to Buckingham not to repeat the same mistakes with other women that he made with Nicks. Like is often the case when it comes to navigating the dating world, recording the song itself "was a bitch," according to *Rumours* co-producer Ken Caillat. In 2012, Caillat explained that the song's chords required that Buckingham restring his guitar every twenty to thirty minutes in order to achieve the best possible sound on his picking parts.[10] Regardless, the work that Caillat and Buckingham put into recording "Never Going Back Again" contributed to the album's polished sound and sonic results that the BBC's Daryl Easlea would laud as "near perfect... like a thousand angels kissing you sweetly on the forehead" in 2007—an incredible 30 years after *Rumours* was originally released.[11]

Since 1977, "Never Going Back Again"—like Nicks's "Dreams"—has become a concert staple for Buckingham while performing with Fleetwood Mac or otherwise. Several other acts have covered Buckingham's breakup ballad since its initial release as well, including Matchbox Twenty for the album *Legacy: A Tribute to Fleetwood Mac's Rumours* and Colin Reid for his 2001 album, *Tilt.* Despite performing the song outside of Fleetwood Mac when demoing the track on solo tours or while promoting his solo material, Buckingham has still sometimes enlisted Nicks to provide backup vocals during these live performances, demonstrating that though "Never Going Back Again" is predominantly considered to be a Fleetwood Mac classic, what gives the song its greatest significance is Buckingham's talent and his own history with the Welsh Witch herself.

Finally, four songs into *Rumours,* fans are treated to the sugary, saccharine voice of Christine McVie as she teams up with Buckingham for "Don't Stop," an upbeat anthem that is often considered to be a vast thematic departure from the rest of *Rumours*—for obvious reasons. Unlike Buckingham or Nicks's moody material, "Don't Stop" shows that McVie had reasons to smile in the wake of her divorce from bassist John McVie. For one, she'd recently started dating the band's "handsome and debonaire" lighting director Curry

Grant.[12] She was also good at managing the tension that her new relationship caused the band, casually flaunting her optimism during recordings of "Don't Stop" while ex-husband John McVie watched from only feet away as she shot Grant adoring glances that were once reserved only for her husband.[13]

The song was released as the third *Rumours* single after "Go Your Own Way" and "Dreams." Like the album's first two singles, Buckingham also helped to produce "Don't Stop" in one way or another. "Don't Stop," like preceding singles, managed to land within the US *Billboard* Hot 100 top ten before the end of the year—it was obvious by now that Buckingham had a knack for production and a keen sense of marketability. This, coupled with Christine McVie's vibrant vocals on "Don't Stop," would prove to be one of *Rumours'* greatest selling points. Not only that, but "Don't Stop" also helped to keep the album from becoming what might've been little more than a depressing slew of back-to-back-to-back breakup songs.

In keeping with the tempo set by McVie's "Don't Stop," Lindsey Buckingham's "Go Your Own Way" begins to draw side one of *Rumours* to a close with aggressive lyrics and guitar work. The song, which was written as a direct attack on ex-girlfriend Stevie Nicks, originated in 1976 while the band was staying together in a rental home in Florida.[14] With all of Fleetwood Mac cooped up in one place, tensions were high, and Buckingham's anger and angst can be heard in the lyrics of "Go Your Own Way," in which he describes the disintegration of his relationship with Nicks.

Just before a harsh, thunderous drumbeat begins, Buckingham explains that maybe he could give Nicks his world—if only she'd take it from him. The drumbeat that ensues was one that Buckingham had engineered as a variation of the one from the Rolling Stones' song "Street Fighting Man," a beat which Buckingham enthusiastically demonstrated to drummer Mick Fleetwood several times over on—among other props—Kleenex boxes. Though initially Fleetwood wasn't sure that he'd be able to satisfy Lindsey's desires, he was eventually able to devise his own, similar rhythm that he used when recording "Go Your Own Way."[15] As with Fleetwood, Buckingham also had plans for bassist John McVie as well, whose original recordings had unintentionally given "Go Your Own Way" a more country-oriented sound. Again, to McVie's frustration, he was directed to play to Buckingham's standards.[16]

The song marked a significant departure from the soft rock that had defined the band's "White Album." As history would have it, this was a good thing for Fleetwood Mac: within a year of the release of "Go Your Own Way" as *Rumours'* first single, the track became the band's first top ten hit in the United States and was an instant success with critics. "Go Your Own Way" also received a substantial amount of airplay following its release in December 1976. Though the popularity of the song alone would have been a sweet enough success story for Buckingham in the aftermath of his breakup with Nicks, perhaps the greatest one-up he'd pulled on his ex-girlfriend following their split was the fact that her retaliatory "Silver Springs" had been left off the album, only to be released as the B-side to Buckingham's smash hit.[17]

As the chaos of "Go Your Own Way" finally winds down, Christine McVie's "Songbird" begins to play. "Songbird," which signals the end of *Rumours'* first half, has an eerily beautiful and hollow sound to it. When the song's vocals kick in, and the recently divorced McVie gently begins to carol about songbirds singing "as if they knew the score," it becomes clear that "Songbird" hadn't been recorded in some stuffy studio. Rather, the song had been recorded live at the University of California's Zellerbach Stadium, where *Rumours* producer Ken Caillat used fifteen classic tube microphones scattered around the auditorium to capture McVie's vocals to give "Songbird" a more stripped-down, concert-recital sound.[18]

The song had come to McVie in the middle of the night while the band was still working to record *Rumours*. She'd woken up at three a.m. with the lyrics already in mind,[19] and within 30 minutes had fleshed "Songbird" out into a fully realized work of art complete with the melodies and chords that would later be recorded live. Lindsey Buckingham is the only other personnel credited with having contributed to the track with his acoustic guitar work that was also recorded live.[20] Come the 1980s, McVie would be the Mac's saving grace commercially by contributing tracks like "Hold Me" to 1982's *Mirage* and "Everywhere" and "Little Lies" to 1987's *Tango in the Night*. Likewise, in 1977, she plays just as critical a role in helping to make Fleetwood Mac's *Rumours* one of the best-selling albums of the decade: her songs are rays of light amongst *Rumours'* bitterness, and "Songbird" serves as an excellent segue into the album's second half, which attempts to maintain the lighter mood that McVie sets in motion with her emotional ballad.[21]

Given the circumstances, it was incredible that the band managed to produce anything in the little over six months that it took to record *Rumours*, let alone tracks like Buckingham's "Go Your Own Way" or Nicks's "Dreams." In the months leading up to the February 1977 release of *Rumours*, estranged lovers and current bandmates refused to socialize outside of their studio in Sausalito. Even in the studio, the McVies were hesitant to speak to one another and Buckingham and Nicks were only ever civil while working together on Nicks's songs. Though there had been some hope on Nicks's part for reconciliation with Buckingham before the two finally called it quits—for real—around December 1976, by then the two hadn't been on speaking terms for weeks. (Not to mention that, by this time, Buckingham had also already struck up a relationship with a woman named Carol Ann Harris, who he'd met only a few months after his split with Nicks.)[22]

However, to say that Fleetwood Mac was in dire straits midway through recording *Rumours* is to say nothing of the shared cocaine habit that each member of the band was beginning to develop by the mid-seventies.

Early on, with tensions high and emotions hard to sustain, cocaine had become a way for Fleetwood Mac to keep spirits high. In the beginning, bags of coke were kept around the studio as an open invitation to anyone looking to take their mind off the constant strain of recording or the pain of heartbreak.[23] By the late seventies, in fact, cocaine had taken over the music industry as a whole and was being pitched to supergroups like Fleetwood Mac as non-addictive, recreational, and safe to use. Under the impression that cocaine was just another way to take a load off, the band had become overindulgent—that is, until spending hours in the studio drinking and snorting cocaine until around three or four a.m. every morning had become the status quo.[24]

While recording *Rumours*, Stevie Nicks and Christine McVie, who by this time had already developed a friendship that would last the better part of the next half-century, lived in nearby condos; the boys in the band, meanwhile, had set up shop in a complex adjacent to Fleetwood Mac's recording studio.[25] Only a few months into recording the album, Fleetwood, John McVie, and

Buckingham had begun hosting huge parties in their home-away-from-home in Sausalito—parties which continued to normalize the band's excessive drug use, so much so that by late 1976 each member of the band had embraced a "when in Rome" attitude and were taking drugs often enough to be considered addicts.[26] Though no one within the Mac's inner circle would dare admit to it then, unfortunately, by the time *Rumours* was released in early 1977, there was no denying that this is exactly what they had become.

BEHIND THE MASK
1977–1978

Fleetwood Mac's latest album is hardly a slow burn: unlike 1972's *Bare Trees* or even 1975's *Fleetwood Mac*, *Rumours* is an instant hit. Only a month after the release of the album, as the band's "White Album" is still steadily working its way up the charts, *Rumours* goes platinum. While *Fleetwood Mac* continues to methodically introduce fans to the band's new line-up and reinvigorated sound, by the end of March, *Rumours* is everywhere. Key to *Rumours'* frenzied popularity is that:

American radio was going to town with the record, playing it almost constantly, as it became the soundtrack of nearly everyone's lives (whether they liked it or not) during this intense period… [*Rumours*] could not have been more perfect as a product for the new radio dimension: FM radio may as well have been named after Fleetwood Mac at that point."[1]

As the money rolls in, the band goes wild: Fleetwood, Buckingham, Nicks, and both McVies purchase expensive homes in and around Malibu and Beverly Hills. John McVie also buys himself a boat.[2] Meanwhile, his ex-wife Christine buys herself a new Rolls Royce, which she drives straight off the showroom floor.[3]

The band tracks the skyrocketing success of *Rumours* while taking in cliffside views from the comfort of their new homes (and boats), though their financial successes belie unfortunate interpersonal and physical turmoil. The dangerous drug habits and vicious infighting that began with the production of *Fleetwood Mac* and were exacerbated while recording *Rumours* are beginning to boil over. Even though Buckingham, Nicks, and the band have already seen their fair share of low points, the band's success with *Rumours* temporarily disguises the reality that the worst is yet to come.

Side two of the album responsible for thrusting Fleetwood Mac into the throes of rock and roll legendry opens with "The Chain," the only song in Fleetwood Mac's history for which all members of the band are credited. The track itself is incredibly complex and began as a Christine McVie demo entitled, "Keep Me There."[4] However, McVie's abandoned track wasn't the only basis on which "The Chain" was formed: previously rejected solo work by Buckingham and Nicks was also used to create the song's basic structure, including the intro to "Lola (My Love)" from *Buckingham Nicks*. Meanwhile, John McVie and Mick Fleetwood created the song's "finale," which begins with a gradual bass progression, while Nicks supplied a majority of the song's lyrics.[5] These bits and pieces were often assembled manually by splicing tapes from earlier sessions and albums with a razor blade and rearranging them.

As a result, like much of *Rumours*, the song contains a variety of hard rock, country, and folk influences and was created by combining different vocal and instrumental snippets post-recording— rather than via a single collaborative effort in studio. Regardless, despite the song's origin as a mess of rejected material, the end result is one of Fleetwood Mac's greatest hits, something that's even more impressive given that the song was never released as a single. In fact, "The Chain" has since become one of the band's most popular hits to perform live and has been included on several of the band's "greatest hits" compilations, including 1995's *25 Years – The Chain* and 2002's *The Very Best of Fleetwood Mac.* The song has also continued to garner attention in the UK more than 30 years after its initial release thanks to the BBC, which for years used "The Chain" as the opening theme for its television coverage of the popular racing series Formula 1.[6]

The song has not only become a smash hit since its release in 1977 but has also come to represent the enduring nature of Fleetwood Mac. Its lyrics damning love and damning lies undoubtedly have their roots in the band's romantic falling outs, but "The Chain's" message about keeping together what is essentially a marriage among the members of Fleetwood Mac is what makes the song such a triumph. In fact, "The Chain" gives listeners an early, intimate insight into a reality that the quintet will struggle to come to terms with for years to come: the reality that, despite their differences, Fleetwood Mac has a whole greater than the sum of its parts. In fact, in the more than 40 years since the "new" Fleetwood Mac was formed in early 1975, perhaps nothing is more a testament to the band's longevity and inner turmoil than "The Chain."

Once "The Chain" comes to an end (the actual end, after you've already been tricked by the eerie silence preceding Buckingham's haunting guitar solo), Christine McVie again returns to the spotlight with another optimistic track about loving someone other than her ex-husband. Though "You Make Loving Fun" isn't McVie's first bouncy, bittersweet single from *Rumours*, it is the first to have been written solely about McVie's new love interest Curry Grant. According to *Rumours* producer Ken Caillat, Christine had initially explained to her ex-husband John that "You Make Loving Fun" was about her dog, rather than about another man. Regardless, heightened tensions between the two proved to be inevitable after John was quick to realize the truth not long after the track was initially recorded.[7]

"You Make Loving Fun" would be released as the fourth single from *Rumours* and would peak at #9 on the US *Billboard* Hot 100, making it the band's fourth top-ten single in a little over nine months. Unlike most of the other tracks on *Rumours*, Buckingham played a minor role in helping to shape "You Make Loving Fun"—the album's final single—into a success. Instead, Buckingham was absent for most of the single's early tracking process, meaning that McVie herself was able to take several liberties with the track's sound and creative direction without interference. Though, like his bandmates, Buckingham would eventually add his respective sound to "You Make Loving Fun," the track is unmistakably McVie's, thanks to the groundwork she'd managed to lay early in the song's production.[8]

Ironically, the track that succeeds McVie's "You Make Loving Fun"—Buckingham and Nicks's "I Don't Want to Know"—is lyrically one of the least vengeful recordings featured on *Rumours*, despite it being one of the most controversial tracks included on the album. The track, a bubbly, country-rock breakup song written by Nicks prior to her split with Buckingham,[9] isn't controversial because of its sound or lyrics—which feature harmonies about crying spirits and emotions that have got Nicks "rockin' and a-reeling"—but because it was the track that the band had chosen for inclusion on *Rumours* over Nicks's "Silver Springs."

There had been great debate over who would be the one to break the news to Nicks. Not only was she in love with "Silver Springs," but she had also signed over the song's publishing rights to her mother, Barbara, to ensure that her mother would benefit from *Rumours'* album sales—as if she were a member of Fleetwood Mac herself.[10] In the end, it was decided that Fleetwood should be the one to inform Nicks that "Silver Springs" had gotten the axe. After all, he was still the one in charge of making any big decisions for the band. Fleetwood approached Nicks just after Buckingham had finished recording vocals for "I Don't Want to Know," which was recorded in Nicks's absence (although she had been the one to write the up-tempo breakup ballad). In justifying the exclusion of "Silver Springs," Fleetwood argued that there wouldn't be enough room on the LP for Nicks's ballad, even if the song—which was originally over ten minutes in length[11]—was trimmed down by five minutes or if tracks like the seven-minute "Gold Dust Woman" were shortened in order to compensate for Nicks's epic.[12] Nicks was furious but would eventually relent, and though the decision to include "I Don't Want to Know" on *Rumours* would inspire deeper tensions between Nicks and her bandmates for several years to come, the song was received with critical acclaim and does well to showcase the power of Nicks's vocals and Buckingham's abilities with an acoustic guitar.[13]

Rumours' official end product, then, allowed Buckingham to serve Nicks what he felt were her just desserts: while scathing tracks like "Second Hand News" or "Go Your Own Way" would make up a third of the album's first half, Nicks was forced to bite her tongue after the bittersweet "Silver Springs" was discarded in favor of the more light-hearted, conciliatory anthem, "I Don't Want to Know."

Following up Buckingham and Nicks's "I Don't Want to Know" is Christine McVie's "Oh Daddy": a dark, haunting ballad about being torn down but never wanting to break away. Though there are varying accounts regarding the song's meaning, those close to the band, including Buckingham's girlfriend at the time Carol Ann Harris, have claimed that the song—like McVie's

"You Make Loving Fun"—was written about Fleetwood Mac lighting director and notorious playboy Curry Grant. In 2009, Harris wrote:

> During *Rumours* Christine was [Grant's] conquest, and it was for him that she wrote the breathtaking "Songbird," then--when she discovered his infidelities—"Oh Daddy," not, as fans mistakenly speculate, for John. Years later, after both songs were beloved by millions, she would say that "Songbird" was written for and dedicated to "everyone" and that "Oh Daddy" was about Mick.[14]

Regardless of where the song's true inspiration lies (Fleetwood *has* claimed that the song was written about him, as he was the only member of the band who was a father around the time the song was written),[15] "Oh Daddy" quickly became a hit when *Rumours* was released in early 1977, and Fleetwood Mac has since performed the song on several of the band's subsequent tours, including their 1997 *The Dance* tour.

In addition to critics' praises, both Fleetwood and Nicks have described "Oh Daddy" as being one of their favorite Fleetwood Mac songs of all time.[16] *Rumours* producer Ken Caillat also described "Oh Daddy" as a "beautiful, airy song" in his 2012 book, *Making Rumours: The Inside Story of the Classic Fleetwood Mac Album*.[17] Though never released as a single in the US, the song was released as a single in Japan in 1978 with Nicks's "I Don't Want to Know" as the song's B-side. The song was also later recorded in 1998 by Tallulah for inclusion on the album *Legacy: A Tribute to Fleetwood Mac's Rumours*. The track, like all of those included on *Rumours*, is a result of years of drug, alcohol, and emotional abuse, and has since helped to define the band's legacy.

The airiness of *Rumours'* second-to-last track establishes an excellent segue into Stevie Nicks's album-closing "Gold Dust Woman," a spooky ballad with an origin and a meaning even more unclear than that of McVie's "Oh Daddy." Though "Gold Dust Woman" is often celebrated by critics as being one of the Mac's greatest studio efforts, the song's true meaning has long been debated by bandmates and listeners alike. Somewhat conclusively, however, Nicks has claimed in interviews with *Rolling Stone* and *VH1* that the song is about the "ritual" of using cocaine, despite the song having been written early in Nicks's tenure with Fleetwood Mac, just before the band's cocaine usage had become out of control.[18]

Like *Rumours'* other tracks, "Gold Dust Woman" was recorded late at night under dimmed lights in the band's recording studio. The song's hazy vocals took several takes to get right, due to Nicks's exhaustion and her budding addiction to cocaine.[19] Still under the impression that their habits were nothing more than recreational, however, it wasn't obvious to the band in the late seventies that the difficulties that they had faced in getting "Gold Dust Woman" recorded would serve as a precursor to their troubled *Tango in the Night* sessions—during which the band would discover that, for them, getting sober had become more difficult than producing platinum-selling records. Despite what was to come, however, Nicks's "Gold Dust Woman" offers a lightweight, radio-friendly insight into addiction and serves as an excellent end to the band's magnum-opus *Rumours.*

Though early on *Rumours'* second half seems to exude a more upbeat tone than the first half of the album—thanks to tracks like McVie's "You Make Loving Fun" or Buckingham and Nicks's bubbly "I Don't Want to Know"—big trouble was brewing beneath the surface not just for the drug-addled Nicks, but namely for Buckingham as well.

Aside from his ongoing feud with Nicks and his own developing drug addiction, Buckingham felt he had plenty of reasons to be angry come the late 1970s. For one, he was already beginning to feel imprisoned within Fleetwood Mac by the time *Rumours* was released. While bands like the Beach Boys, the Talking Heads, and the Who were stepping outside of the box with albums like the avant-garde *Smiley Smile* or the abandoned rock opera *Lifehouse*,[20] Fleetwood Mac and Warner Bros. were content having committed themselves to a best-selling soft-rock formula. Buckingham, meanwhile, was becoming drawn to the experimental, post-punk style of the late 1970s, an interest that no one else in the band—or in Burbank—would dare pursue after the success of *Fleetwood Mac* in 1975.

Not quite ready to take the money and run just yet, Buckingham continued to appease Warner Bros.' wishes by temporarily putting a lid on his obsession with the experimental and avant-garde even after working conditions in the band's Sausalito studio had become almost unbearably toxic by the mid-seventies. In fact, even as the band was coming close to declaring *Rumours* a wrap, John McVie was still reluctant to let Buckingham take more than his fair share of creative liberties with the band's sound. At the same time, a grudge was beginning to form between Buckingham and Fleetwood, who Buckingham suspected was becoming romantically involved with his ex-girlfriend Stevie Nicks.[21] Though there wasn't any real evidence that the two were fooling around, jealousy was beginning to get the better of Buckingham, who was still sore after his split with Nicks and couldn't bear the thought of his ex-love getting cozy with another man just yet.

Buckingham had brought to the band a style that at times mimicked that of Buddy Holly, the Beach Boys, and the Beatles, among others. He had brought a unique finger-picking style and a knack for transforming his bandmates' unfinished, unpolished, or unrefined demos into smash hits. Not only that, but Buckingham had brought with him a keen sense of style and a flair for theatrics—

after all, he had literally brought the extraordinary Stevie Nicks along with him, whose ability to write hits and please a crowd after only months into her tenure with Fleetwood Mac seemed worthy of warranting Nicks her own one-woman show. However, despite all of Buckingham's influence and abilities, his bandmates were beginning to raise concerns that maybe Fleetwood Mac wasn't a good fit for Buckingham. In fact, after the release of *Rumours* in early 1977, Mick Fleetwood suggested that maybe Buckingham shouldn't be in a band at all.[22]

It would seem that Fleetwood was right, given that Buckingham ended up suffering a breakdown shortly after the start of the band's *Rumours* tour; a breakdown that doctors would attribute to an onset of mild epilepsy.[23] Buckingham's medical drama hadn't come from out of the blue, however: while on tour, he had been working exhaustively on new material that he planned to include on the band's upcoming effort, *Tusk*. Unfortunately, writing, recording, and producing music while on the road put a massive strain on Buckingham, and he had begun to have trouble making his music sound the way he wanted—not unlike the way things had been early on while recording *Rumours*. It seemed that by late 1977, Buckingham's creative tendencies were beginning to get the better of him.

After all, as a member of Fleetwood Mac, Buckingham wasn't being allowed room to grow as an artist, and more so than ever by early 1978, it was becoming apparent that despite the band's recent successes, the stress of having to conform to Fleetwood Mac's standards was becoming a pill too hard for Buckingham to swallow. Not only was he never going to be allowed to be the center of attention within Fleetwood Mac, but despite being a central component to Fleetwood Mac's newfound success, Buckingham hadn't even been included on the cover of *Rumours*; instead, photographer Herbert "Herbie" Worthington had insisted that the album's cover feature Buckingham's ex-girlfriend Nicks holding hands with none other than Fleetwood himself.[24]

A falling out seemed inevitable.

CAN'T GO BACK
1978–1980

Shortly after the release of *Rumours*, Buckingham takes to using an eight-track Tascam tape recorder while on tour with Fleetwood Mac to record new material that is all his own.[1] Using Kleenex boxes as snare drums, Buckingham begins to lay the groundwork for the band's follow-up to *Rumours*—1979's *Tusk*—all the while developing an experimental, eccentric style that would lead to the production of tracks like "That's Enough for Me," "Save Me a Place," and "The Ledge." Each of these songs would be recorded solely by Buckingham. He's only recently had a falling out with Mick Fleetwood about whether or not being in a band would be the right move for him going forward. Regardless, the band manages to convince Buckingham to maintain his relationship with Fleetwood Mac, now knee-deep in their year-long *Rumours* tour.

Though Buckingham and the band are selling out stadiums and moving records by the millions while on their world tour, Buckingham's mind is elsewhere. He's fallen in love with the post-punk style of bands like the Talking Heads and is determined to make Fleetwood Mac relevant in the ever-expanding "post-punk world."[2] In between concerts, as he's recording his demos and knocking around Kleenex boxes, he's putting together a proposal for Fleetwood. Buckingham doesn't want his bandmates' opinions and doubts to intimidate him or coerce him into making a "*Rumours Part II.*" Instead, he's planning on suggesting that he be allowed to record his contributions to the band's next album not in some stuffy studio, but from the comfort of his own home.[3]

His idea has its fair share of cons, sure, but Buckingham's got answers to his critics' objections. This is an important step forward for Buckingham, after all. The others might not like it, but if worse comes to worst, Buckingham is confident in his bandmates' ability to "do their own thing." Christine McVie, for example, can carry over her pop-rock sound from tracks like "You Make Loving Fun" while Nicks can bring the sweetness of "Dreams" or "Rhiannon" along with her. If anything, McVie and Nicks will ensure that there's at least *some* continuity between *Rumours* and its successor. Regardless, Buckingham's positive that he won't be bringing that same L.A. soft-rock sound that had made *Rumours* such a success with him. Instead, he'll be attempting to embrace a more brash style, one that'll immediately let listeners know that Fleetwood Mac is a band with a knack not only for writing radio-friendly records like *Rumours* but for producing avant-garde pop art as well.

Rumours was released on February 4, 1977 for $7.98, a dollar more than the industry standard of $6.98 for single-disc albums.[4] It would seem that by early 1977, Lindsey Buckingham and his Fleetwood Mac bandmates were now considered to be "established artists," sharing the same rarified airspace as bands like Pink Floyd and Queen, whose respective albums *Animals* and *A Day at the Races* were also being priced accordingly by their own record labels, Columbia and Elektra.[5]

By March of 1978, *Rumours* had become Fleetwood Mac's second record to top the US *Billboard* Hot 200. Also, by early 1978, the album had managed to become the band's first #1 album in the UK and had won the 1978 Grammy Award for Album of the Year. Not only that, but *Rumours* had also sold over 10 million copies worldwide only a little over a year after the album's initial release, far exceeding Warner Bros.' expectations for the band's follow-up to 1975's *Fleetwood Mac*. After six grueling months of screaming matches and cocaine-fueled all-nighters in Sausalito, Fleetwood Mac had done it again: *Rumours* was a smash hit. So then where do you go when you're already at the top?

To the men and women in Burbank, Fleetwood Mac's next move seemed like a no-brainer. Likewise, Christine McVie and Stevie Nicks were keen to build off the success of *Rumours* by creating a radio-friendly soft-rock album that would again dominate the sales charts at home and abroad. However, these thoughts never occurred to Buckingham, who was determined from the get-go to create an album that sounded nothing like its predecessor. To achieve this, Buckingham decided to up the ante, creating songs that needed to be pieced together or by recording fragmented demos and experimenting on them by turning knobs or changing their pitch until he was satisfied with what he had created. As a result, several of Buckingham's songs would come off as half-formed, fuzzy, and incoherent messes, just as he had planned.[6]

After a year of recording, the end result was 1979's *Tusk*, a highly experimental double album that was the embodiment of Warner Bros.' worst nightmare.

The album's first of four sides contains tracks like Christine McVie's "Think About Me" and Stevie Nicks's "Sara," two tracks that would be released as singles within months of the album's initial release in September 1979. These tracks are classic Fleetwood Mac, and the fact that each song would manage to crack the US *Billboard* 100's top ten shortly after being lifted off the album as singles is proof enough of that. McVie's "Think About Me" is a bouncy, upbeat tune that helps *Tusk* maintain a fragile resemblance to its predecessor *Rumours*. Likewise, Nicks's "Sara" is a lyrically intricate ballad about heartbreak that concludes with Nicks's cries as she calls out for "the poet of her heart."

However, Nicks's "Sara" serves as more than just a saving grace for "classic" Fleetwood Mac fans not quite ready to embrace *Tusk* and all its quirks. In fact, "Sara" can be defined as the epitome of "classic" Fleetwood Mac, having since become one of the most popular works that the band has ever produced following the song's original release as a single in December 1979. The song, written about a child Nicks had planned to have with Don Henley of Eagles fame prior to the disintegration of their relationship in the late-1970s,[7] tells a poignant story of heartbreak and of what "could've been"—themes that the band had embraced while writing and recording *Rumours*, their most emotionally raw and successful album to date.

"Sara" also includes lyrics that point out the comfort that Nicks was seeking in her company with Mick Fleetwood following her breakup from Lindsey Buckingham, a hint early on that the scars from *Rumours* were still raw—something that later recording sessions for *Tusk* would reveal as well.

In between Christine McVie's gentle album opener "Over and Over" and Nicks's "Sara" are two tracks by Buckingham, which right off the bat give audiences a taste of what's to come. First up is "The Ledge," an erratic ode to Buckingham's relationship with Nicks. In between Buckingham's brash, screeching vocals are harsh, rumbling instrumentals—a product of Buckingham trying to create a conceptual piece similar to his other contributions to *Tusk*. In a similar vein, "Save Me a Place" is an eerie, haunting track about loneliness that was also recorded solely by Buckingham.[8] Though "Save Me a Place" was hardly considered by Warner Bros. to be a track worthy of hitting the airwaves of FM radio in late 1979, the song, like Buckingham's other frantic, jumpy, and disjointed contributions to *Tusk*, is nonetheless a testament to the versatility of both Buckingham and Fleetwood Mac and to the power and potency of the "post-punk" movement of the late 1970s.

The album's second quarter begins with Buckingham's "What Makes You Think You're the One," a loud, drum-beat-driven track that manages to encapsulate a wild, snaring garage band-like sound.[9] In fact, probably more so than any other track on *Tusk*, "What Makes You Think You're the One" manages to send a message to Warner Bros. and longtime fans of the band that Lindsey Buckingham does not and will not conform to any commercial standards. One of Buckingham's proudest works, the song was created by him in collaboration with Mick Fleetwood and was the product of a late-night jam session spent in the band's new recording studio, Studio D (also known as the Village Recorder) in Los Angeles.[10]

The follow-up to Buckingham's "What Makes You Think You're the One" is Stevie Nicks's "Storms." The song's gentle vocals and guitar work belie its heavy lyricism, perhaps putting at ease any listeners who've suddenly realized six tracks into *Tusk* that this album is hardly a "*Rumours Part II*". While the track's lyrics on their own lament Nicks's turbulent relationship and subsequent falling-out with Mick Fleetwood, recording the song was a source of drama in and of itself. When Nicks presented "Storms" to the band, unsurprisingly, hearing the song's lyrics about Nicks's doomed relationship with Fleetwood opened old wounds for Buckingham, who was still coming to terms with his own breakup with Nicks. Suddenly, the civility that the two often managed to uphold while collaborating in the studio vanished, and Buckingham lashed out at Nicks, suggesting that, without him, she'd never have any decent material.[11]

Nicks retaliated, and a screaming match ensued. The two exchanged verbal blows, using knowledge of each other's histories as sources of ammunition. However, in the end, the song would become one of the album's most beautifully poignant tracks, despite it having incited such a brutal toxicity between Buckingham and Nicks.

After only a few months spent in the studio recording the band's follow-up to 1977's *Rumours*, it seemed that even after several years, there was still plenty of unresolved tension between the two. These tensions were no doubt spurred on by the band's continuing drug habits and partner-swapping in the aftermath of *Rumours*.

Following "Storms" is Buckingham's "That's All for Everyone." "That's All" is one of the best examples of how Buckingham's sound and style had been influenced by albums like the Beach Boys' abandoned *Smile*,[12] in that it features a complex arrangement and exudes a distinct strangeness. Though the song listens like a fuzzy compilation of overlapping vocals and half-formed instrumentals, "That's All for Everyone" is essential Fleetwood Mac, as it perfectly encapsulates the experimental sound that Buckingham had hoped to achieve on *Tusk*. The song's lyrics, like its bizarre instrumentation, make just as strong a statement about his developing need for creative freedom within Fleetwood Mac, featuring a pleading Buckingham desperate for "somewhere to go."

Much more frenzied than the comparatively tame "That's All for Everyone," Buckingham's "Not That Funny" and Nicks's "Sisters of the Moon" round out the album's first half. "Not That Funny" is yet another product of Buckingham spending hours at a time in the basement of his own home, scribbling lyrics and fiddling with tapes until he'd emerge from the darkness only to find himself still completely immersed in his work. Nicks's "Sisters of the Moon," meanwhile, is a rarity on *Tusk*. For one, it was the result of a jam session held in the band's primary recording studio, rather than a product of any of the long, manic sessions held in Buckingham's basement. Two, the song is a product of Nicks finally acquiescing to the "strangeness" of *Tusk*. While several of Nicks's other songs on the album boast lyrics derived from heartbreak or emotional trauma, "Sisters of the Moon" is a gnarly, guitar-driven epic that Nicks has since claimed in interviews "makes no sense."[13]

Though these songs were only able to achieve moderate success upon their release as singles in early 1980, both tracks have managed to maintain significant longevity thanks to the band's legendary live performances of "Not That Funny" and "Sisters of the Moon." These tracks, when presented in concert, often extend far beyond their original runtimes of three and four minutes, respectively. In fact, a nearly ten-minute version of Buckingham's "Not That Funny"—featuring several minutes of extended instrumentals—would later be included on Fleetwood Mac's 1980 album *Live*, recorded during the band's year-long *Tusk* tour.

The second half of *Tusk* opens with Nicks's "Angel," a track that serves as both a precursor to country-rock-inspired tracks like Nicks's "That's Alright" from 1982's *Mirage* as well as a throwback to the days of *Buckingham Nicks*. On the album, the song is *partly* a duet between Buckingham and Nicks, though while on stage during the band's subsequent *Tusk* tour, "Angel" would be much more of a collaborative effort between the two.[14] In fact, the track was one that Buckingham and Nicks would often perform as an affectionate duo for the sake of putting on a good show for audiences, though to anyone familiar with the band's history, it was obvious that, all the while, the two were gritting their teeth.

"That's Enough for Me" is another track written and recorded solely by Buckingham. Once this fast-paced number about the "same old way" and "same old pain" comes to an abrupt end after a little under two minutes, listeners are finally treated to not one, but two tracks by Christine McVie, who hasn't made an appearance on *Tusk* since side one's "Think About Me." The first track by McVie, "Brown Eyes," features former

Fleetwood Mac frontman Peter Green on guitar.[15] Like McVie's tracks on *Rumours*, "Brown Eyes" helps to give *Tusk* a more positive, upbeat sound, and McVie's "Never Make Me Cry" is an optimistic piece about love and happiness. Though neither song ever quite reaches the same fever pitch as "Don't Stop," or "Songbird," "Brown Eyes" and "Never Make Me Cry" are two classic anthems that exude positivity among a slew of raunchy, clattered tracks produced by Buckingham.

The first track on side four of *Tusk*, Christine McVie's "Honey Hi" and the final song on the album's third side, Lindsey Buckingham's "I Know I'm Not Wrong," amp up the album's airiness. In fact, both tracks almost come off as out of place on *Tusk*, with the upbeat tempo of "I'm Know I'm Not Wrong" and the aloof lyrics of "Honey Hi" being a far departure from the heaviness of songs like "Not That Funny" or the weariness of "Storms." Regardless, *Tusk* is all the better for it, and McVie and Buckingham's contributions to the album this late in the game only help to further shape *Tusk* into the genre-bending roller coaster it was destined to become. Like Buckingham's "The Ledge," side three's "I Know I'm Not Wrong" was a track that Buckingham heavily experimented with, again using objects like Kleenex boxes to help him achieve, among other things, an "elusive" drumming effect.[16]

Nicks makes a one-off return in the album's fourth quarter to remind listeners that the recording for sessions for *Tusk* were nothing short of toxic with "Beautiful Child," a heartbreaking ballad presented as a gorgeous mix of angelic vocals, acoustics, and instrumentals. Though the song—in which Nicks sings about an ill-fated relationship, growing out of childhood, and being "too trusting"—has origins that are long debated (some claim that the song is about Buckingham, Fleetwood, or even Beatles' road manager Derek Taylor),[17] "Beautiful Child" nonetheless remains one of Fleetwood Mac's most gorgeously composed and meticulously arranged works, from *Tusk* or otherwise. Unfortunately, the song's exclusion from albums like 1988's *Greatest Hits* or 2002's *The Very Best of Fleetwood Mac* meant that "Beautiful Child" would largely remain a novelty up until its inclusion on the track listing for the 2004 DVD release of Fleetwood Mac's *Live in Boston*, 25 years after its original release.

Like Nicks's "Beautiful Child," Buckingham's "Walk a Thin Line" is a somber ode to recovery and solitude. The song's impressive lyricism and haunting vocal arrangements allow the track to fit right in with other Buckingham-led compositions from *Tusk*, like side one's "The Ledge" or "Save Me a Place." Though midway through the album's final quarter Nicks's "Beautiful Child" and the similarly solemn "Walk a Thin Line" have established a delicate sense of continuity, *Tusk* isn't done springing surprises. While listeners would hardly expect the album to throw out any sense of coordination or progression this late in the game, that's exactly what *Tusk* does.

Anyone who has managed to stick it out this long might have thought they had *Tusk* all figured out. The truth? Nothing they'd already heard could've prepared them for *Tusk*'s animalistic title track, which is prepared to throw listeners' preconceptions right out the window.

The three-and-half minute mess of drumming, slapping, chanting, and screeching has since been described by *Rolling Stone* as a "landmark of badass rock & roll bravado,"[18] and was created by Buckingham and Fleetwood in collaboration with *Tusk* producers Ken Caillat and Richard Dashut. To lay the groundwork for "Tusk," Buckingham and Dashut took a drum riff that Fleetwood often used as a warm-up prior to live performances and combined it with a guitar riff that Buckingham often performed during sound checks. A percussion-driven production, Fleetwood added the use of tribal drums and tissue boxes—among other oddities—to help "Tusk" achieve a more raw, untamed sound.[19]

In addition to playing guitar on "Tusk," Buckingham also wrote the track's interrogative lyrics, which beg to know "who's on the phone" and "the latest on his throne." Recorded live at Dodger Stadium in L.A., *Tusk*'s most flamboyant track also features the University of Southern

California's Trojan Marching Band. The band provides "Tusk" with a screeching horn section that oddly enough manages to compliment Fleetwood's kooky percussive effects and the band's vocals, which quickly evolve into a war-cry of sorts by "Tusk's" conclusion. The performance at Dodger Stadium was also videotaped and would eventually be released as "Tusk's" official music video.

The video features the USC Marching Band performing in formation and Fleetwood Mac bandmates Buckingham, Nicks, Christine McVie, and Mick Fleetwood in various stages of the recording process. In fact, the video for "Tusk" is equally as curious as the song itself, featuring Nicks twirling batons, McVie and Fleetwood playfully modeling Trojan Marching Band attire, and each member of the band taking turns carrying around a cardboard cutout of John McVie—who was away in Tahiti during the video's recording.[20] "Tusk" was released as the album's first single in September 1979, and the track would manage to peak at #9 on the US *Billboard* Hot 100 and #6 on the UK Singles Chart before the end of the year.

Finally, Christine McVie's "Never Forget" manages to bring *Tusk* full circle. Of course, because it's a track by McVie, "Never Forget" is an upbeat album closer and has an airy, cheerfulness about it, not unlike her other contributions to *Tusk*. A lighthearted ballad reminiscent of a truly wonderful night, McVie sings about shining stars and a love that's as good as gold. These sprightly high points are few and far between on the band's moody follow-up to *Rumours*, and McVie's work undoubtedly helps to make *Tusk* the wonderfully diverse mess that it is. In fact, had this song been penned by Buckingham or Nicks, "Never Forget" might've just been another track about a cocaine-fueled rage or late-night screaming match.

Now that would've made for a great "*Rumours Part II.*"

Though the album's self-titled first single "Tusk" managed to achieve some success in the late 1970s, the album itself wouldn't fare as well.

Like 1975's *Fleetwood Mac*, *Tusk*'s early sales numbers were slow coming but began to climb steadily once the band embarked on a world tour in support of the album, which included stops in cities like New York, Tokyo, Melbourne, and Munich, among others. While on tour, live performances of tracks like Nicks's "Rhiannon," Buckingham's "Not That Funny," and Christine McVie's "Don't Stop" were recorded for inclusion on an album Fleetwood Mac released in late 1980 simply entitled *Live*. This album, which was released in hopes of further securing *Tusk* greater sales numbers, also included original recordings, like a cover of the Beach Boys' "The Farmer's Daughter," McVie's "One More Night," and Nicks's "Fireflies," the latter of which—like

1977's "The Chain"—pays homage to the longevity of the band.[21]

Their efforts paid off, and by the early 1980s *Tusk* had managed to sell four million copies worldwide. For any other band that wasn't Fleetwood Mac, these sales numbers would've been more than enough to secure any record company's commendations. However, compared to 1977's *Rumours*, which by 1978 had sold over 10 million copies, *Tusk* had tanked. As such, the album was dismissed by Warner Bros. as a commercial failure within months of its initial release. Mick Fleetwood initially pinned blame for the album's "failure" on a botched attempt by Warner Bros. to promote the album, writing in 1990 that:

> With as much hype as possible, *Tusk* was broadcast in its entirety on the Westwood One rock radio network, which comprised most of America's FM radio stations in major markets. This was an unmitigated disaster, as millions stayed home that night and *taped* the whole album, avoiding record stores completely.[22]

Despite this, in the ensuing fallout, blame for the album's disappointing performance was laid squarely on Buckingham, the chief architect behind the "commercial suicide" that was *Tusk*. Critics were quick to shame the album's quirks and declare Buckingham self-indulgent.[23]

Despite the success of the band's subsequent tour in support of *Tusk*, there were still further signs of trouble while on the road as criticism of Buckingham, his controlling nature, and *Tusk* began to weigh on the mastermind behind Fleetwood Mac's recent "flop." In March of 1980, while the band was on tour in Wellington, New Zealand, things came to a nasty head: three songs into the band's setlist, Nicks began to dominate the stage. Her moves and ability to enchant a crowd with a chiffon scarf ensured that all eyes were on her even when ex Lindsey Buckingham or gal pal Christine McVie were meant to be the main attractions while performing lead vocals on tracks like "Go Your Own Way" or "Say You Love Me." Nicks's performance didn't have everyone swooning, however. Unsurprisingly, Buckingham could hardly stand to see his ex-girlfriend owning the spotlight.

Maybe it was *Tusk*'s lagging sales numbers or maybe it was the onslaught of critics who'd taken to challenging his creative direction, but Buckingham's temper would get the better of him. Not long after the show opened with McVie's "Say You Love Me," Buckingham began to intentionally play out of tune, disrupting Nicks's performances before trying to trip her as she limped through a rendition of "Rhiannon" without the full support of her guitarist. Then, in an alcohol-fueled stunt aimed at bagging himself some attention from the crowd of around 60,000 fans, Buckingham mocked Nicks's moves as she attempted to keep the audience's eyes on her. Ultimately, when he realized that his initial stunts weren't earning him enough attention, Buckingham furiously pitched a Les Paul guitar at his ex-girlfriend's head. Shortly after, the show came to a painfully awkward end. This time around, it was the traditionally serene Christine McVie that Buckingham had managed to rile up with his antics. Following the show, she found Buckingham backstage in the men's dressing room and smacked him across the face.[24] It was an embarrassing night for Fleetwood Mac and just one of many cocaine and alcohol-induced breakdowns to come.

Though Mick Fleetwood had suggested making *Tusk* a double album early on in order to give the band's three songwriters "more space,"[25] it seemed as though being given room to explore new sounds and recording techniques had actually been detrimental to Buckingham. While *Tusk* would eventually become one of Fleetwood Mac's most celebrated works—garnering several positive retrospective reviews from critics 10, 20, and even 30 years after its initial release[26]— Buckingham's genius having initially gone unrecognized meant that he would be forced to bear the burden of the band's lagging sales for the time being. However, as his efforts within Fleetwood Mac continued to go unappreciated, Buckingham was beginning to look elsewhere for a way to satisfy his creative urges.

Specifically, by mid-1980, Buckingham's aspirations were beginning to take shape in the form of a potential solo career. This way, without his bandmates or any expectations to live up to, Buckingham would be able to write the rulebook and do as he damn well pleased. Sure, going solo had its fair share of risks, but albums like *Fleetwood Mac* or *Rumours* hadn't become smash hits because Buckingham had played it safe—not to mention that his ex-girlfriend Stevie Nicks had also recently mentioned her interest in potentially going solo.

S T R A I G H T   B A C K

1 9 8 1 – 1 9 8 2

OCTOBER 3, 1981

Lindsey Buckingham releases his first solo album *Law and Order* with American record label Asylum—known for having previously signed artists like Linda Ronstadt, Bob Dylan, and Creedence Clearwater Revival frontman John Fogerty. Recorded in less than a year, the album is Buckingham's first foray into making music outside of Fleetwood Mac since the early seventies. At first glance, *Law and Order* seems like a direct response to fellow Fleetwood Mac bandmate Stevie Nicks's debut album, *Bella Donna*, which was released only a few months earlier in July.

However, while *Bella Donna* managed to reach #1 on the US charts only a month prior to the release of *Law and Order* in September 1981, Buckingham isn't as liable as critics to draw comparisons between the two. In fact, he knows that at this point, he's far from achieving stardom as a solo artist.

More so than anything else, *Law and Order* is Buckingham's way of proving to himself that he can create a work of art that is distinctly his own. Across the album, he draws inspiration from a variety of 50s and 60s rock and pop classics, and even includes covers of Gary Paxton's "It Was I," and Kurt Weill and Maxwell Anderson's "September Song."[1] Of course, *Law and Order* also includes several experimental tracks not unlike those that Buckingham had recorded for Fleetwood Mac's *Tusk* two years prior, including the song, "I'll Tell You Now."

In February 1982, a few months after the release of *Law and Order*, Buckingham would perform as the musical guest on *Saturday Night Live* in an effort to promote his first-ever solo album. In collaboration with Mick Fleetwood, Buckingham performed the songs "Trouble" and "Bwana."

Despite releasing *Law and Order* as a way to prove to himself that he had the chops to go solo, Buckingham's debut album still managed to sell a couple hundred thousand copies, which is no small feat for *anyone* trying to make it in the music industry. In fact, the album's lead single "Trouble" would manage to peak at #9 on the US Hot 100, while the album itself would peak at #32 on the US *Billboard* Hot 200 by the end of the year, bringing it within striking distance of albums like Pat Benatar's *Precious Time* and Billy Squier's *Don't Say No*. Though Buckingham is never completely divorced from Fleetwood Mac during his first stint as a solo artist, having enlisted the help of bandmates Christine McVie on "Shadow of the West" and Mick Fleetwood on "Trouble," *Law and Order* is still a considerable success for Buckingham, who is only just beginning to experiment with going solo.

After being blamed for the "failure" that was 1979's *Tusk*, Buckingham decided to take some time for himself. He deserved it, after all. For the last five years, he'd been helping to shape Fleetwood Mac into a rock and roll legend capable of selling albums by the millions and filling stadiums and arenas meant to accommodate thousands of adoring fans to full capacity. So, rather than take it slow by shipping off to an island somewhere to play golf and chug martinis, Buckingham returned to the studio to further experiment with the new-wave, post-punk sound that he had fallen in love with prior to recording *Tusk*. In between sessions at Wally Heider Studios in San Francisco and Larrabee Sound Studios in Southern California, Buckingham was able to piece together a body of work that would eventually become his debut album, *Law and Order*.

It isn't just because Buckingham had recorded *Law and Order* while bouncing around California that the album listens like a collection of bits and pieces rather than a cohesive, commercially satisfying work of pop art. Rather, it's the unleashing of Buckingham's creative tendencies that makes his debut album such a mixed bag of styles and sounds, which is far from a bad thing. Though the album opener "Bwana" maintains a similar sound to songs like *Tusk*'s "I Know I'm Not Wrong" or "The Ledge," Buckingham takes much greater risks deeper into *Law and Order*.

The album's first of four singles, "Trouble," was released in November 1981. If nothing else, "Trouble" was proof that despite his experimental tendencies, Buckingham could still whip up radio-friendly hits on a whim, as "Trouble" would manage to peak at #9 on the US *Billboard* Hot 100 and at #32 on the UK Singles Chart. The track features Mick Fleetwood on drums and George Hawkins on bass guitar, though Buckingham would later overdub some of his own drum and percussion work on "Trouble" to give the track a more "live feel."[2] A star-studded music video featuring Fleetwood, Walter Egan, and former Mac guitarists Bob Weston and Bob Welch was also recorded to accompany the song's release as a single.

Other standouts that emphasize the album's faint lo-fi/new-wave theme, for example, include original recordings like "Shadow of the West," which combines country-like instrumentals with airy vocals, and "Love from Here, Love from There," which features similar instrumental work, albeit with a few more tics to it. "Johnny Stew," meanwhile—like "Bwana" and several of Buckingham's contributions to *Tusk*—features Buckingham's layered vocals and a panicked rhythm section. Among original material composed by Buckingham, *Law and Order* also includes faithful renditions of the antsy "It Was I" and Walter Huston's "September Song," an uncharacteristically mellow lull that rolls around midway through the album. However, despite the inclusion of tracks like "September Song," much of the instrumental work on Buckingham's debut album works to maintain a constantly frantic fever pitch that would also define the sound and style of his 1984 solo project, *Go Insane*.

If *Law and Order*'s ability to uphold similar pitch and tone from track to track seems almost uncanny, it's because nearly all the album's instrumental work was performed solely by Buckingham. In fact, he provided all the instrumental and vocal work on every track featured on *Law and Order* aside from on "Trouble" (which featured Mick Fleetwood on drums), "It Was I" (a duet between Buckingham and then-girlfriend Carol Ann Harris), and "Shadow of the West" (on which Christine McVie provided backup vocals). Though not entirely "free" from Fleetwood Mac, *Law and Order* was proof that Buckingham could still take charge of his own creative destiny.

Only a few months before *Law and Order* was set to be released, Fleetwood Mac had reconvened after a little over a year apart. Though Buckingham, Nicks, and Fleetwood had been hard at work on their own solo projects (none of which had been released by the time the band began recording *Mirage*), the quintet made a unanimous decision from the get-go to make *Mirage* a "true" Fleetwood Mac album—a sort of "homage" to *Rumours*.[3] Who could blame them, after all? After spending some time apart and not yet having seen their solo efforts come to fruition following *Tusk*'s disappointing debut two years earlier, the band was eager to pick up where they'd left off with *Rumours*. Buckingham specifically was keen to relinquish the leadership role he'd maintained while recording *Tusk* and put Fleetwood Mac's future back into the hands of his bandmates.[4]

Mirage was recorded at Château d'Hérouville in France, where fellow superstars like Elton John and David Bowie had previously recorded albums like 1972's *Honky Château* and 1973's *Pin Ups*, respectively. Maybe it's because the album was recorded a mere 20 miles from Paris, or maybe it's because the band was dedicated to recreating the infectious soft-rock sound of their 1977 smash hit, but Fleetwood Mac's *Mirage* actually manages to recapture some of the magic of *Rumours*. In fact, the band's follow-up to *Tusk* incorporates both the theatrics and magic of *Rumours* as well as the hard-hitting lyricism of *Tusk*. None of the songs on *Mirage* are ever as instrumentally bare-bones or frantic as anything featured on 1979's *Tusk*, however. As such, the band makes it clear with *Mirage* that they're well-equipped to adapt and respond to their fans' recent demands.

The album's first two tracks, for example, Christine McVie's "Love in Store" and Lindsey Buckingham's "Can't Go Back," are tracks that easily could've found a place on *Rumours*. McVie's album opener is a traditionally upbeat, bubbly pop ballad about the feeling of falling in love, while Buckingham's follow-up sports lyrics laced with regret—specifically, "Can't Go Back" is a reminiscence about the man Buckingham "used to be." However, like *Rumours'* "Go Your Own Way" or *Fleetwood Mac's* "Monday Morning," Buckingham's wounded lyrics are betrayed by "Can't Go Back's" effervescent instrumentals and high-pitched vocals.

Nicks's "That's Alright" is a smooth, soft-rock ballad not unlike *Tusk's* "Angel." Though the track takes on a much more country-rock-inspired sound than anything Nicks had created for *Rumours*, the song is remarkably similar to Nicks's "Dreams," in that "That's Alright" manages to tackle the subject of her and Buckingham's breakup without so much as a hint of bitterness. In fact, Nicks's ability to keep coy could be considered even more impressive come the early 80s, given the implied competition between her and Buckingham as budding solo artists and the fact that, at the time, both of them were engaged in serious relationships outside of Fleetwood Mac (Buckingham was still dating longtime girlfriend Carol Ann Harris while Nicks had recently struck up a relationship with *Bella Donna* producer Jimmy Iovine).

Following "That's Alright," Buckingham returns to the spotlight with another track about loneliness and falling out of love. Like Buckingham's "Can't Go Back," *Mirage*'s "Book of Love" sets a theme that dominates the album from beginning to end. Like *Rumours*, *Mirage* listens like a roadmap of bandmates' pasts, presents, and futures. Buckingham's first two features on *Mirage* talk about the disintegration of relationships—with Nicks and others—while McVie's "Love in Store" and "Only Over You"[5] embrace the prospects of finding new love and "watching love grow." While early on both Buckingham and McVie are essential in developing *Mirage* into a worthy successor to *Rumours*, it is Nicks who owns the album's first half with "Gypsy," a shimmering ode to her life before becoming a rock star.

Initially released as a single in September 1982, Nicks's "Gypsy" is a beautifully arranged ballad containing her best lyricism to date, detailing a time in her life long before she'd managed to establish herself as a formidable tour de force in the world of rock and roll. For the most part, however, like many of the Buckingham/Nicks penned tracks contained on *Mirage*, Nicks's "Gypsy" was largely written about the duo's ill-fated relationship. Specifically, the nearly four-and-a-half-minute ballad is about Nick's life before she and Buckingham had managed to "make it big" with Fleetwood Mac—about the days when the duo lived in a small, dimly lit apartment and slept on a single, king-sized bed surrounded by "some lace and paper flowers."

Interestingly, though the song had initially been recorded in the early eighties largely as an ode to Nicks's relationship with Buckingham and early life as a "gypsy" living in San Francisco, the song's lyrics would eventually take on yet another meaning for Nicks in the months following the release of *Mirage* in late 1982, when, two months into the band's tour of the same name, Nicks would learn that her longtime friend Robin Anderson had died of leukemia.[6] "Gypsy's" lyrics beginning in the song's second quarter and especially in the song's closing stages best reflect Anderson's passing, with Nicks making reference to still being able to see Anderson's "bright eyes."

After the song's initial release as a single, "Gypsy" would peak at #12 on the US *Billboard*

Hot 100 by the end of the year. The song would also be released with an accompanying music video, which at the time of its release was the most expensive music video ever produced.[7] Recorded over a three-day period, the elaborate video—which was also the first-ever "World Premiere Video" to be featured on MTV—contained several scenes set in various locations, including city streets, a forest, and a cabaret club, among others. Of course, "Gypsy's" music video couldn't be considered a genuine Fleetwood Mac production if the process of recording the video had been anything less than a drama-filled shit show.

For one, in order to keep the video's recording schedule on track, Nicks had been forced to leave rehab (which she had entered a few weeks earlier in an effort to ward off her cocaine addiction.) As a result, Nicks maintained a short temper and suffered from severe symptoms of withdrawal throughout the production of "Gypsy's" music video.[8] Nicks wasn't the only one uncomfortable while recording the elaborate film, however. In fact, the entire band struggled with being asked to maintain close contact with one another. In one of the video's earliest scenes, for example, John and Christine McVie are featured dining in each other's company while Buckingham and Nicks are shown sharing an idyllic ballroom dance. Unsurprisingly, Nicks found the experience of having to dance with her ex-boyfriend Buckingham extremely uncomfortable.[9]

The album's B-side contains just as many hits as *Mirage*'s stellar first half, beginning with Buckingham's "Empire State" and Nicks's "Straight Back." Both are equally as enchanting. "Empire State" is at times erratic (though never enough to warrant it inclusion on an album like *Tusk*) and features Buckingham's vocals drenched in an echo effect, while Nicks's follow-up chronicles her one-off relationship with *Bella Donna* producer Jimmy Iovine.[10] Even though Buckingham's intro to *Mirage*'s B-side is much bouncier than Nicks's haunting "Straight Back," both songs are an excellent segue into what would become the album's biggest hit, "Hold Me," a piping duet between Buckingham and Christine McVie.

Written by McVie and English singer-songwriter Robbie Patton,[11] "Hold Me" was the first single released from *Mirage* and was one of two tracks from the album—the other being Nicks's "Gypsy"—to become top 20 hits in the US. Like "Gypsy," "Hold Me" was released with an accompanying music video. Remarkably, "Hold Me's" music video actually manages to one-up "Gypsy's" with a setting even more exotic than an enchanted forest or cabaret club: the Mojave Desert. Though asking rock and roll divas like Stevie Nicks to hike up and down sand dunes in platforms while maintaining close contact with two of her ex-boyfriends was already an awful idea, this was just the tip of the iceberg.

By the time the video was recorded, the entire band was still committed to a vicious cycle that involved any one of them sleeping with someone they shouldn't have, being bitter about someone having slept with someone else, and then drinking or drugging themselves to the point of numbness. In addition to ongoing feuds like those between the McVies or Buckingham and Nicks, Mick Fleetwood, fresh off his *Tusk*-era affair with Nicks, had been sleeping with one of Nicks's best friends, much to the witchy woman's fury.[12] As a result, much like the process of filming the music video for "Gypsy," recording "Hold Me's" music video was a complete nightmare, one that was further complicated by the sky-high temperatures of the Mojave, which were well over 100 degrees throughout filming.[13]

Snuggled up in between McVie's "Hold Me" and album closers, "Eyes of the World" and "Wish You Were Here," is what is perhaps one of most underrated tracks ever produced by Lindsey Buckingham in his time with Fleetwood Mac or otherwise, despite it being the first single from *Mirage* to crack the top ten of the UK Singles Chart in 1983.

Written in Hérouville, Buckingham's "Oh Diane" best exemplifies the Palo Alto native's return to form as a 1950s classic rock-inspired musician.[14] "Oh Diane" also best represents Buckingham's willingness to recommit himself to Fleetwood Mac, at least for the time being. Maybe it had been the way critics had torn apart *Tusk* or how little attention the folks in Burbank had paid to 1981's *Law and Order*, but if he hadn't already proved it with side one's "Can't Go Back" or "Empire State," "Oh Diane" all but confirms Buckingham's having pledged himself to the same soft-rock sound that had helped to make him and his bandmates millionaires by the early eighties. As a result, "Oh Diane" helps to distinguish an important turning point in Fleetwood Mac's history: though *Mirage* would help to win back fans who had been put off by 1979's *Tusk*, for most of the band, the album would promote a shared disinterest in Fleetwood Mac.[15]

Once completed, *Mirage* was released on June 18, 1982, and succeeded in topping the US *Billboard* Hot 200 within months of its initial release. It was the first time an album by Fleetwood Mac had managed to top the US charts since *Rumours*, and the album's extended life on the US *Billboard* 200 chart meant that for several weeks *Mirage* remained within the same rarefied airspace as albums like John Cougar's *American Fool* as well as Men at Work's *Business as Usual*, among others. Again, though the album signaled Fleetwood Mac's return to a classic soft-rock style and sound, perhaps no other album in the band's history has been as divisive as *Mirage*.

Though while recording *Mirage* there were fewer screaming matches, cocaine-fueled rages, or alcohol-induced breakdowns than there had been during recording sessions for *Rumours* or *Tusk*, bandmates Buckingham, Nicks and Christine McVie were content as ever to separate following the conclusion of their year-long North American *Mirage* tour. By the time the tour had been declared a wrap by late 1982 in Austin, Texas, it had already been a year since Nicks's *Bella Donna* had usurped Foreigner's *4* as #1 on the US *Billboard* 200 chart and been certified platinum by the RIAA. Unsurprisingly, eager to build off *Bella Donna*'s success, by late 1982 Nicks had already begun recording demos and writing songs for inclusion on a follow-up album that would later become 1983's *The Wild Heart*.

Nicks of course wasn't the only one looking to build off her prior success as a solo artist. While she was working to make a name for herself outside of Fleetwood Mac, Buckingham, inspired by his deteriorating relationship with longtime girlfriend Carol Ann Harris, would soon begin work on his second solo effort as well, 1984's *Go Insane*, while Fleetwood Mac bandmate Christine McVie would take to the studio less than a year after the release of *Mirage* to record her second self-titled album, a follow-up to 1970's *Christine Perfect*. In fact, within a year of *Mirage*'s release, it seemed like Fleetwood Mac might never reconvene despite years of success as a quintet. After all, why would they?

For one, Nicks had already established herself as a force to be reckoned with in the world of rock and roll with the release of *Bella Donna*.

Buckingham, meanwhile, was back to his old ways after he'd conformed to Warner Bros.' standards for the last time to create what would prove to be Fleetwood Mac's final bubbly collection of radio-friendly pop songs. Even Christine McVie, who hadn't released an album outside of Fleetwood Mac in more than ten years, would manage to crack the top ten of the US *Billboard*'s Hot 100 chart with her 1984 album's lead single, "Got a Hold on Me."[16]

Buckingham's girlfriend during the band's *Mirage* tour, Carol Ann Harris, later wrote in 2009 that:

> With the exception of Mick and John, nobody wanted to be on the road... By Halloween, Stevie, Lindsey, and Christine had told John and Mick that after next month's U.S. tour dates were completed the *Mirage* tour was over. There would be no European or Far East tour. With *Mirage* at number one for two straight months, the band was over it. They wanted to pursue their solo projects.[17]

However, despite the odds and the band's shifting interests, Buckingham's influence would once again prove to be Fleetwood Mac's saving grace: by the end of the decade, he would manage to finally combine his own kooky methods of music-making with his bandmates' to create what would prove to be one of Fleetwood Mac's greatest contributions to the world of rock and roll.

DON'T LOOK DOWN
1982–1986

A few months after the conclusion of Fleetwood Mac's *Mirage* tour and in between recording sessions for what would become 1984's *Go Insane*, Lindsey Buckingham is approached by American actor, director, and writer Harold Ramis, who asks Buckingham to record two songs for inclusion on the soundtrack for the 1983 film *National Lampoon's Vacation*. Buckingham is hesitant at first, believing that soundtrack work is out of his wheelhouse. Despite his reservations, Buckingham ultimately agrees and records two songs for the movie's soundtrack: "Dancin' Across the USA" and "Holiday Road," the latter of which he would release as a single a few months later in the summer of 1983.[1] "Holiday Road" would peak at #82 on the US *Billboard* Hot 100 chart in early August. The song's release and Buckingham's contributions to the *Vacation* soundtrack are just a few of many exciting highs he's experiencing in his career in the aftermath of *Mirage*.

For Buckingham, *Mirage* had felt like nothing more than a remake of *Rumours*. After the disaster that was *Tusk*'s dismal debut, however, he and the band had been left with little choice other than to cling to the same soft-rock and pop formula that made *Rumours* such a success. With Buckingham, Fleetwood, and Christine McVie working on writing, recording, and releasing solo albums throughout the mid-1980s and Nicks planning to release and tour *two* solo albums in the span of two years—albums that would become 1983's *The Wild Heart* and 1985's *Rock a Little*—Fleetwood Mac's fate would remain uncertain until late 1985.

When Lindsey Buckingham, John McVie, and Mick Fleetwood were recruited in early 1985 to supply the instrumentation for a cover of Elvis Presley's "Can't Help Falling in Love" by Christine McVie, the quartet was unknowingly laying the groundwork for the band's follow-up to 1982's *Mirage*. Once the bandmates reestablished contact with one another and with Richard Dashut—who had been contracted to produce McVie's cover of the lead single from Presley's *Blue in Hawaii*—Mick Fleetwood and Warner Bros. began to sense blood in the water. Even though *Tusk* and its successor *Mirage* hadn't sold nearly as many units in their respective debuts as *Rumours* had, Warner Bros. was still eager to milk the cash cow that by 1985 was essentially Lindsey Buckingham's Fleetwood Mac. They were quick to suggest that Buckingham drop his solo schtick in favor of getting the band back together again.

After his breakup with Stevie Nicks in 1976, Lindsey Buckingham hadn't had any trouble finding women willing to take her place. After all, he was an attractive Southern California kid with a knack for writing love songs and guitar solos—not to mention that by the mid-seventies he was part of a band that was quickly becoming one of the biggest names in rock and roll. In fact, it wasn't long before Buckingham met a woman who would prove to be more than just another one of the Fleetwood Mac guitarist's many "conquests."[2] When the couple met, Carol Ann Harris was working as a studio manager at Producer's Workshop—a recording studio in Hollywood—while Buckingham was working to put the finishing touches on what would become Fleetwood Mac's magnum opus, *Rumours*.[3]

Immediately, the two hit it off and for years were inseparable. Following the release of *Rumours*, the two moved in together, and Harris often accompanied Buckingham and the band on tours, trips to the studio, and parties all over the country. Unfortunately for Harris, dating Buckingham during his post-punk/new wave phase was nearly as stressful as being one of his bandmates. While recording *Tusk*, for example, Buckingham would often spend hours on end holed up in the couple's basement, hardly ever coming up for air.[4] Likewise, while recording 1981's *Law and Order* or *Mirage* a year later, Buckingham was intense: while he was capable of intimacy and affection, he could also become cold and detached in an instant.

Regardless, the two were an excellent match early on. Harris, even when she couldn't physically be with her boyfriend in the studio or on tour, was Buckingham's anchor. In addition to the constant emotional support she provided, Harris's influence and consistent presence also helped to keep Buckingham grounded and from indulging in the same self-destructive lifestyle that would cause Mick Fleetwood to declare bankruptcy in the mid-eighties.[5] By late 1978, those close to Buckingham, including his bandmates and *Rumours* co-producer Richard Dashut, could tell that Buckingham was incredibly happy with Harris—perhaps more so than he had ever been before.

Despite the couple's promising start, Buckingham and Harris's relationship had begun to deteriorate by the early 1980s. Much like Buckingham's relationship with Nicks, his lengthy courtship with Harris was ended partially thanks to the influence of rock and roll and hard drugs. A beautiful blonde girl from the small town of Tulsa,

Oklahoma, there was no way that Harris could've predicted what she'd gotten herself into when she'd fallen for Buckingham back in the mid-seventies. Perhaps predictably, like Buckingham's bandmates, Harris would find herself addicted to cocaine and struggling to differentiate between fantasy and reality only a little over a year into her relationship with Fleetwood Mac's lead guitarist.[6]

Eventually, with her mental and physical health crumbling and Buckingham more on edge than ever, it was up to Harris to make a decision: should she continue to risk it all for Buckingham's sake or split from Fleetwood Mac before it was too late? Like Nicks in the late-1980s, Harris was tempting fate by fooling around with Fleetwood Mac and the music industry's most popular poison. Within a few months, Harris had made up her mind. Unfortunately for Buckingham, the choice had been clear, and the two split not long after he and the band released *Mirage* in mid-1982.

Following their separation, Harris remarked:

> It was very lonely… I think I lived my life for Lindsey. I really felt it was important for me to be there for him, whether or not he was there physically, but for him to know I was there at home. He needed me there emotionally. It was rough. I don't think I can remember relaxing the whole time I was with him.[7]

Despite the circumstances that had led to the couple's split, Buckingham and Harris's breakup wasn't nearly as bitter as Buckingham's prior split with Nicks. In fact, Buckingham not only agreed to continue financially supporting Harris in the months following the couple's unanimous split, but he also helped find her a place to live after she moved out of his Los Angeles estate in 1984.[8] Naturally, though his separation from Harris ended in fewer fireworks than his split with Nicks had in the mid-seventies, the sudden deterioration of the couple's relationship still took its toll on Buckingham.

Where else would he go to gather his thoughts?

In early 1984, Buckingham took to Cherokee Studios in Los Angeles to record a new album inspired by his recent breakup with Harris. Like 1981's *Law and Order*, Buckingham's next solo effort was set to be as out-of-the-box as possible and he proves his intentions right off the bat with "I Want You," an album opener that features kooky sound effects coupled with dark, brooding vocals. Though the song does well to demonstrate Buckingham's flair for theatrics, its lyrics are quick to remind listeners why *Go Insane* was recorded in the first place. "I was someone hard to lose," Buckingham sings, amid a flurry of lyrics reminiscent of those to 1975's "I'm So Afraid." Buckingham's lyricism here is as poignant as ever, and the song's lonely lyrics coupled with the track's erratic mid-section work to make "I Want You" a suitable precursor to 1987's "Big Love."

Incredibly, the album's title track "Go Insane" immediately one-ups the chaos of "I Want You" with its classic, over-synthesized 1980s sound. Though "Go Insane's" lyrics are similar to its predecessor's, it has a much grander arrangement, which, like most of the other tracks on the album, features Buckingham on all instruments aside from bass guitar. Though the track to some might listen like little more than an erratic mess of frantic vocals and overlapping percussive effects, it well-represents the process of recording the album in the wake of both Buckingham's split with Harris as well as the compartmentalization of his feelings in the early eighties.

Aside from the obvious refrain of "go insane," Buckingham sings about the troubles of "living," "dying," and "rumors flying," clear references to his time not only with Harris and Nicks but with Fleetwood Mac as well. While putting the finishing touches on *Go Insane*, Buckingham wasn't sure that he'd ever return to the band, a prospect that wouldn't have been the end of the world—especially if his newest album were to become a hit. In fact, he was positive that the band would be quick to move on without him should *Go Insane* manage to top the charts, claiming in a 1984 interview with *Rolling Stone*'s Michael Goldberg that he'd heard "rumors" that the band was "going to seek out somebody else" if he wasn't willing to make another Fleetwood Mac album in the months following the release of his second solo album.[9]

That's not the only evidence that points to Buckingham having Fleetwood Mac on the brain in late 1984, despite what he might've wanted critics to believe. As the title track comes to a close, Buckingham makes yet another reference to his history with Nicks, something still ever apparent even after their split almost ten years ago, by using the final verse of "Go Insane" to liken Harris to Nicks.

Because it's the title track and a perfect fit for 1980s FM radio, "Go Insane" was released as the first single off Buckingham's second solo album. The song would manage to peak at #23 on the US charts, thus becoming Buckingham's second top 40 hit of his solo career, while the album itself would peak at #45 in the US, failing to chart as high as its predecessor, *Law and Order*. Only two tracks into *Go Insane*, it's obvious that Buckingham is a skilled musician and songwriter on his own. Yet, it is also obvious by this point that his creation was destined to become just another mildly successful studio effort, at best. Perhaps *AllMusic* critic William Ruhlmann said it best in his retrospective review of *Go Insane*, writing that:

> at least at this point it appeared that
> Buckingham's solo albums were going
> to serve as laboratory experiments in
> which he tried out new musical ideas

before bringing them to greater popular attention through Fleetwood Mac.[10]

Other standouts from Buckingham's second solo effort include the album's second single, "Slow Dancing,"[11] the two-part epic "Play in the Rain,"[12] and the dynamic album closer "D.W. Suite," a tribute to the Beach Boys' Dennis Wilson.

Buckingham seemed to have accomplished what he set out to do. For one, the album was a far departure from his work with Fleetwood Mac, ripe with material that DJs in the mid-eighties would never dare play on top 40 or FM radio in general. In fact, by the time Buckingham released *Go Insane*, it had been nearly two years since he'd seen any of his former bandmates in the flesh. Though trying to branch out and make a name for himself outside of Fleetwood Mac was a valid excuse for having distanced himself from his bandmates in the mid-1980s, there was no denying that the relationship between Buckingham and the band had soured drastically since the release of *Rumours* in 1977.

Sure, no one would've expected Buckingham and Nicks to be best friends years or even decades after their nasty split in the mid-seventies, but even while recording *Rumours* or *Tusk*, there had never been any real kinship between Buckingham and *anyone* in the band. Having only ever bonded together over a shared interest in making music, the quintet had never really engaged with one another outside of a recording studio.[13] No, in the decade since Buckingham had joined the band, he had never invited Fleetwood out for drinks or gone to see a movie with either of the McVies, and now that Fleetwood Mac had disbanded for a while, leaving time for each of them to develop their own unique sounds, the fragile creative bond holding the band together had been severed.

With no concrete plans to return to Fleetwood Mac and not having fully conquered his demons with *Go Insane*, Buckingham took to the studio again in 1985 with the intention of recording a third solo album.[14] While *Go Insane* and *Law and Order* had been well-received critically, they hadn't been as commercially successful as Buckingham would've liked. Regardless, he still had high hopes for his follow-up to *Go Insane*, which was meant to feature songs like "Big Love," "Caroline," and "Tango in the Night"—three tracks inspired by the aftermath of his breakup with longtime girlfriend Carol Ann Harris in 1984.

Though it finally seemed as if the seas were beginning to part for Buckingham in early 1985, escaping Fleetwood Mac would prove inevitable for the aspiring solo artist only weeks into recording his planned follow-up to *Go Insane*. After being coerced into collaborating with Fleetwood and John McVie to form the rhythm section for a Christine McVie-led cover of Elvis Presley's "Can't Help Falling in Love"[15]—which

McVie had been asked to record for inclusion on the soundtrack for the 1986 film *A Fine Mess*[16]— Buckingham couldn't help but admit that he and his former bandmates sounded great together. After spending the last couple of years keeping strictly to himself, there was no denying that he enjoyed the company, too.

If Buckingham wasn't willing to listen to his heart in early 1985, Mick Fleetwood was dead set on ensuring that Buckingham would listen with his ears. Shortly after completing work on McVie's "Falling in Love," Buckingham learned that McVie had been working on much more than just Elvis Presley cover songs. In fact, when Fleetwood played some of McVie's recently recorded demos for Buckingham, it was one of the first times that tracks like "Everywhere," "Little Lies," and "Isn't It Midnight" had ever seen the light of day.

Though it was impossible to tell so early on that these tracks by McVie would become three of the band's biggest hits, Buckingham had nearly been sold on the spot. He needed some time to think Fleetwood's offer over first. To help him decide, Fleetwood was keenly quick to remind Buckingham that thanks to McVie, the band already had enough material and momentum to move on without him, should they need to.[17]

Only a few weeks later, Buckingham made up his mind.

Sessions for the newly minted Fleetwood Mac project *Tango in the Night* originally took place at

Rumbo Recorders in Canoga Park, California without Stevie Nicks, who was busy on tour to promote her 1985 album *Rock a Little*. Eventually, the sessions moved to Lindsey Buckingham's garage studio in late 1985,[18] around the same time Nicks managed to catch wind of the project.

Like Buckingham, Nicks was sold upon hearing Fleetwood Mac's most recent material—including tracks like McVie's "Little Lies" and Buckingham's "Big Love." Feeling as though her bandmates had cooked up something capable of returning Fleetwood Mac to the top of the charts, she set about recording her own material while on tour, including rough, early demos for tracks like "Welcome to the Room Sara" and "When I See You Again." These tapes were sent to Buckingham and the band for them to tinker with in Nicks's absence.[19] Though Nicks had already established herself as a powerhouse solo act outside of Fleetwood Mac, after she'd heard what her bandmates were doing in L.A., there was no way that she wasn't going to be a part of something that had the potential to reestablish Fleetwood Mac as premier rock and roll royalty.

There was great potential: McVie and Buckingham were doing some of their best work in years, while Nicks, despite her success abroad, was willing to contribute to the album, which Warner Bros. was hoping would finally rival the success of *Rumours*. Unfortunately for Fleetwood Mac, there was trouble brewing as well. The band, though they had never been entirely free from the clutches of hard drugs and financial and personal dissension, had suffered a severe relapse: Buckingham, for one, had become increasingly volatile and was quick to snap at bandmates and critics alike, while Nicks, just beginning to get clean after years of substance abuse, had recently developed an addiction to Klonopin, a tranquilizer even more dangerous than the drug it had been prescribed to treat.[20] Meanwhile, Mick Fleetwood was also at an all-time low, having recently declared bankruptcy.

Remarkably, the band's drug habits would be among the least of their worries this time around, with the quintet's personal inner turmoil being what would most inspire the toxicity of the late eighties' *Tango in the Night* sessions.

Regardless, Fleetwood Mac had faced this level of adversity before. In fact, better yet, this time around, Lindsey Buckingham was already well-versed in creating masterpieces amid controversy and his bandmates' bullshit.

Though Buckingham would manage to pull Fleetwood Mac back from the brink one last time before the early nineties rolled around, the eventual success of *Tango in the Night* would beg the question: with half the album made up of tracks written and recorded by Buckingham, what would've become of his ill-fated solo effort?[21]

There's no way of knowing, of course. However, it's possible that, had Buckingham's solo effort been released as intended, history might remember him as a superstar of the late-1980s, rather than Fleetwood Mac.

1986–1987

Fleetwood Mac is beginning to wrap up production on their fifth studio album set to be released since the start of its Buckingham Nicks era in early 1975. Interestingly, unlike on any of the band's prior albums, little of the material set to be included on 1987's *Tango in the Night* is being recorded collaboratively (or in a studio, for that matter). Instead, the band is distant, taking turns recording their parts one at a time inside a giant RV parked in Lindsey Buckingham's driveway.[1] Nicks, meanwhile, has hardly ever been present to begin with. Instead, she's been on the road for the last two years, working to promote her most recent solo effort, *Rock a Little*. However, to ensure that she'll still be represented on the album, she's been sending demos that she's recorded while on tour to the band back in L.A. for the last couple of months.

By now, Buckingham's used to working on his bandmates' music. After all, he's been doing it for a little over ten years. However, recording *Tango in the Night* had been a whole different ballgame. For one, when Nicks had actually been in L.A. to record, she, like most of her bandmates, hadn't been happy to be there. Still working to recover from a decade-long drug addiction, she'd picked up a habit of downing several shots of brandy before recording any of her vocals. Likewise, Mick Fleetwood, still heavily addicted to the drug-fueled party lifestyle that the band adopted in the late seventies, had recently declared bankruptcy, and like Nicks, could barely keep conscious long enough to produce anything album-worthy. More than 25 years later, Buckingham would recount in an interview with *Something Else!* that, "by the time we did *Tango in the Night,* everybody was leading their lives in a way that they would not be too proud of today. It was difficult for everybody."[2]

Perhaps no single instance better represents the struggle of producing *Tango in the Night* more so than "When I See You Again," a track on *Tango*'s B-side that. While written by Nicks, the song features Buckingham's vocals rather than Nicks's for almost the entirety of the song's second half. More casual listeners might chalk this up to a creative decision on Buckingham's part, though in reality, it had been Nicks's newly developed addiction to Klonopin[3]—the very drug she had been prescribed to help treat her cocaine addiction—that had forced Buckingham's hand, or rather, voice. In fact, the two-and-a-half minutes which actually feature Nicks's vocals were created by Buckingham re-assembling separately recorded takes to create the illusion that Nicks had at least been well enough to record *something* worth presenting to the folks in Burbank.[4]

By late March of 1987, more so than ever before, it's up to Buckingham to pick up the pieces and create an album worthy of selling a couple million copies or so, at least.

Though the band's recording sessions for *Rumours* would become the subject of several documentaries, books, and television programs in the years following the album's initial release in early 1977, the band's much less-publicized *Tango in the Night* sessions were just as (if not more) fascinatingly brutal.

Stevie Nicks's absence for much of the recording and production process would undoubtedly prove to be a source of drama in the album's later stages, while on the opposite end of the spectrum, Buckingham was as obsessive as ever, consistently making a habit of spending entire days at a time in the studio, subjecting co-producer Richard Dashut and engineer Greg Droman to hours upon hours of tedium until they'd achieved nothing short of perfection.

Despite the drama, however, Buckingham's efforts would pay off, big time. As was the case with 1975's *Fleetwood Mac*, the band was certain early on that they had something special in *Tango in the Night*. Though there was no way that any one of them could've predicted just *how well* the album would perform commercially, perhaps the writing had been on the wall all along, seeing as, from the get-go, *Tango in the Night* features some of the best material ever recorded in the band's more than 50-year history.

First up is Buckingham, who sets the mood with "Big Love," a track that was inspired by his breakup with Carol Ann Harris in the mid-eighties. As someone who had managed to maintain constant companionship throughout the mid-seventies and early eighties, Buckingham's split with Harris had hit hard. The track opens with an obvious reference to Buckingham's two-million-dollar L.A. estate—which is nothing more than an impressive bachelor pad to Buckingham now that he's rolling solo[5]—and a subsequent promise to make a kingdom out of his "house on a hill" for any woman willing to take him on as their man.

"Big Love" was released as the first single from *Tango in the Night* in late March 1987. It was a promising start: "Big Love" would manage to reach #5 on the US *Billboard* Hot 100 by the summer of '87 and was the first of four US top 20 hits that the band would release in the span of eight months. If nothing else, *Tango in the Night*'s lead single is a product of Buckingham finally managing to strike a perfect balance between his own style and the soft rock/pop sounds of Fleetwood Mac. Of course, "Big Love" is much more than glittery FM radio fodder. In fact, an all-around Buckingham masterclass, the track easily manages to go above and beyond its purpose of setting the tone of *Tango in the Night* as a shimmering ode to the lush, glam rock of the 1980s—not to mention that the track has since become not only one of Fleetwood Mac's biggest hits but one of the most popular tracks of the entire decade.

It's not surprising how well "Big Love" performed commercially in the months following its release as a single in the late eighties given the song's damn near flawless production values.[6] Though the wildly popular album opener had been written and demoed by Buckingham years before the idea for *Tango in the Night* had ever been conceived, several hours were still dedicated to polishing up the song's arrangement and sound during the album's production in the late-1980s. In fact, Buckingham, Dashut, and Droman—the latter of which had engineered Buckingham's recording of "Time Bomb Town" for the *Back to the Future* soundtrack in 1985[7]—spent so much time reworking *Tango*'s lead single that by the time the song had made its way to the airwaves of FM radio, Droman had long had his fill of "Big Love."[8]

Remarkably, despite the stress and strain that working with Buckingham had put on the relatively inexperienced Droman, there were no hard feelings between the two following the release of *Tango in the Night* in the late-1980s. In fact, it wouldn't be long before Buckingham and Droman would join forces again to collaborate on Buckingham's third solo album, *Out of the Cradle*, in the early 1990s.

Buckingham's "Big Love" segues well into Nicks's "Seven Wonders," the first of only three tracks on *Tango in the Night* to be credited to Nicks. There are several things that make "Seven Wonders" one of the most curious recordings ever released by Fleetwood Mac. For one, the song is one of few tracks in the band's history that doesn't have an identical singer and songwriter in Stevie Nicks. While Nicks is credited with having co-written "Seven Wonders" merely because she misheard one of the song's early lyrics—"all the way down the line" as "all the way down to Emmaline"[9]—the vast majority of the song was actually written by Sandy Stewart,[10] a singer-songwriter famous for having worked with Nicks before on her 1983 album *The Wild Heart* and for her own 1984 album, *Cat Dancer*.[11]

The band's second top 20 single of the late-1980s is also an anomaly given the fact that Nicks's ability to lay down such stunning vocals for the track was nothing short of a miracle, mostly due in part to her extended absence during *Tango*'s recording sessions, her excessive drinking habits in the late-1980s and the influence of Klonopin. Remarkably, thanks to the power of Nicks's voice, the harmony-soaked "Seven Wonders" manages to carry on the lush, exotic tone set forth by Buckingham's "Big Love," and ensures that the band is two-for-two in the lead-up to Christine McVie's equally as dazzling "Everywhere."

Remarkably, while their bandmates were going bankrupt and trying to strangle one another, the McVies were stirring up little to no drama in the late-1980s. Christine McVie, instead, was busy writing and recording hit after hit and is perhaps the most responsible for Fleetwood Mac's return to the forefront of rock and roll over a decade after the release of *Rumours* in 1977.

McVie makes her debut on the album with "Everywhere," a glimmering demand for a lover's undivided attention which features vocal harmonies so gorgeous that they rival those of the Bee Gees' or Eagles'. Interestingly, controversy over these harmonies would be what would finally get McVie ensnared in some good old fashion Fleetwood Mac drama: when Stevie Nicks made a trip to the band's San Francisco studio amid her *Rock a Little* tour to check in on the band's progress, she was distraught to find that her harmonies hadn't been included on McVie's "Everywhere."

Though most of the physical and verbal violence that took place during the production of

Tango in the Night stemmed from conflicts between Buckingham and Nicks, this time it was McVie who lashed out at Nicks after the solo star had dared to criticize the creative decisions that McVie and the band had been making in her absence. Though Nicks's vocals would be added to "Everywhere" before the track's eventual release as *Tango in the Night*'s fourth single in November 1987, McVie was quick to remind Nicks that the band had been working hard to include her on *Tango* despite her constant absence. McVie explained to Nicks that if she didn't like the way that the others were handling things, then perhaps she should have been more of a team-player from the get-go, telling Nicks, "I wanted you to sing on it, too… but you weren't there… Now why don't you tell us you're sorry and we'll work it out."[12]

Ultimately, "Everywhere" would manage to reach #14 on the US *Billboard* Hot 100 chart, and like *Tango*'s three prior singles, "Big Love," "Seven Wonders," and "Little Lies," was released alongside an accompanying music video. Critics have often praised the song's harmonies and lyricism as two of the biggest reasons the song has managed to uphold such an enduring legacy. Further indicative of McVie's impeccable songwriting abilities is that "Everywhere" has maintained a consistent radio presence more than 20 years after its initial release—and that several popular artists, including Chaka Khan, Indigo and Paramore[13] have also recorded covers of McVie's

"Everywhere," either in concert or for inclusion on albums of their own.[14]

In the late fifties and early sixties, much of the music industry shared a similar mentality: that there was little money to be made in albums and that singles were king. In fact, once renowned (and now disgraced) American record producer and songwriter Phil Spector once remarked that albums were nothing more than "two hits and ten pieces of junk."[15] Though perceptions had changed drastically by the early seventies, Fleetwood Mac's *Tango in the Night* is a compelling rebuttal to this argument in and of itself.

The first non-singles to appear on *Tango*'s tracklist are Buckingham's "Caroline," "Tango in the Night" and "Mystified." Though technically a co-write between Buckingham and Christine McVie, "Mystified," just like Buckingham's "Caroline" and "Tango," is an obvious product of the experimental freedom Buckingham had had in the studio thanks to Nicks's absence for a majority of *Tango in the Night*'s recording process.

Each of the three tracks that close the album's A-side, despite never being released as singles, serve as showcases of Buckingham's capabilities in the studio. For one, "Caroline"—a track with a clear inspiration—contains Buckingham's best lyricism since 1977's "Go Your Own Way."[16] Early on, Buckingham sings of a "fatal fury" and "cutting cords," effectively summarizing his early eighties split with Harris in less than 60 seconds.

Meanwhile, the album's title track not only features more of the Fleetwood Mac frontman's impeccable lyricism but also a thunderous guitar solo as well, one that seems to come to an end just a bit too soon—yet is still one of Buckingham's greatest of all time.

Finally, Buckingham and McVie's "Mystified" is the peak of *Tango in the Night*'s often borderline over-extravagance, thanks to the track's high-gloss instrumentation and McVie's saccharine vocals. More than just a piece of ear candy, "Mystified" is an excellent precursor to the kind of magic that Buckingham and McVie would later create together on their 2017 self-titled studio effort, *Lindsey Buckingham/Christine McVie*.

Though all the tracks on *Tango*'s A-side are well-deserving of inclusion on the album, fans would later discover that several tracks that *didn't* make the cut were just as impressive.

Buckingham's "Down Endless Street," for example, is one of the greatest studio efforts by the band that was nearly lost to time. Almost 30 years after *Tango in the Night*'s initial release, the song was featured on a 2017 deluxe reissue of the album.[17] If there had been a Fleetwood Mac album released in between 1982's *Mirage* and *Tango in the Night*, perhaps that's where "Down Endless Street" would have fit in best, with its upbeat, airy instrumentals that are just a smidge too tame for

Tango in the Night and its strong, clear vocals that are just a bit too masculine for *Mirage.*

Likewise, Christine McVie's "Ricky" is another tune that was left off the album and instead was used as the B-side to one of the band's bigger hits, "Little Lies." Unlike "Down Endless Street," "Ricky" is a track that would have been a perfect fit for the peculiarly sultry *Tango in the Night.* Namely, it's McVie's uncharacteristically lunging vocals paired with a thunderous drum beat and glittering backing instrumentals that give the track a distinctly exotic feel that tracks like *Tango*'s "Family Man" or "Welcome to the Room Sara" aren't quite able to pull off as well.

Even more obscure are the outtakes and demos for "Ooh My Love," "Where We Belong," the instrumental "Book of Miracles" and Nicks's "Juliet," the latter of which would later be re-recorded for inclusion on Nicks's 1989 solo album, *The Other Side of the Mirror.*[18] Of these, it's "Juliet" that would have sounded the most out of place on *Tango in the Night,* namely because of its hard-rock sound and Nicks's explicitly narrative lyricism that is often characteristic of her solo work. Regardless, the track, both as a rough, unedited album reject and as a Nicks solo feature, is a fantastic track that is one of the witchy woman's most underrated masterpieces.

It's clear from the very beginning that Fleetwood Mac's newest album features some of the band's finest work to date. However, *Tango in the Night* can hardly be considered a "return to form" for the fiery five-some.

Instead, perhaps the album's superb A-side is even more impressive considering that the band isn't playing off the sounds and success of *Rumours* like they had with *Mirage* or clinging to any of *Tusk*'s strengths. Rather, it's clear that, early on, Fleetwood Mac has achieved something uniquely special in *Tango* by creating an album that manages to incorporate new sounds, styles, and direction without *completely* neglecting any of the band's earlier works or influences.

Even more impressive—though hardly surprising—is that *Tango in the Night* is the first Fleetwood Mac album to *finally* credit Lindsey Buckingham by name as one of its producers, and it shows: *Tango in the Night* contains gorgeously arranged hit after hit and listens like a cohesive piece of exotic pop-art perfectly suited for the 1980s and beyond—and that's only to speak of the album's first half.

As was the case with *Rumours*, however, the glitzy, polished, made-for-pop-radio sounds of *Tango in the Night* belie a bubbling tension among members of the band that was set to come to a head just before recording sessions would be declared a wrap in early 1987.

WAIT FOR YOU
1987–1988

Fleetwood Mac is live at San Francisco's Cow Palace, embroiled in a passionate performance of Christine McVie's "Isn't It Midnight," a song that would eventually be released as a single from the band's most recent studio effort, *Tango in the Night*. Though "Isn't It Midnight" has been a concert staple for the band ever since they set out on tour in late September, this performance is special for several reasons. For one, it's being recorded for a VHS concert special set to be released in an effort to bolster *Tango in the Night*'s sales numbers.[1] However, most notably, this performance of "Isn't It Midnight" is a highly publicized outing for two new members of the band: Billy Burnette and Rick Vito.

Burnette, a rockabilly singer and guitarist, and Vito, a popular session musician known for working with the likes of Bob Seger and Jackson Browne, are owning the stage as if they've been a part of Fleetwood Mac since the very beginning. Vito, the band's new lead guitarist, bobs his head under the glow of purple stage lights, while, in collaboration with Burnette, also lends his vocals to "Isn't It Midnight's" haunting, self-identifying refrain. The band sounds great, and their performance is energized. Regardless, it's a strange sight for longtime Fleetwood Mac fans, who have become accustomed to seeing Lindsey Buckingham slaying heavy guitar-driven tracks like McVie's "Midnight."

Unfortunately for longtime fans of Lindsey Buckingham, the band's *Tango in the Night* tour— also known as the Shake the Cage tour—is just the beginning of a new era for Fleetwood Mac. In fact, after leaving the band behind in late August 1987, Buckingham had unknowingly set in motion a devastating domino effect—one that would ultimately culminate in an unprecedented low point for Fleetwood Mac. However, because the band seems to be in such high spirits tonight, it's impossible to know what's to come. What's obvious for classic fans of the band, however, is that this "new" Fleetwood Mac is something that will take some getting used to.[2]

Tango in the Night's B-side is much more than just the place where tracks like McVie's sensational "Little Lies" or the album's mildly successful fifth single, "Family Man" find a home.[3] In fact, much of the material included on the second half of the band's wildly popular 1987 release would prove to be the source of most of the drama that plagued *Tango*'s grueling recording sessions. Tracks like Nicks's "When I See You Again," for example, managed to put a further strain on Buckingham and Nicks's relationship, thanks to the number of creative liberties Buckingham would be forced to take in order to make the song worthy of inclusion on the album to begin with. Meanwhile, tracks like Nicks's other B-side contribution, "Welcome to the Room Sara," detail the band's inner turmoil via its autobiographical lyrics.

Tango in the Night's B-side opens with Christine McVie's "Little Lies," a track that is undoubtedly one of the greatest Fleetwood Mac songs to be released in the 1980s (or ever, for that matter). The song, which features a simple refrain and minimal lyricism, has since become one of the Mac's biggest hits simply because of how catchy it is. For the most part, it's McVie and Nicks's stellar vocal work on "Little Lies" that has helped the US top 10 hit to maintain a consistent FM radio presence more than 30 years after its initial release in August 1987.

Interestingly, however, not all of the track's success can be contributed solely to members of Fleetwood Mac, as "Little Lies'" success as a single is also due in part to McVie's husband Eddy Quintela, who she married in 1986. Quintela, McVie's co-write for "Little Lies," would also manage to play a similar role in engineering one of Fleetwood Mac's other great hits of the late-1980s, McVie's "Isn't It Midnight." The couple would remain a formidable songwriting duo up until their eventual divorce in 2003.[4]

McVie's smash hit is followed up by Buckingham's "Family Man" and Nicks's "Welcome to the Room Sara," the former of which would be released as *Tango in the Night*'s fifth single in late 1987 to very mild success. While Buckingham's "Family Man" is yet another shimmering, up-tempo ode to Buckingham's impressive lyrical skills, Nicks's "Welcome to the Room" is a slow-moving ballad that tackles much more serious subject matter. Specifically, the song details a recent visit by Nicks to the Betty Ford Center in Rancho Mirage, California, where she was treated for her more than decade-long addiction to cocaine.[5]

Though "Welcome to the Room Sara" comes off a bit sluggish when compared to the rest of *Tango*'s tracklist—which features upbeat anthems like Buckingham's "Big Love" or McVie's "Little Lies"—Nicks's solemn reflection on her time in rehab is still an important contribution to the album. For one, the gloomy track manages to establish *Tango in the Night* as more than just a collection of bubbly 1980s pop-rock ballads as it brings to light the inner turmoil that Nicks faced throughout the mid-to-late eighties. Not only that, but the song also marks an important turning point in the rock and roll legend's life, as it signaled the end of her devastating addiction to cocaine—an addiction that had nearly claimed her life several times in the years leading up to the release of *Tango in the Night*.[6]

Christine McVie's "Isn't It Midnight," famous for its fantastic lyricism as well as its guitar work by Buckingham, was released as the final single from *Tango in the Night* in June of 1988.[7] The song, co-written by McVie, Quintela, and Buckingham, is a hard-rock anthem featuring McVie on lead vocals, who, via her performance, manages to prove that she's a versatile vocalist, able to tackle any genre of music with ease.

Thanks to the track's heavy, guitar-driven style and brash sound uncharacteristic of any of *Tango in the Night*'s prior singles, "Isn't It Midnight" would quickly become a live concert staple for the band in the late eighties and early nineties, consistently finding a place on the tracklists for Fleetwood Mac's *Tango in the Night* and subsequent *Behind the Mask* tours. Regardless of its many accolades, however, if nothing else, "Isn't It Midnight" serves as a further testament to Christine McVie's role as Fleetwood Mac's driving creative force in the late-1980s. In fact, many contemporary critics contend that McVie—rather than *Tango in the Night* co-producer Lindsey Buckingham—was most responsible for the band's success in the late eighties. *NME* posthumously wrote in 2022 that:

> following the continued success of the more experimental 'Tusk' (1979) and consolidatory 'Mirage' (1982)… it was again McVie's songs which would epitomise the synthetic pop sounds of Fleetwood Mac's second biggest record 'Tango In The Night' in 1987, and which would make the most lasting mark. 'Everywhere', particularly, became a DJ staple as the 1980s revival kicked off in earnest in the mid- to late-'00s… her 1980s masterpieces 'Everywhere' and 'Little Lies' [were] effectively the bedrocks of the '80s revivalism which has set the tone for so much 21st century music.[8]

Finally, *Tango in the Night* wraps up with Nicks's "When I See You Again" (a track infamous for its nasally vocals), and "You and I, Part II," the third and final co-write between Buckingham and McVie to be featured on the album. The latter of the two tracks, Buckingham and McVie's "You and I, Part II," would later be released by the band in 2017 as a full-length track featuring the song's initially discarded first half.[9] Regardless, even in its original, partial form, "You and I, Part II" is a strong end to *Tango in the Night,* an album that is by far one of the band's greatest triumphs to date.

Tango in the Night would become the band's second best-selling album of all time following its release in April 1987, eventually managing to outsell both of its recent predecessors *Mirage* and *Tusk.* Initially peaking at #7 on the US *Billboard* Hot 200 charts, the album would spend more than 10 months within the *Billboard* top 40. Even for the band that had managed to top the *Billboard* 200 charts for more than 30 non-consecutive weeks following the release of *Rumours* in 1977,[10] this was an impressive feat.

The album would spawn four top 20 singles in the US and three top 10 hits in the UK, where it would also manage to top the charts three times within one year of its initial release. To this day, *Tango in the Night* remains one of the UK's best-selling albums of all time, while tracks like McVie's "Everywhere," "Little Lies," and Nicks's "Seven Wonders" are often considered to be classics of the era in and of themselves.

Unfortunately for Fleetwood Mac, despite having finally established themselves as premiere rock and roll icons of the 1980s, there was little time to celebrate their return to the top. After the stress of recording the album, Buckingham was exhausted. By the time *Tango in the Night* hit shelves, his relationship with Nicks was as sour as ever, not to mention that Nicks's ongoing addiction to Klonopin meant that she had hit a bitter low point—one that would last for the better part of eight, long years.[11] Fed up with his bandmates' bullshit and not willing to witness Nicks continue down such a devastating path of self-destruction, Buckingham decided to distance himself from Fleetwood Mac. As Mick Fleetwood wrote in 2014:

> *Tango in the Night* came out in the spring and jumped into the Top 10 on both sides of the Atlantic. In the UK it even reached number 1 and sold more than two million copies. The next logical step was to tour the record. Everyone was ready to go, except for Lindsey. He wanted to stay home and finish his solo record, which ostensibly would put an end to this cycle of Fleetwood Mac.[12]

As history would have it, of course, Buckingham ultimately resigned from the band in August 1987, a little over a month before the band was set to begin their *Tango in the Night* tour.

Buckingham's departure dealt a great blow to the band, who owed a lot of *Tango in the Night*'s success to their former guitarist. Regardless, with Buckingham dead set on going solo for the foreseeable future, Fleetwood Mac would recover—temporarily—to save their upcoming tour from the clutches of purgatory by adding not one, but two guitarists to the band's lineup in an effort to replace Buckingham.

Rick Vito, a handsome slide guitarist and singer best known for having been featured on albums like Todd Rundgren's third studio album *Something/Anything?* in 1970 and Bonnie Raitt's *Green Light* in 1982, was hired by Mick Fleetwood only weeks after Buckingham's departure as the band's new lead guitarist without so much as an audition.

Likewise, Billy Burnette, a former member of Mick Fleetwood's Zoo,[13] was also hired without an audition based on the singer/songwriter's impressive credentials. In addition to his earlier work with Fleetwood, Burnette's resume included a catalog of five solo albums that the rock and roller had released prior to 1987, including 1986's *Soldier of Love*.[14]

After touring for a little less than a year as a newly minted sextet in support of 1987's *Tango in the Night*, the band eventually returned to L.A. in late 1989 sans Buckingham to record *Behind the Mask*—the only Fleetwood Mac album ever released to feature the unique lineup of Burnette, Vito, Nicks, Fleetwood, and the McVies.

Despite the band's early crisis control, fans of Fleetwood Mac could see that disaster was inevitable come the early 1990s. For one, Buckingham seemed to be doing just fine on his own, using his breakup with Nicks and recent departure from the band to his advantage to create a poignant solo album aptly entitled, *Out of the Cradle.*[15]

Meanwhile, back on the band's home front, sales would quickly begin to dissipate following the release of 1990's *Behind the Mask*, the band's first and last studio album of the nineties to feature either Stevie Nicks or Rick Vito, who would each resign from Fleetwood Mac within weeks of wrapping up the band's nearly nine-month-long tour of the same name.

Despite the obvious signs of trouble that would arise in the aftermath of Buckingham's sudden departure in the late eighties, perhaps nothing is more indicative of how much the band relied on Buckingham for its success than the release of Fleetwood Mac's *Greatest Hits* album in 1988.

Using 1975's *Fleetwood Mac* as its starting point, the 1988 US release of *Greatest Hits* is a compilation album that spans an over 10-year period of the band's greatest commercial success. Plans for the album were initially drawn up just before the summer of 1988. *Greatest Hits* would include liner notes from the band's former road manager John Courage and be:

> a compilation of the current band's best
> songs, augmented by new tracks from

Stevie and Christine... [and] released for the holidays in all three formats: compact disc, vinyl, and cassette. Warner Bros... ordered a huge advance pressing.[16]

The album contains tracks like Nicks's "Rhiannon" (from *Fleetwood Mac*) and McVie's "You Make Loving Fun" (from *Rumours*), as well as several tracks from 1979's *Tusk* and its successors *Mirage* and *Tango in the Night*. Despite there also being two new tracks on the album, including McVie's "As Long as You Follow"—which would be released as a single to promote the album in late November 1988[17]—there's no denying that it contains an overwhelmingly large number of tracks either written, recorded, or produced by Lindsey Buckingham.

Despite having been long gone by the time *Greatest Hits* would be released in the late-1980s, Buckingham manages to maintain a sizeable presence on the album. In fact, if it seems as though Buckingham's influence is ever-present from the album's start to finish, it's because it is. Even if it's not a Buckingham-penned track like "Big Love," on which he's the main attraction, his incredible instrumental work speaks for itself on tracks like McVie's "Hold Me" or Nicks's "Gypsy," while his glimmering production values are perhaps why tracks like 1977's "Dreams" or 1979's "Tusk" were even able to manage a place on the album to begin with.

Having to hire two musicians to do the job of one Lindsey Buckingham had already cast a shadow of doubt over Fleetwood Mac's aspirations heading into the early nineties. However, perhaps it was 1988's *Greatest Hits* that had been the most frightening sign of things to come.

After all, without Lindsey Buckingham, the architect behind much of Fleetwood Mac's success in the late seventies and eighties, how likely was it that the band would be able to emulate a similar level of success in his absence?

Only *Time* would tell.

F I R E F L I E S

1990–1996

Fleetwood Mac release *25 Years – The Chain*, a box set containing four CDs featuring more than 40 hit songs released by the band since its formation in 1967. The set contains tracks like Peter Green's "Black Magic Woman," several previously unreleased tracks from albums like 1982's *Mirage*, and Stevie Nicks's "Silver Springs," the latter of which had been previously left off of 1977's *Rumours* because of space limitations on the band's smash-hit LP, much to Nicks's fury. However, it's the song's inclusion on

25 Years – The Chain that's managed to infuriate Nicks this time around, who'd been informed by Mick Fleetwood one year earlier that because "Silver Springs" was *technically* a Fleetwood Mac song, it wouldn't be appropriate for the song to also be included on Nicks's 1991 album, *Timespace: The Best of Stevie Nicks*.[1]

As a result, by the time *25 Years – The Chain* was released in late 1992, several of the band's biggest names—including Buckingham and Nicks—had jumped ship, leaving behind a band that now, at best, was little more than a shell of its former self. Still, the band would soldier on through the mid-nineties to release the ill-fated album *Time*, featuring a line-up consisting of Mick Fleetwood, John and Christine McVie, Billy Burnette, and newcomer to the band Bekka Bramlett—a former member of Mick Fleetwood's early nineties band, The Zoo. The album would prove to be the worst-performing album in the band's history, and only months after *Time*'s initial release in late 1995, Christine McVie, Burnette, and Bramlett would each announce their resignation from Fleetwood Mac.

By early 1996, Fleetwood Mac had been completely disbanded less than 10 years after Lindsey Buckingham's sudden departure from the band in the late-1980s. There are two things that might be attributed to Lindsey Buckingham: the enduring, internal chaos of Fleetwood Mac, and the band's immense commercial success. In the aftermath of *Time*, however, it's clear that even without Buckingham, the band is destined to fight and feud regardless. It's also clear, though, that without Buckingham, Fleetwood Mac is a far cry from a multimillion-dollar money maker capable of producing platinum albums like *Rumours* or *Tango in the Night*. All of this means to say, of course, that come the mid-nineties, it's abundantly clear that the band is much more reliant on Buckingham for its success, rather than its drama, and that the reality was this: if there was ever going to be a Fleetwood Mac again, Buckingham would have to be the one to bring the band back from the dead.

Fleetwood Mac didn't immediately crumble in the aftermath of Lindsey Buckingham's departure, of course. In fact, the chemistry among new and old band members was promising. Billy Burnette would later remark that:

> When I joined the band, I already felt like part of the family. So it was easy. I'll never forget the first day of rehearsal when Stevie walked up to me in the parking lot. We rehearsed at this place where I had filmed a movie before. She walked up and goes, "Sounds like Fleetwood Mac to me."
>
> We rehearsed the songs. Everyone got along great. We did our first date in Kansas City. It was fantastic. I don't

think we got a bad review on that *Tango in the Night* tour until we got to Pittsburgh.[2]

The band's live performances went off without a hitch in the immediate aftermath of Buckingham's exit—including a sold-out show at Wembley Stadium in late 1987.[3] Even the band's next studio album, 1990's *Behind the Mask*—the first Fleetwood Mac album recorded and released without Buckingham since 1974's *Heroes Are Hard to Find*—was also a hit. Ultimately, the album would peak at #18 on the US *Billboard* Hot 200 and at #1 on the UK Albums Chart by the end of May 1990. *Behind the Mask* was co-produced by Greg Ladanyi,[4] best known for his earlier production and engineering work with Jackson Browne, Don Henley, and Kansas on albums like 1977's *Running on Empty* and 1989's *The End of Innocence*. The album spawned three singles in the US: Christine McVie's "Save Me" and "Skies the Limit," as well as "Love is Dangerous," a duet between Nicks and new Fleetwood Mac lead guitarist Rick Vito.

"Save Me"—a product of Christine McVie and Eddy Quintela looking to carry their success as a songwriting duo over from the band's *Tango in the Night* sessions—was the album's most successful single, managing to crack the US Top 40. The song, not unlike McVie and Quintela's other collaborative efforts, features a catchy chorus as well as some searing guitar work by Vito.

While much less successful than their predecessor, the album's other two singles still achieved moderate airplay on US FM radio in the early 1990s.[5] Meanwhile, other standouts from the album include Burnette's "In the Back of My Mind" and Nicks's "Affairs of the Heart."

While his former bandmates were busy recording, releasing, and touring their new album in the early 1990s, Lindsey Buckingham was spending most of his time in recording studios as well, working with former Fleetwood Mac producer Richard Dashut to engineer what would finally become his third solo album, *Out of the Cradle.*

Though the album features a variety of genres, including hard-rock numbers and poignant pop anthems, Buckingham's third solo album, released in June 1992, actually best suits the early nineties grunge movement that had peaked just the year before with the release of albums like Nirvana's *Nevermind* and Pearl Jam's *Ten.*

Out of the Cradle features a whopping 16 tracks—three of which are instrumental or spoken introductions to a subsequent track. Standouts from the album include a cover of The Kingston Trio's "All My Sorrows" as well as Buckingham's "Wrong," "Soul Drifter," "Street of Dreams," "You Do or You Don't," and "Turn It On."

Specifically of note here is that while Buckingham again performs most of the instrumental work on the album, *Out of the Cradle* does—like 1981's *Law and Order*—feature some big-name guest personnel, including Larry Klein[6] on bass (on tracks like "Wrong" and "This is the Time") and producer Mitchell Froom,[7] who plays the organ for track #14 on the album, "Turn It On." Additionally, Buckingham's cover of "All My Sorrows" and original recording "Street of Dreams" feature Buell Neidlinger, a "versatile genre- and style-hopping bassist, composer, and music teacher."[8]

Also of note, of course, is the familiar inspiration for Buckingham's "Street of Dreams": Fleetwood Mac—the same group that inspired Buckingham to write track #3 on the album, "Wrong." Specifically, "Street of Dreams" was inspired by Buckingham's desperate search for creative freedom and liberty throughout the late 1970s and 1980s, particularly in the aftermath of *Tusk*'s supposedly disastrous debut. Written during the period immediately following his split with Fleetwood Mac in the late 1980s, Buckingham's "Street of Dreams" is "about the exercise and the discipline… of dreaming dreams and acting on those and how lonely that can be," Buckingham would later explain, noting that "Street of Dreams" is also about "how satisfying it can be ultimately, but how it takes a certain amount of wherewithal to do that."[9]

Particularly poignant is the song's bridge, where Buckingham sings, "There's a shadow on my daddy's stone, where he was laid, laid to rest / I ask him is this just a dream, or is it just another test?"[10] Buckingham would explain that in the song's bridge:

> I'm imagining myself at the cemetery where my father is buried and talking to him... asking him, "Will I ever stop trying to attain this particular sensibility?" In my head, he's looking at me going, "No, you're always going to be that person, dummy." That's what the song is about... in the midst of all that you're... looking for someone to share that sensibility... which for many years was not that easy to find.[11]

Speaking of sensibility, Buckingham's "Wrong" also makes reference to Fleetwood Mac—or, in particular—to Mick Fleetwood himself. In the song, Buckingham croons, "Everybody's heard it / How everything went wrong / Advance was spent some time ago."[12] A thinly veiled dig at Mick Fleetwood, Buckingham's "Wrong" was inspired by Mick's 1990 memoir, *Fleetwood: My Life and Adventures in Fleetwood Mac*: a book that, despite its fun title, was nothing more than pitiful self-promotion on Fleetwood's part, according to Buckingham. Buckingham would also claim that Fleetwood's book features several falsified scenes, including one in which Buckingham allegedly attempted to physically assault Stevie Nicks during the band's tense recording sessions for *Tango in the Night*.[13] "[It was] just kind of a real trashy thing," Buckingham would later remark dryly, also explaining that Fleetwood "doesn't have a mechanism for self-editing... or perhaps discerning where the line is."[14]

"Wrong" was released as the album's second single in August of 1992, one month after *Out of the Cradle*'s first single "Countdown" was released. These two singles were ultimately followed by "Soul Drifter" in November 1992—a song with an "Americana kind of feel" that Buckingham would label in 2021 as his "most romantic song"[15]—and the album's fourth and final single, "Don't Look Down," which would be released in April 1993. While none of the singles from *Out of the Cradle* managed to crack the US Hot 100 Chart or UK Singles Chart, all four songs did peak within the top 60 on Canada's Top 100 Chart.

Despite the variety of genres represented on the album, *Out of the Cradle* manages to maintain a consistent theme, one well-representative of Buckingham's feelings following his split not only from Nicks in the late-1970s but in the aftermath of his recent falling out with Fleetwood Mac as well.

Perhaps that is *Out of the Cradle*'s greatest strength.

Something that seems to plague a majority of recording artists that decide to branch out into solo careers is blandness: think Ringo Starr's

"Sentimental Journey"—an album described as "horrendous" by *Rolling Stone* critic Greil Marcus[16]—or Christine McVie's 1984 self-titled solo effort—an album likewise deemed by the publication as "a little on the tame side."[17]

However, Buckingham's one and only solo album of the 1990s succeeds in defying this trend, in that *Out of the Cradle* is an album that manages to listen like a collection of 16 diverse tracks, each of which sounds far different from the last. Whether it's the drastic change in tempo that occurs in between "All My Sorrows" and "Soul Drifter" or the dramatic change in pace that becomes apparent as "You Do or You Don't" transitions into "Street of Dreams," Buckingham achieves something that many equally as well-established artists have tried and failed to accomplish.

Though what Buckingham is able to achieve on *Out of the Cradle* might seem like a remarkably minor feat, it's important to remember that variety was something that had come much more easily to Buckingham while working with Fleetwood Mac. After all, the band had featured three singer-songwriters, each with their own distinct sense of style—which means to say that, for example, in the band's entire history, no one has ever listened to "Never Going Back Again" and "Don't Stop" back-to-back and thought that the two tracks were indistinguishable.

For Buckingham to emulate the same kind of diverse sound on his own album makes *Out of the*

Cradle one of his best solo efforts to date, not to mention that the album's ability to chart within the top 200 on both the US and UK Albums charts is equally as impressive. Unsurprisingly, given the strength of the album as a whole, Buckingham would later label *Out of the Cradle* his most "fulfilling solo work"[18] and one of his favorite albums.[19] Meanwhile, record label and production company Rhino would also retrospectively deem the album "a creative triumph" and "a gorgeously produced album filled with some of the strongest music of [Buckingham's] career as a solo artist."[20]

In early 1993, only a few months after Buckingham released the incredible *Out of the Cradle*, a special voice came calling for the reunification of Fleetwood Mac. While a call from the band's longtime record label Warner Bros. might have fallen on deaf ears, a request from then-president-elect Bill Clinton succeeded in capturing the band's attention.

Unwilling to give up such an opportunity, the band decided to put their differences aside for a one-off live performance of what had been the theme song for Clinton's presidential campaign: "Don't Stop"—a song that had "played in a seemingly endless loop from the night of Clinton's nomination at the 1992 Democratic National Convention that previous summer through to election night in November."[21]

Even though it had been more than five years since the band's *"Rumours 5"* line-up shared a stage, their performance at Clinton's inaugural gala was a hit: by the time their sensational live performance of "Don't Stop" concluded, the famous five-some had been joined on stage by the First Family and several other special guests, including Michael Jackson and Chuck Berry.[22]

It was a big night for the band, whose performance at the president's Inaugural Ball would spark a revived public interest in Fleetwood Mac. Despite the free outpouring of publicity, the band still had no plans to reunite again for the foreseeable future. Given what was to come, however, perhaps the band should have made a case for Buckingham's immediate reinstatement that very night.

1994 was the beginning of a historic low point for Fleetwood Mac, who began production on their follow-up to 1990's *Behind the Mask* shortly after vocalists Stevie Nicks and Rick Vito departed the band in late 1991. To replace Nicks and Vito, the band added country vocalist Bekka Bramlett and former Traffic guitarist Dave Mason to its lineup prior to Fleetwood Mac's Another Link in the Chain tour in 1994.

A precursor to what was to come, the lengthy world tour was an embarrassing couple of months for Fleetwood Mac, who while on the road were tasked with opening for Crosby, Stills and Nash before being forced to tour as a part of a package deal that also included REO Speedwagon and Pat Benatar in 1995.[23] Though while on tour the band was able to consistently perform several of Fleetwood Mac's greatest hits in concert, the tour was still a far cry from the days when the band was selling out stadiums and headlining their own shows.

A month after the band's "Chain" tour was declared a wrap in early September 1995, the band's new lineup consisting of Bramlett, Mason, Billy Burnette, and Fleetwood Mac namesakes John McVie and Mick Fleetwood—as well as Christine McVie, who had been absent during the band's most recent world tour—released Fleetwood Mac's 16th studio effort overall, *Time*.

The album is ironically a production that might as well have been lost to its namesake. Of the 13 tracks included on the album, only Christine McVie's "I Do"—a co-write between her and husband Quintela—was released as a single, to remarkably little success.[24]

Unfortunately, not only would the failure of *Time*'s first single signal what was an apparent, significant decline in Fleetwood Mac's popularity by the mid-1990s, but it would also serve as evidence that not even McVie's knack for writing catchy pop songs would be able to save the band now.

In addition to McVie's "I Do," other standouts from the album include Dave Mason's "Blow by Blow" and Mick Fleetwood's "These Strange

Times," which unfortunately are *Time*'s greatest standouts for all the wrong reasons.

What's immediately apparent is that Mason's work with Fleetwood Mac is hardly comparable to the type of work he'd been doing with Traffic on and off in the late sixties and early seventies. Even at its best, Mason's "Blow by Blow" is little more than middle-ground soft rock that might be remembered as one of the band's biggest hits only if Fleetwood Mac had still been relative unknowns trying to make it in the music industry by the mid-1990s.

Equally if not more disturbing than Mason's "Blow by Blow" is the album closer "These Strange Times," a track with lead vocals performed by none other than Mick Fleetwood himself. A spoken-word piece just over seven minutes in length, "These Strange Times" several times over alludes to Fleetwood's ex-bandmate Peter Green and the former Fleetwood Mac frontman's descent into madness in the late 1960s. Interestingly, "These Strange Times" is the second track to be released by the band in the 1990s that features Fleetwood on lead vocals—the first of which, "Lizard People," had been the B-side to the 1990 single "In the Back of My Mind."

Unsurprisingly, the album was torn apart upon its debut by critics and fans alike, who lambasted *Time* as an odd, subdued effort that hardly deserved to have been released under the banner of Fleetwood Mac. While the album is able to manage a few high points here and there, such as Bramlett's "Dreamin' the Dream" and McVie's "All Over Again,"[25] in the end, *Time* just wasn't what fans had come to expect from the band responsible for albums like 1975's *Fleetwood Mac* and the 1977 smash-hit *Rumours*.

Perhaps there was no one breathing a bigger sigh of relief in the wake of *Time*'s disastrous debut than Stevie Nicks, who by 1995 had already released three solo albums in five years, each of which sold more copies within one year of their respective releases than *Time* has since managed to sell in its entire lifetime. While *Time* also struggled to claw its way to #47 on the UK Albums Chart and completely failed to make it anywhere close to charting in the US, all three of Nicks's solo efforts—including 1989's *The Other Side of the Mirror* and 1994's *Street Angel*—charted in both territories, with her 1989 solo effort having peaked at #10 on the US *Billboard* Hot 200 in the summer of 1989.

In the aftermath of *Time*'s disastrous debut, most of the band elected to follow Nicks's early lead and jump ship with what little of their dignity they had left. Christine McVie, for example, who deserved to be a part of something better than what was little more than a Fleetwood Mac cover band by late 1995, was quick to inform her bandmates that *Time* would be her last album with Fleetwood Mac.[26] Likewise, Burnette and Bramlett, never truly having been welcomed into the band by longtime Fleetwood Mac fans, decided to make a go of it on their own soon after the release of *Time*, subsequently forming a country music duo called Bekka & Billy in late 1996. Interestingly, the duo would eventually release their own self-titled debut in 1997 to mild critical acclaim,[27] only to break up a year later, however.[28]

As for Dave Mason and John McVie, they too were forced to look for jobs elsewhere following the complete disbandment of Fleetwood Mac by Mick Fleetwood in the mid-1990s, a move which brought to a head an incredible turn of events: remarkably, only months after the release of their 16th studio effort, the wildly popular rock and roll band Fleetwood Mac suddenly ceased to exist.

Despite its flaws, if nothing else, *Time* retrospectively exists as an accurate foretelling of what was to become of the band in late 1995 via the lyrics to Christine McVie's "All Over Again," which suggest that come the mid-1990s, it was finally time for the band to "break the chain" once and for all.

The beloved *Rumours*-era Fleetwood Mac is back and live on stage at Warner Bros. Studios in Burbank, California. A little over halfway through their performance, which is being recorded for the *MTV* television special, *The Dance*, the band has already covered some of their greatest hits live, including Nicks's "Dreams," McVie's "Say You Love Me," and Buckingham's "I'm So Afraid," as well as previously unreleased material like McVie's sprightly "Temporary One." Among these new and recently unearthed tracks by the band is Stevie

Nicks's "Silver Springs," a track largely unheard of after it had been axed from the band's magnum opus *Rumours* and instead released as a B-side to Buckingham's hit single, "Go Your Own Way" in 1976.

Nicks of course is the star once "Silver Springs" begins about an hour into the band's lengthy setlist, but she's willing to share the spotlight with her guitarist by the time the song's chorus comes around. While in perfect harmony with Buckingham, Nicks stares her ex-boyfriend down as she promises that her voice will forever haunt him. The onstage tension between the two continues through the song's dramatic conclusion, as Nicks reaches a fever pitch fans have rarely seen on stage since her violent early performances of "Rhiannon" in the late-1970s. A potent response to Buckingham's "Go Your Own Way," Nicks is finally getting to tell her side of the story, while all her bandmates can do is sit back and watch the drama unfold.

By the end of the show, which would also include passionate renditions of the band's hit singles "Don't Stop" and "Tusk" performed in conjunction with the USC Marching Band, it's clear that Fleetwood Mac is finally back in business after almost an entire decade apart. Fleetwood Mac fans, happy to have their favorite band of the late seventies and eighties back together, went wild over *The Dance*, and unsurprisingly, the album debuted at #1 on the US *Billboard* Hot 200 in early September 1997 and sold over a million copies in less than nine weeks in the US alone. Needless to say, 1997's *The Dance* gave Fleetwood Mac more than enough momentum to build off of heading into the early 21st century. And despite having already been a formidable force in the world of rock and roll for more than 20 years by the early 2000s, it was obvious with the release of *The Dance* that Fleetwood Mac was still far from ready to start taking things slow.

Following the disastrous release of *Time* and the subsequent disbandment of Fleetwood Mac in late 1995, Lindsey Buckingham invited Mick Fleetwood and John McVie—the Mac's former rhythm section—to perform on one of his upcoming solo efforts. At the time, the album was still in its very early stages, yet, perhaps because Fleetwood Mac had officially been dismantled only a year earlier, Buckingham thought that this time, he would be safe from falling back into the clutches of Fleetwood Mac and Warner Bros.—even despite Warner Bros.' well-established willingness to bring the band's old lineup back together at any given minute.

Soon after Buckingham also asked Christine McVie to participate in his solo album sessions in mid-1996, however, Fleetwood Mac was back from the dead—almost. Ultimately, with Stevie Nicks fresh off the release of 1994's *Street Angel*—her first solo effort not to be certified platinum in the US or crack the US *Billboard* Hot 200's top 20 upon its release[1]—reuniting the whole of the band's most successful iteration wouldn't be too difficult come early 1997. (Not to mention that Buckingham and Nicks already collaborated a year earlier on the song "Twisted," which Nicks had been recording for inclusion on the *Twister* soundtrack.)[2]

Perhaps it was because they were all willing to cash in on Fleetwood Mac's greatest hits after such a trying decade, or maybe it was because there was no expectation that they'd have to work in a studio with one another again any time soon, or maybe their coming together really was—as Buckingham would later recount—just an "organic thing" that "felt good,"[3] but the band, including Nicks, officially reunited in March 1997. Two months later, in May of the same year, they were live on stage again, performing as a five-some for the first time in more than 10 years.

Only a few months after *Rumours* celebrated its 20th anniversary, the band took to Warner Bros. Studios in Burbank, California on May 23, 1997 to give a live performance that would be recorded and released not only as Fleetwood Mac's first live album since 1980, but the band's first-ever *MTV* television special.[4] Knowing that the concert would be released commercially from the get-go, the band was determined to make *The Dance* more than just another greatest hits package. From the start, it was clear that if the band's most recent studio effort had left a bad taste in fans' mouths, *The Dance* was going to be quick in righting all of *Time*'s wrongs.

Under elaborate dancing lights and a giant glowing halo spanning the length of the stage, *The Dance* opens with a passionate rendition of "The Chain," sending a message to new and long-time fans of the band alike: Fleetwood Mac—*the* Fleetwood Mac—was back, and stronger than ever.

From there, the band is sure to check several boxes right off the bat. Following "The Chain" is Nicks's "Dreams," McVie's "Everywhere," and another performance by Nicks, who gives an appropriately haunting rendition of "Gold Dust Woman," as if fans needed reminding how Fleetwood Mac had come to be one of the best-selling rock and roll bands of all time by the late-1990s. After Buckingham nails an extended performance of his 1975 guitar-solo-showcase classic "I'm So Afraid," the band proves that they aren't just resting on their laurels: now that they've jogged your memory with some essential Fleetwood Mac, they spring McVie's "Temporary One" on audience goers, knowing that fans never would've objected to hearing some of the Mac's best new music in years.

"Temporary One" is another bouncy ballad written by McVie and husband Eddy Quintela, the duo responsible for hits like *Tango in the Night*'s

"Little Lies" and "Isn't It Midnight," as well as what little redeemable material had been included on 1990's *Behind the Mask* and 1995's *Time.* Interestingly, like McVie's "All Over Again" from *Time,* "Temporary One's" lyrics are almost autobiographical, with the track's chorus suggesting that should anything as insurmountable as a sea ever divide Fleetwood Mac, there's no need to fret, as such a blockade is merely a "temporary one."

Luckily for Fleetwood Mac fans, *The Dance* takes on a persona like that of 1977's *Elvis in Concert* or Tom Waits' *Glitter and Doom Live* in that it features humorous commentary among bandmates in between select tracks. Following "Temporary One," for example, Buckingham takes a moment to explain how *The Dance* came to be, a discussion that segues into his introduction to "Temporary One's" successor "Bleed to Love Her":

> I had asked Mick to play drums on a solo album I was working on—still working on, actually—but… one thing led to another and suddenly there we were in the studio saying, "gee, this feels pretty good." Isn't that weird?[5]

"Bleed to Love Her" is, unsurprisingly, a track that was meant to be included on Buckingham's planned follow-up to 1992's *Out of the Cradle*— yet another unnamed solo effort he had been forced to put on hold early in its development thanks to the seemingly inescapable force of Fleetwood Mac.[6]

Fleetwood Mac fans are treated to another lucky break that Buckingham's "Bleed to Love Her" debuted sooner on *The Dance* rather than later on one of Buckingham's solo efforts. Though of course the track probably would've included backing vocals provided by McVie, Nicks, or both had it been featured on Buckingham's temporarily shelved solo effort anyway, the band's live rendition of "Bleed to Love Her" makes for a gorgeous addition to *The Dance*'s setlist, and it's a track that segues well into another shimmering Mac ballad in Nicks's "Gypsy."

After Nicks wraps up a tame performance of her 1982 classic, Buckingham retakes center stage to perform unique renditions of "Big Love" from 1987's *Tango in the Night* and "Go Insane" from his 1984 solo album of the same name. As all other stage lights dim aside from a single spotlight bearing down on Buckingham, it becomes apparent that both renditions are going to be toned-down, acoustic performances of tracks that were originally products of 1980s over-production and an almost over-excessive use of echoing vocal effects and synthesizers. Naturally, there's great risk in debuting such drastically altered renditions of some of Buckingham's best works in a live performance that will soon be broadcast to millions of viewers.

Regardless (or perhaps unsurprisingly), Buckingham nails each of the strenuous back-to-back performances, which, because they've been drastically toned down instrumentally, now require greater vocalization to give them the same "punch" they packed with their initial releases in the mid-to-late eighties. Buckingham manages to step up to the plate both vocally and instrumentally, using his finger-picking skills to establish these new takes on old classics as masterpieces in their own right. In fact, five years after the release of *The Dance* in 1997, these acoustic versions of "Big Love" and "Go Insane"—rather than their original counterparts—would land a place on 2002's *The Very Best of Fleetwood Mac*,[7] a testament to Buckingham's vocal and instrumental versatility.

Among the best of the rest is a Nicks-led performance of 1975's "Landslide"—a recording which would later be released as *The Dance*'s fourth and final single in 1998 as a follow-up to McVie's "Temporary One," "The Chain," and Nicks's "Silver Springs"—and a banjo-based rendition of McVie's "Say You Love Me," a track which "for the first time ever" features John McVie on back-up vocals, at the request of his ex-wife.[8]

Before the show is declared a wrap, in addition to a show-stopping performance of Nicks's "Silver Springs," the band's setlist also includes two more new tracks debuted by Buckingham and Nicks, with Buckingham taking the lead first on "My Little Demon," a track that was a standout during rehearsals for *The Dance* but was largely neglected by fans following the album's release and was later replaced by classic Mac tracks like "Second Hand News" on the band's subsequent *Dance* tour.[9] Later, Nicks assumes center stage with "Sweet Girl,"[10] a track that, like Buckingham's "Demon," has yet to be released on any other Fleetwood Mac album aside from 1997's *The Dance*. To round out the mix, the band performed four of Fleetwood Mac's most enduring tracks of all time, including three of *Rumours'* greatest hits.

Though *The Dance* stands as one of Fleetwood Mac's greatest triumphs because it signals a rare, complete reunification of one of rock and roll's most beloved fivesomes, perhaps it is because the band closes the show in a way that pays homage to Fleetwood Mac's enduring history that makes *The Dance* one of the band's most celebrated contributions to the world of rock and roll.

Specifically, it's the dramatic introduction of the University of Southern California's Marching Band to the stage following an unforgettable performance of Buckingham's "Go Your Own Way" that in and of itself is one of *The Dance*'s greatest accolades. In their glimmering costumes, the marching band takes the stage to recreate the magic of "Tusk's" original 1979 recording just two songs shy of McVie's concert-closing "Songbird." However, it's not just "Tusk" that's complemented by the USC Marching Band's thunderous drumbeats and huge horn section.

After "Tusk" comes to a sudden, slamming halt, for the first time ever, the University of Southern California's Marching Band is featured in a dazzling, one-off performance of McVie's "Don't Stop" to create a rendition that extends several minutes over the track's original runtime thanks to a dramatic encore by the band's brass section. In fact, by the time the band is long gone and McVie's wrapped up a quiet, concluding performance of the sweet "Songbird," it's clear that *The Dance* had been more than just a quick cash grab by the band, it had been—and still remains—a testament to Fleetwood Mac's remarkable legacy and longevity.

In the aftermath of *The Dance*, despite some reservations, not one member of Fleetwood Mac was willing to give up the opportunity to ride the wave of success created by the album's debut in the spring of 1997. As a result, from mid-September to late November of 1997, the band embarked on a 44-date tour across the US, making stops in states like Ohio, Tennessee, and New York, among others. Though much of the band's setlist while on tour was identical to what they'd performed while on *The Dance,* there were some notable additions and exemptions to the band's touring catalog.

For one, the band was sure to include a cover of the Beach Boys' "Farmer's Daughter" and Buckingham's "Not That Funny," two tracks made popular on the band's *Tusk* tour in the late-

1970s. Additionally, the band was finally willing to include tracks like Nicks's solo smash hit "Stand Back" from her 1983 album *The Wild Heart* while on tour. Interestingly, though the track had been included on the band's 1987 *Tango in the Night* tour, its inclusion on the bands' setlist back then had in fact been one of the reasons Buckingham refused to tour with the band into the late eighties.[11]

Fleetwood Mac's—or rather Buckingham's—willingness to include Nicks's solo work on the band's setlists come the late 1990s seemed to mark an important turning point in the history of Fleetwood Mac. Finally, it seemed as though the band was working as a team for the first time since the release of their self-titled debut in 1975. Further evidence that the band was more buddy-buddy than ever just prior to the onset of the new millennium was the fact that the band's most recent effort, *The Dance*, was the first album ever released by Fleetwood Mac to contain all five members of the band on its cover—something that Buckingham had been wishing for since the release of *Rumours* more than 20 years earlier.[12]

Though more so than ever it seemed like the band was finally getting along and was prepared to launch into the 21st century with a head full of steam, as history would have it, this just wasn't the case.

Despite the massive success of *The Dance*, which would be certified 5x platinum in the years following its initial release, the band quickly fell back apart by late 1998, only a few months after Fleetwood Mac was inducted into the Rock & Roll Hall of Fame in late January.[13] Remarkably, it was one of the band's most historically committed members, Christine McVie, who would be the one responsible for "breaking the chain" this time around, deciding to resign from the band just before the start of the new millennium largely in part due to homesickness and a fear of flying.[14]

Though Fleetwood Mac was still a formidable presence in the world of rock and roll by the late-1990s, McVie's move wasn't completely unjustified. After all, by 1998, she had been a member of the band for the better part of the last 28 years, and, as is the case for most musicians with careers spanning one, two, or three decades even, for McVie, this meant that she'd largely missed out on being able to live a "normal, domestic life."[15]

As a result, by the time the early 2000s rolled around, McVie was already several thousand miles removed from Fleetwood Mac, Los Angeles, and her millions of adoring fans, having settled down in Kent, England, in a neat little fixer-upper. Now that she'd left her hectic life as a rock and roller behind, McVie was looking forward to spending plenty of time playing around with her newest pet project.[16]

In the years following McVie's departure, the band, namely Nicks, was positive that McVie would never be back.[17]

Even in the wake of McVie's departure, several major pieces of the Fleetwood Mac puzzle were still in place by the late-1990s, giving fans hope that perhaps the band had something more up their sleeve following *The Dance*'s debut in 1997. However, any hopes for a new Fleetwood Mac album or world tour would be quickly squashed by Buckingham, who only a few weeks after McVie's resignation from the band in 1998 adamantly declared that Fleetwood Mac had *never* truly been "back together" ever since their initial split back in the late-1980s,[18] despite the band's famous, much-publicized "reunion" in March of 1997.

Buckingham's sentiments were a huge blow to Fleetwood Mac fans as well as to bandmate Stevie Nicks, who by the early 2000s was tired of being kept in the dark regarding the future of Fleetwood Mac.[19] True to his word and eager to get back to work on his abandoned solo effort, soon after McVie's departure from Fleetwood Mac, Buckingham elected to follow suit, leaving the band behind for the second time in a little over ten years.

Though his departure from the band in 1998 might've been upsetting to fans, Buckingham, on the other hand, had a lot to celebrate in the wake of the band's *Dance* tour and his decision to go solo. On the home front, Buckingham welcomed his first-ever child with longtime girlfriend Kristen Messner on July 8, 1998. *Billboard* magazine's "Lifelines" section excitedly noted the birth of Buckingham's first child:

> Boy, William Gregory, to Kristen Messner and Lindsey Buckingham, July 8 in Los Angeles. Father is a vocalist/ guitarist/songwriter for Fleetwood Mac and is currently working on a new solo album for Reprise Records.[20]

Two years later, Buckingham married Messner, a photographer and interior designer he met in the late 1990s. The couple welcomed a daughter, Leelee Buckingham, that same year.[21]

Meanwhile, picking up where he'd left off back in 1995, Buckingham would also finally complete work on an album he'd taken to calling *Gift of Screws* by 2001—an album featuring some of Buckingham's hardest rock numbers to date as well as an expertly arranged studio recording of *The Dance*'s "Bleed to Love Her."

In creating his first solo album since 1992's *Out of the Cradle,* Buckingham pulled out all the stops in order to create yet another well-developed, fully fleshed-out studio effort worthy of bearing his name. To that end, by 2001, Buckingham had already written and recorded several of what would later become some of Fleetwood Mac's greatest hits of the 21st century, including

"Miranda," "Come," and "Peacekeeper."[22] Unfortunately, perhaps it's all too easy to predict what happened when Buckingham presented his hard work to the folks in Burbank in late 2001, while the massive success of Fleetwood Mac's most recent album was still fresh in the minds of Warner Bros. executives.

DESTINY RULES
2003–2009

SEPTEMBER 23, 2003

Fleetwood Mac is live in Boston, Massachusetts, engaged in a concert performance set to be released as a live album and DVD music video sometime late next year. The show—one of many stops included on the band's *Say You Will* tour—is special for several reasons. Perhaps because it's the spiritual successor to the band's epic 1970 live album of the same name, 2003's *Live in Boston* features some of the most passionate performances bandmates Buckingham and Nicks have put on in years. First, Nicks, engaged in a wild rendition of

"Rhiannon," succeeds in properly channeling her inner Welsh witch on stage again for the first time in decades.

Then, Buckingham, eager to show off some material from the band's most recent studio effort, gives his all while performing one of Fleetwood Mac's newest guitar-driven, heavy-hitting rock anthems, "Come." The song starts off slow, with Buckingham's quiet vocals leading up to a sudden explosion of sound, a dramatic transition in style characteristic of many of Buckingham's solo works. So goes the entire show, with Buckingham and Nicks trading off vocal duties until it comes time for the two to split the bill on "Don't Stop," a track they've got to perform because it's trademark Fleetwood Mac, even though Christine McVie—the voice behind the original powerhouse anthem—is several thousand miles away, content with having left her bandmates behind in exchange for a quiet life in the English countryside... for now.

Despite McVie's absence, Fleetwood Mac's *Live in Boston* is a hit—just one of many strides that the band has already made since the start of the new millennium. After all, much of the material being performed tonight is being sampled from their first ever album released in the 21st century, 2003's *Say You Will*, an album that—like 1987's *Tango in the Night*—has its origins in an abandoned Buckingham solo effort. It's impossible to predict how well the band best known for its work in the seventies and eighties might've fared come the early 2000s if not for Lindsey Buckingham's dynamic style and influence. However, it's safe to say that by the early 21st century, Buckingham's enduring presence had played a major role in extending Fleetwood Mac's shelf life well beyond what anyone would've predicted it to be back in 1975: back when a sprightly California couple joined forces with an old blues band with no guarantee that any one of them would end up as anything more than just a few starving artists trying to make it big in the supposed "City of Angels."

2003's *Say You Will* begins with three tracks that are quick to remind listeners that the fun of the seventies and eighties is long gone. Specifically, the album opens with Buckingham's "What's the World Coming To" and "Murrow Turning Over in his Grave" as well as Nicks's "Illume," the latter of which details Nicks's witnessing of the events of 9/11 two years prior to the release of the album. In a 2003 interview with *USA Today*, Nicks, who was staying in New York's Waldorf Astoria Hotel on 9/11, recounted having watched "people jumping [from the World Trade Center] on a Mexican TV channel," and having to put "wet towels in the windows to keep out the burning iron smell."[1]

Meanwhile, Buckingham's "Murrow Turning Over in his Grave" is a heavily overdubbed, stormy-guitar-driven track inspired by iconic mid-20th-century journalist Edward R. Murrow, who

Buckingham believed would be incredibly disheartened by the state of the news and media come the early 21st century.[2] The album-opening "What's the World Coming To" is written in a similar vein, though its meaning is a bit more obvious than its successor's. Thus begins a unique Fleetwood Mac album, in that the often-intimate love songs that the band has long built their success upon have taken a backseat to tracks with much more serious subject matter.

Two of *Say You Will*'s greatest features are Nicks's "Thrown Down" and its follow-up, Buckingham's "Miranda." For one, Stevie Nicks's "Thrown Down," despite being more than 20 years removed from the release of *Rumours*, actually sounds as though it might've made a fine addition to the band's magnum opus—or to *Tusk*, at least. Nicks had originally written the song in 1997 about Buckingham and had considered including it on her 2001 solo album *Trouble in Shangri-La*.[3] However, Buckingham would later explain that the song had already been worked on by three producers by the time *Say You Will* was recorded and that the song was only perfected once he added a guitar riff in its chorus. "It was a fairly simple thing," Buckingham explained, clearly alluding to his historied working relationship with Nicks, "there seems to be an understanding between us as to what to do."[4]

Featuring Buckingham's added riff, "Thrown Down" is considerably moodier than anything the band had included on *Mirage* or *Tango in the Night*, though the song fits in well on *Say You Will* among tracks like its predecessor "Illume" or later tracks "Come" and "Silver Girl." Nicks's lyricism is incredibly strong here, as she brings the band back to its roots with lyrics about a faltering relationship and having your faith in a lover shaken.

Just as Nicks's "Thrown Down" manages to establish *some* continuity between *Say You Will* and Fleetwood Mac's prior studio efforts, Buckingham quickly breaks this streak with "Miranda." It's not surprising, of course. After all, "Miranda" had been written for inclusion on Buckingham's solo effort *Gift of Screws* before the project had been reworked into a Fleetwood Mac album.[5] Though "Miranda" doesn't adhere to most of Fleetwood Mac's rhythmical or lyrical standards, the song is still a standout from the album, even though it's technically one of Buckingham's strongest tracks to date, rather than one of Fleetwood Mac's.

"Miranda" features some of the best instrumental work of Buckingham's career and is an incredible example of how well Buckingham is able to take various styles and influences and combine them to create a single gnawing, genre-bending piece of pop art. In fact, thanks to Buckingham's instrumental work, "Miranda" would still be one of *Say You Will*'s greatest standouts even if the song's lyrics were complete rubbish. Remarkably, however, it *is* the track's lyrics, above all else, that are "Miranda's" greatest asset. In fact, it would be almost impossible to believe that Buckingham had come this far as a songwriter by 2003 if not for tracks still yet to come, like the seemingly instant Hollywood love-story soundtrack staple, "Steal Your Heart Away."

Both of *Say You Will*'s singles follow up "Red Rover," a Buckingham finger-picking masterclass with a haunting, self-identifying refrain that makes for a dramatic transition into the album's bubbly title track.

While "Say You Will" isn't quite able to achieve the same sugary, saccharine sound of Christine McVie's "Hold Me" or "Little Lies," it manages to come close. Released as *Say You Will*'s second single in June 2003, the album's title track seems destined for FM radio waves from the get-go (at least more so than anything else on the album up to this point) with its upbeat tempo and bouncy lyrics about the feeling of falling in love with someone new and dancing away old wounds. *Say You Will*'s title track, which also features Sheryl Crow, John McVie's daughter Molly, and Stevie Nicks's niece Jessica on backing vocals,[6] would debut to mild success, managing to peak at #17 on the US Adult Contemporary Charts by the fall of 2003.

Buckingham's "Peacekeeper," meanwhile, would become the more successful of the two tracks lifted from the album, entering at #93 on the US *Billboard* Hot 100 in March of 2003 before managing to peak at #80 in the US by late spring. Unmistakably different from its predecessor, "Peacekeeper" brings the album back to its roots as a clear, politically driven message about desensitization to violence and themes of war and peace. Despite its bleak subject matter, "Peacekeeper" was well-deserving of its place on the *Billboard* Charts and is simultaneously one of Fleetwood Mac's greatest hits of the 21st century as well as one of the biggest reasons why *Say You Will* listens like an album even more fragmented than 1979's *Tusk*—which critics had lambasted as a disjointed effort that sounded as if it had been the work of three solo artists.[7]

Despite its refusal to adhere to any kind of collective standard, *Say You Will* is still one of the Mac's greatest albums of all time, largely in part thanks to "Peacekeeper," which features some of Buckingham's best vocal and instrumental work to date, even at age 54. Interestingly, as yet another one of the tracks Buckingham had planned to include on his abandoned *Gift of Screws* album, "Peacekeeper" again raises the question of "what if?"

This question of "what if" wouldn't be answered—somewhat—until late 2008, more than five years after the release of *Say You Will,* when Buckingham's *Gift of Screws* would finally see the light of day.

One of Buckingham's most straight-up rock and roll-oriented albums, *Gift of Screws*[8] would manage to peak at #48 on the US *Billboard* Charts within a month of its initial release and at #15 on the *Billboard* Rock Albums Chart. By the time *Gift of Screws* was finally released in September 2008, the album was hardly the same one Buckingham had pitched to Warner Bros. back in 2001. In fact, Buckingham had used most of the material planned for *Gift of Screws* not only on 2003's *Say You Will,* but also on his 2006 solo album *Under the Skin.* This meant that hardly anything from the album's early stages—aside from the album's title track—survived long enough to make it onto the finished product.

Perhaps because some of *Gift of Screws'* greatest hits had been released on 2003's *Say You Will* under the Fleetwood Mac banner, it's impossible to know if the album (had it been released as intended) would've been the one to finally catapult Buckingham into solo stardom. Because some of Buckingham's best solo work had again been attributed to Fleetwood Mac's legacy rather than his own, it's impossible to truly answer the question of "what if?" Regardless, it would seem as though—like in the case of his abandoned late eighties solo effort and 1992's *Out of the Cradle*—that Buckingham would once again just miss out on making a name for himself as a solo artist with *Gift of Screws.*

After track #9 on *Say You Will*—Buckingham's borderline heavy-metal epic "Come"—draws to a thunderous close, there's not one, not two, but *nine* more songs left on the album's tracklist. While for most bands of the early 2000s "Come" would've been an excellent album closer, Buckingham's guitar-driven heavy-hitter merely marks the midway point for *Say You Will*. In fact, Buckingham was the one who'd campaigned for the creation of a double album shortly after work on *Say You Will* had begun in late 2001, despite Nicks and his bandmates' claims that doing so would be "career suicide," given young peoples' lessening interest in buying albums come the early 2000s.[9]

Buckingham fought back fiercely, with his chief argument being that there wouldn't have been an album to begin with if not for him, after all. Of course, in the end, Buckingham would get his way, though this dispute would prove to be merely the first of many to go down in between the band's early studio sessions and the eventual release of *Say You Will* in early 2003. In fact, conflicts between Fleetwood Mac bandmates this time around would range from explosive arguments over the album's tracklist and style to more minor back-and-forths, including petty arguments concerning Nicks's inconsistent use of pronouns in her lyrics for "Thrown Down" and who the band should get to mix *Say You Will*'s songs.[10]

Despite the band's constant feuding, which by 2003 was practically one of Fleetwood Mac's trademarks, *Say You Will* soldiers on with Stevie

Nicks's "Smile at You," "Running Through the Garden," and "Silver Girl," three tracks that each contribute to a sort of lull that begins at the start of the album's second half. While "Smile at You"—originally a reject from the band's *Tusk* and *Mirage* sessions[11]—sports great lyrics and Nicks's incredible cascading vocals, its successors just don't quite hit the same mark. Luckily, "Running Through the Garden" and "Silver Girl" segue into several tracks that are some of *Say You Will*'s best, including Buckingham's "Steal Your Heart Away" and two more tracks by Nicks: "Everybody Finds Out" and "Destiny Rules."

"Steal Your Heart Away" is an instant soft-rock classic that, since its release, has been wildly underappreciated by fans and critics alike, who often fail to recognize that the song is not only one of Fleetwood Mac's best recordings of all time but also one of Buckingham's. Buckingham's guitar work on "Steal Your Heart Away" is a thing of beauty, while his lyrics and flow are perhaps the best of his entire career. Nicks's vocals, of course, as they have for years, gorgeously complement Buckingham's. Yet, despite "Steal Your Heart Away" having all the characteristics of a timeless love song, the track was remarkably never released as a single. *Say You Will* was a modest success given Fleetwood Mac's standards, but perhaps had "Steal Your Heart Away" been given proper commercial promotion, history might remember the album as one of Fleetwood Mac's greatest.

After Buckingham's studio recording of *The Dance*'s "Bleed to Love Her," Nicks manages to get in two of her greatest contributions to the album: the dramatic, four-and-a-half minute "Everybody Finds Out" as well as the more subdued "Destiny Rules."

"Everybody Finds Out" is a compact track that doesn't feature an instrumental break until the song's final minutes, a break that follows Nicks's demonstrating that even at age 55, she's still got one hell of a voice. It's the song's lyrics, vocals, and instrumental work that make "Everybody Finds Out" such a triumph, however, as the three work together to create a compelling and remarkably telling narrative: "When love starts out in the darkness / It doesn't do well in the light," Nicks sings, "Affairs of the heart / That start out in the dark / Usually stay with the night."[12]

Though "Destiny Rules" doesn't contain vocal or instrumental work nearly as brash or orchestral as what's featured on "Everybody Finds Out," what may as well be *Say You Will*'s penultimate track still manages to tell a story just as scandalous as its predecessor's. In the song, Nicks argues that perhaps a particular ill-fated relationship of hers was doomed from the start, much in part due to "ruthless spirits" and the "paths they choose."

Finally, *Say You Will* wraps up with two appropriately titled tracks: Buckingham's "Say Goodbye" and Nicks's "Goodbye Baby," the latter of which is largely a duet between the two former lovers. Though "Goodbye Baby" is a strong track by Nicks, it's "Say Goodbye's" lyrics—which tell of letting old loves slip away and coming to terms with reality—that make the song a more fitting end to *Say You Will*, Fleetwood Mac's final studio album ever.[13]

The album debuted at #3 on the *Billboard* Hot 200, becoming the first Fleetwood Mac album to peak in the top three in the US since 1982's *Mirage*. Soon after the album's release, the band embarked on a year-long world tour in support of *Say You Will* in May of 2003, a tour that featured stops in Washington, D.C. and Boston, Massachusetts, as well as in Berlin, Germany, London, England, and Sydney, Australia. By the time the tour was declared a wrap in September 2004, the band had grossed nearly 70 million dollars in the US alone.[14] Playing music from their newest album as well as material from the last 30 years, Fleetwood Mac's *Say You Will* tour managed to establish the band as a multi-faceted tour de force relevant even three decades removed from their debut into the world of rock and roll.

The band's tour in support of their newest studio effort concluded in 2004. Buckingham explained later that:

When [Fleetwood Mac] got off the road after the *Say You Will* tour in 2004, I said to the band, 'Look, don't bother me for three or four years, because I really want to put out two albums in relatively short order for me and tour behind both of them.'[15]

As a result, two years after Fleetwood Mac's *Say You Will* tour was declared a wrap, Buckingham released 2006's *Under the Skin*, his fourth solo album of all time and first in more than ten years. Though primarily an album with a focus on acoustics that from the get-go listens like a subdued *Law and Order* or bridled *Go Insane*, *Under the Skin* features three tracks that allow for a bit of country-rock-inspired wildness: "To Try for the Sun" (a cover of Scottish singer-songwriter Donovan's original), "Down on Rodeo," and "Someone's Gotta Change Your Mind." Interestingly, these three tracks were taken from Buckingham's early *Gift of Screws* sessions, which is perhaps why they're a bit (if only slightly) harder rocking than the rest of *Under the Skin*.[16]

It is "To Try for the Sun," "Down on Rodeo," and "Someone's Gotta Change Your Mind" as well as lead single "Show You How" that are *Under the Skin*'s greatest triumphs, in fact. Specifically, "Show You How" and the three tracks lifted from the temporarily shelved *Gift of Screws* stand out from the album because they feature *Under the Skin*'s most poignant lyricism and untamed vocal work, and serve as effective showcases of Buckingham's raw, unfiltered talent.

"Down on Rodeo," for instance, features a chorus with long, drawn-out vocals and was originally written about a woman Buckingham had been dating for about a year by the time *Under the Skin* was completed. Buckingham would also later remark that the song "more broadly" is about "people who spend all their time window shopping through their life… [and] being down on Rodeo Drive in Beverly Hills and window shopping."[17] Unsurprisingly, given Buckingham's habit of safeguarding his solo albums from others' creative influence, "Down on Rodeo" and "Someone's Gotta Change Your Mind" were the only two songs on *Under the Skin* to feature outside artists— the familiar faces of John McVie and Mick Fleetwood.

Though of these four tracks only "Show You How" would be released as a single,[18] 2006's *Under the Skin* would prove to be yet another mildly successful Buckingham solo effort, peaking at #80 in the US in October of 2006.

In the aftermath of *Under the Skin*, Buckingham and his backing band embarked on a tour in support of the album. While on tour, Buckingham recorded a live album later entitled *Live at the Bass Performance Hall*. The album, which was recorded in Fort Worth, Texas, features live renditions of songs from Fleetwood Mac's "White Album," *Rumours*, and *Tango in the Night* as well as from several of Buckingham's solo works, including 1984's *Go Insane* and, of course,

Under the Skin. The album was released in early 2008 and ultimately peaked at #186 on the US *Billboard* 200 Chart.

That same year, Buckingham also finally released *Gift of Screws.* By the time he released his long-delayed fifth solo effort, Buckingham seemed to have accomplished what he set out to do at the conclusion of Fleetwood Mac's *Say You Will* tour. With one live album and two studio efforts released in the span of only two years, Buckingham would happily put his solo career on hold and rejoin forces with the band for their Unleashed tour in 2009.

Ultimately, the tour would gross over 80 million dollars[19]—meanwhile, Buckingham's solo works had finally provided him with the creative outlet he'd been searching for for years. As such, heading into the early 2010s, it seemed as though Buckingham had finally managed to strike up an almost perfect balance between his solo career and work with Fleetwood Mac.

By this point, of course, it's been well-established that Fleetwood Mac has never been known for their happy endings.

2011–2016

NOVEMBER 22, 2015

Fleetwood Mac concludes their hugely successful On with the Show tour in Auckland, New Zealand, the 120th stop that the band has made in the last 14 months. Now that they're off the road, the band immediately discusses plans to record a new studio album—their first since 2003's *Say You Will*—and takes to recording at The Village Recorder in Los Angeles, the same studio where they recorded *Tusk* in the late 1970s.[1] Despite their grand plans to write, record, and release a "reunion" album, McVie and Buckingham make sure to note to excited fans and journalists that the timetable for recording and releasing their new studio effort largely depends on when they can get Stevie Nicks into the studio,[2] who had embarked on a solo tour a little under a year after the band's On with the Show tour was declared a wrap in late 2015.

While Nicks is busy touring in support of her 2014 solo album *24 Karat Gold*, Buckingham and McVie excitedly boast about how easily they've rekindled their "unbelievable" chemistry in the studio; in fact, only a little over a year after McVie announced her intention to return to the band in 2014, she and Buckingham have put together so much material that Buckingham jokes with journalists that he might be "pushing for a double album."[3]

McVie's return and Fleetwood Mac's sensational On with the Show tour only add to a recent high Buckingham's been riding, kickstarted by the release of a critically and commercially successful solo album, *Seeds We Sow*, three years earlier in 2011. While things are continuing to look up for Buckingham—perhaps he was prophesizing rather than songwriting when he created the lyrics to 2008's "Love Runs Deeper": "You were out of tune / It seemed to suit my dark side / You had a prophet's pose / And two states of mind / Well I was sure I'd go / We were parallel lines."[4]

Around the time Lindsey Buckingham released his fourth solo album *Under the Skin* in 2006, his perspective had begun to shift. He would later explain that "what had changed was I had got married and had kids and had a whole new set of things to write about."[5] Unsurprisingly, 2008's *Gift of Screws*, despite being brasher in tone than 2006's *Under the Skin*, clearly reflects this change in the guitarist's perspective; while the cover of the album features a stone-faced Buckingham (not unlike the covers of several of his previous solo efforts), fans can easily tell that the album is heavily influenced by the guitarist's love for his growing family (including wife Kristen, son Will, and daughters Leelee and Stella): a trend that would continue through the production of Buckingham's follow-up to *Gift of Screws*, 2011's *Seeds We Sow*.

Songwriting credits for two tracks from *Gift of Screws*, "Did You Miss Me" and "Love Runs Deeper," for example, are shared between Buckingham and his wife.[6] These two tracks were released as the album's first two singles in July and September 2008, respectively. The lyrics to track #2 on the album, "Time Precious Time" were also inspired by Buckingham's relationship with his wife. As Buckingham would later explain, by the time he met Kristen Messner, he was in his late 40s and had already assumed that, nearing age 50, he'd missed his chance to fall in love, marry, and have children.[7] As such, *Gift of Screws'* "Time Precious Time" addresses Buckingham's having "held off" getting married, having seen "so many people that had gotten married at a more 'normal' age and had screwed it up." "Time Precious Time," then—specifically—is "just about taking the time you need for something but remembering that time is precious," Buckingham would later explain.[8]

While Buckingham's wife received songwriting credits on two tracks from *Gift of Screws,* his son Will received songwriting credits on one: the album-opener "Great Day." In 2008, Buckingham explained that Will:

> was probably around 8... I was down in the studio, he was just walking around with me humming this thing. He was going, "Great day, great day." It was a fully fleshed out chorus and I said, "What is that?" He said, "I don't know, I just made it up." I said, "I'm going to try and make it into a song, is that OK with you?" He said... "Oh yeah, great, great."[9]

Aside from these three tracks, there are two other standouts from the album, the first being track #4, "Wait for You":[10] a "yearning song that The Cars or Cheap Trick would have killed for, but with an added stadium melancholy that only Buckingham can do."[11] The second is track #7, "The Right Place to Fade"[12]—a "great *Rumours* song that never was."[13] Unsurprisingly, the lyrics to these songs also seem to allude to Buckingham's wife and children, particularly the lyrics to "Fade": "How long... we hesitate / Waiting for the light that might light our way,"[14] Buckingham sings.

On September 6, 2011, two years after the conclusion of Fleetwood Mac's wildly successful Unleashed tour and three years after the long-awaited debut of *Gift of Screws*, Lindsey Buckingham's sixth solo album, *Seeds We Sow*, was released.

Kristen Buckingham is credited with having sequenced Buckingham's follow-up to *Gift of Screws*, and though none of his family members would receive songwriting credits this time around, Buckingham's wife and three children are still very much present on the album. Working with a blank slate following the release of the long-delayed *Gift of Screws* in 2008, Buckingham's *Seeds We Sow*, when compared to his earliest solo works, represents a drastic shift in tone for the traditionally "lonely guy."

While *Law and Order*, *Go Insane*, and *Out of the Cradle* were crafted in the immediate aftermath of some of Buckingham's lowest moments—including in the wake of *Tusk*'s dismal debut, his breakup with Carol Ann Harris, and his late eighties split with Fleetwood Mac—*Seeds We Sow* was instead released during a positive period in both Buckingham's personal and professional life.

Perhaps because the album was produced during a time largely free of the toxicity that had dominated the production of his earliest solo works, *Seeds We Sow* listens a lot like Buckingham's solo works from the early 1990s and mid-2000s in that its persona is remarkably tame when compared to works like 1981's *Law and Order* or 1984's *Go Insane.* This is hardly a bad thing: beginning with 1992's *Out of the Cradle,* Buckingham's shift in style from experimental to more acoustic-based works began allowing his instrumental ability to shine through much more clearly—his work on *Seeds We Sow* is no exception. In fact, from the get-go, Buckingham's 2011 solo effort is one of the best of his career in terms of how well its tracklist showcases his almost other-worldly finger-picking and instrumental capabilities. The album's opening title track and first single,[15] for example, sports an instrumental interlude reminiscent of that of Jefferson Airplane's "Embryonic Journey." Though having even one track on the album comparable to anything from *Surrealistic Pillow* is a triumph in and of itself, Buckingham isn't ready to stop impressing just yet.

"That's the Way That Love Goes" and "When She Comes Down" are also exceptionally poignant, the former of which features a chorus so infectiously catchy that one might mistakenly believe it had been written by Fleetwood Mac hitmaker Christine McVie. Likewise, "In Our Own Time," which was released as the album's second single in July 2011, features a swift, slick chorus that you can't help but get stuck in your head no matter how many times you hear it.

Other standouts from *Seeds We Sow* include Buckingham's "Rock Away Blind," a track that the hall-of-famer has since managed to make sound even more kick-ass in live performances, as well as a cover of the Rolling Stones' "She Smiled Sweetly," a track featured on their 1967 album *Between the Buttons*. Of course, Buckingham does the track justice, and his coverage of a track from the Stones' brief psychedelic era[16] ensures that there is at least a bit of experimental-sounding material present on *Seeds We Sow*.

Meanwhile, in addition to the album's title track and the sensational "In Our Own Time," other singles from the LP include "When She Comes Down"—which was released as a single in the UK in August 2011—and "End of Time," which was released as a single at the same time in the US.

Ultimately, *Seeds We Sow*, which Buckingham self-released due to Warner Bros.' unwillingness to fund the creation of promotional materials for the album,[17] peaked at #45 on the US *Billboard* Hot 200, making *Seeds We Sow* Buckingham's second best-performing solo album of all time behind 1981's *Law and Order*.

After releasing his sixth solo effort to critical acclaim, Buckingham embarked on a brief tour in support of *Seeds We Sow* in late 2011 and a solo US tour (without his backing band) a few months later in early May of 2012. These two tours, which featured tracklists containing songs like *Rumours'*

"Go Your Own Way," *Go Insane*'s title track, and even *Buckingham Nicks's* "Stephanie," would result in the release of two live albums. The first was 2011's *Songs from the Small Machine*,[18] which was recorded in late April 2011 at the Saban Theatre in Beverly Hills. The second, 2012's *One Man Show*, is a recording of "a single night in Des Moines, Iowa, taken right off the console mix, with a couple of room mikes added in," Buckingham would later explain. "It's live and raw, with no post-production. I love it!"[19]

Following tours in support of *Seeds We Sow* and the release of *Songs from the Small Machine* and *One Man Show*, Buckingham rejoined with Fleetwood Mac in 2013 for the band's Live world tour, beginning in April at a concert held in Columbus, Ohio.

Unsurprisingly, the tour was a great success for the band, who while on the road would release Fleetwood Mac's first new music since 2003's *Say You Will* via a four-track EP. It featured three new Buckingham-led tracks as well as "Sad Angel," a song which Buckingham had written about Nicks and presented to her just before the band's 2013 tour kicked off in the spring. "Sad Angel," along with "Without You"—a song written by Nicks around the time the two were preparing material for a second *Buckingham Nicks* album in the early 1970s[20]—were often performed by the band while on tour in 2013.

The EP, simply entitled, *Extended Play*, was only released in a digital format and, even without any promotion, managed to peak at #48 on the US *Billboard* 200 Chart following its release. Clearly, the EP was a welcome surprise for long-time Fleetwood Mac fans, though its release in early 2013 was just the start of an exciting sequence of events for fans of the band. This series of events, of course, included an announcement by the band's publicist Liz Rosenberg in early 2014 that fans were beginning to believe might never come: for the first time since the late-1990s, Christine McVie would be returning as a full-time member of Fleetwood Mac.[21]

A few months earlier, McVie had joined the band on stage in London to perform "Don't Stop." Unsurprisingly, the performance proved to be an emotional experience for McVie, the band, and their fans. Despite McVie's sensational surprise appearance, however, the band and its fans had been certain that McVie would still surely never return to Fleetwood Mac full-time.[22]

However, a few months after Rosenberg's announcement, McVie spoke with Carson Daly on the *Today Show*. When asked if the rumors were true about her rejoining Fleetwood Mac, she responded emphatically: "I think that can be said with a definite capital 'Yes'," she answered with a smile.[23]

Unsurprisingly, the band was ecstatic about McVie's return, especially Stevie Nicks, who, more so than anyone else in the band, had been "seriously convinced that [McVie] would never come back."[24] Only a few months after McVie announced her return, she, Buckingham, Mick Fleetwood, John McVie, and Stevie Nicks—the "*Rumours 5*" as fans have come to call the quintet—would embark on a 34-show concert tour across the United States: a tour that would begin in Minneapolis, Minnesota and conclude in Tampa, Florida.

The band's On with the Show tour featuring McVie would officially kick off in late September 2014, not long after Fleetwood Mac's Live tour had made its final stop at Las Vegas's Paris Hotel in January. Featuring several sold-out stops across the US and UK, the band's On with the Show tour was hugely popular and, as a result, was extended in October 2014 by five months, meaning that the tour would ultimately conclude in November 2015.

While on tour, Buckingham announced in an interview with *PBS* that the band would likely use Fleetwood Mac's momentum as a reminted quintet to create a new album that would serve as a "beautiful way to wrap up [Fleetwood Mac's] last act."[25] Though Buckingham's plan seemed like a fitting end for the band, it should be obvious by now that things never quite work out as planned for the problematic five-piece.

The earliest signs of trouble would arise shortly after the band's On with the Show tour had been declared a wrap in late 2015. A little over a year later, in October 2016, despite plans to reconvene in the studio to record Fleetwood Mac's supposed swan song, Stevie Nicks instead took to the road in support of her 2014 solo album, *24 Karat Gold*, embarking on a tour that would last until November 2017. Though the band initially soldiered on without Nicks as they had in their early recording sessions for *Tango in the Night*, eventually Nicks's unwillingness to put her solo career on hold would force Buckingham's hand.

In Buckingham's defense, though by 2017 Nicks had long established herself as one of Fleetwood Mac's greatest assets, the band knew that they were onto something special come the late-2010s. For one, Christine McVie, while living alone in the English countryside for almost 20 years, had thought up enough material to create an album all her own by the time the band had wrapped up their 2015 tour.[26] Likewise, Buckingham was also eager to add to Fleetwood Mac's legacy with some material he'd manufactured in the last couple of years.

By the spring of 2017, it was clear that the band wasn't going to wait on Nicks to participate any longer. It was unanimously decided that all the work the McVies, Buckingham, and Mick Fleetwood had put into what they had intended to be Fleetwood Mac's second studio album of the

21st century would need to see the light of day sooner, rather than later.

——— FEBRUARY 24, 2019 ———

Fleetwood Mac takes a bow after performing live at the Spectrum Center in Charlotte, North Carolina as a part of their yearlong An Evening with Fleetwood Mac tour. The show, which had begun with the band's classic set-opener "The Chain," has come to a close after a little over two hours. Unsurprisingly, even as the band heads backstage, the crowd is still head over heels for Stevie Nicks, who'd managed to steal the show tonight with her dramatic stage presence and powerhouse vocals that somehow still sound the same way they did back in the seventies. Other highlights from the show included a reimagined, 21st-century rendition of Peter Green's "Black Magic Woman" as well as a delightful rendition of "Don't Dream It's Over," a song originally recorded by... Crowded House?

Despite Fleetwood Mac's incredible legacy, perhaps only one man could've done the Crowded House classic proper justice. Luckily, Neil Finn, the man behind "Don't Dream It's Over," had been on stage with the band tonight, and the performance had gone off without a hitch. However, the former Crowded House frontman hadn't been on stage with the band for some sort of one-off collaboration featuring Fleetwood Mac. Rather, by this point, Finn, as well as former Tom Petty & the Heartbreakers guitarist Mike Campbell, have been formal members of Fleetwood Mac for almost an entire year. Reminiscent of what had gone down in the aftermath of *Tango in the Night*'s release in late 1987, the band has again taken on two new members to replace their recently ousted guitarist and sole male vocalist, Lindsey Buckingham.[1]

Buckingham hadn't been the one to make the call this time around, though. In reality, the band had let Buckingham go following a several-month-long dispute between the two parties over what would eventually become the band's "Evening" tour.[2] Though Buckingham later claimed that it was Nicks who had him ousted from the band, the controversy, in essence, was born out of

Buckingham's reluctance to tour with Fleetwood Mac without being given more time to take to the road as a solo act first.[3] No matter what the cause of Buckingham's firing was, however, perhaps the former Fleetwood Mac frontman himself would say it best in a statement released in early 2018, in which he described his firing as a decision that "ends the beautiful 43-year legacy we built together."[4]

On June 9, 2017, Lindsey Buckingham and Christine McVie would finally pull the trigger and release a duet album simply entitled, *Lindsey Buckingham/Christine McVie*. While the album featured Buckingham and McVie as well as Fleetwood Mac's familiar rhythm section of Mick Fleetwood and John McVie, *Lindsey Buckingham/Christine McVie* was not in any way marketed as a Fleetwood Mac album. Despite the band's initial plans to record and release a reunion album featuring the full "*Rumours 5*" line-up, Stevie Nicks's continued unwillingness to participate in the band's studio sessions had led to the creation of *Lindsey Buckingham/Christine McVie*— Buckingham and McVie's first-ever album as a duet.

Upon its debut, *Lindsey Buckingham/Christine McVie* received mostly positive reviews, with outlets like *Rolling Stone* and *Pitchfork* quick to liken the album to the duo's work with Fleetwood Mac. Despite the two's efforts to brand themselves as a duo independent of Fleetwood Mac, *Pitchfork*'s Sean Collins perhaps would say it best in his review of *Lindsey Buckingham/Christine McVie,* in which he labeled the duo's first-ever collaboration "A Fleetwood Mac album in all but name."[5] As critics picked apart the album's tracklist, it became increasingly clear that even without Stevie Nicks, Buckingham's most recent body of work (produced in collaboration with Mitchell Froom and Mark Needham) was—despite what the duo may have wanted you to believe—some of Fleetwood Mac's best work in years.

Whether it's the familiar intertwining of Buckingham and McVie's voices on tracks like "In My World" or "Too Far Gone" or the classic Fleetwood Mac instrumentation on "On with the Show," *Lindsey Buckingham/Christine McVie* does manage to uphold several hallmarks of the band's sound made famous on albums like 1977's *Rumours* and even 1979's *Tusk,* among others. Regardless of whether the duo's first-ever duet album is a triumph all its own or really is just "a Fleetwood Mac album in all but name," 2017's *Lindsey Buckingham/Christine McVie* is still evidence of Buckingham's continued ability to craft something that *sells*,[6] even more than 40 years after his first proper foray into the world of rock and roll.

While the parallels between Buckingham and McVie's duet album and their work with

Fleetwood Mac are there, the album is certainly strong enough to stand on its own. From the very beginning, Buckingham and McVie are set to impress: the album opens with three back-to-back knockouts, including McVie's "Feel About You"—a bubbly song with a "jangly, infectious chorus"[7]—as well as Buckingham's "Sleeping Around the Corner" and "In My World." The first of these two tracks by Buckingham, "Sleeping Around the Corner," was initially included as a bonus track on a digital edition of the guitarist's 2011 solo work, *Seeds We Sow.*[8] Meanwhile, "In My World" was released as the album's first single in April of 2017[9] and would be performed by the duo on *The Tonight Show Starring Jimmy Fallon* only a few weeks after the album's initial release in early June.

Other standouts from the album written by McVie include "Red Sun," which was released in the UK as the album's second single in June of 2017, and "Too Far Gone," a track built around a bluesy guitar riff and percussion breakdown borrowed from "Tusk."[10] "Too Far Gone" is also one of three songs on the album co-written by Buckingham and McVie.[11] Buckingham's "Love is Here to Stay," meanwhile, is a track that, like 2003's "Steal Your Heart Away," seemed almost destined upon its release to find a place on a romantic major motion picture's heart-wrenching soundtrack. Buckingham's vocals are as tender as ever here, and his glimmering, sugary instrumental work is just as likely to satisfy your sweet tooth.

It's for these reasons that Buckingham's "Love is Here to Stay" is perhaps his greatest track on the album.

Likewise, Buckingham's "On with the Show" takes on a similarly moody yet shimmering sound, though the penultimate track's lyrics are much more biting than "Love is Here to Stay's." If it isn't obvious from the track's name and repetitive refrain, "On with the Show's" lyrics detail just that—packing up, moving right along, and leaving those unwilling to "stand with the band" as a distant memory: "There'll come a day / When we all feel the same," Buckingham sings, ultimately urging the band onward, sans Stevie Nicks: "There's nowhere to go / But on down the road / Let's get on with the show."[12]

Finally, Christine McVie's album-closer "Carnival Begin" is perhaps the most satisfying conclusion to any Fleetwood Mac album ever, which is incredible given the fact that *Lindsey Buckingham/Christine McVie* isn't even *technically* a Fleetwood Mac album. The song's lyrics coupled with Buckingham's epic concluding guitar solo are undoubtedly the track's greatest strengths, though McVie's youthful vocals even at age 73 are remarkable as well. Though the album hadn't been manufactured as a "proper" Fleetwood Mac swan song and "Carnival Begin" itself tells a story of a new beginning, perhaps its inclusion as *Lindsey Buckingham/Christine McVie's* album closer warrants enough reason to proclaim the album as an "unofficial" end to the era of what had essentially been Lindsey Buckingham's Fleetwood Mac.

After all, trouble would begin to brew not long after Buckingham and McVie's duet album was released in early June.

At first, things looked good for Fleetwood Mac fans. Not only did Buckingham and McVie embark on an extensive tour in support of their duet album, but in early March 2017, *Billboard* had also announced two classic rock festivals that were to be headlined by two of the biggest bands in rock and roll: Eagles and Fleetwood Mac (*including* Stevie Nicks).[13] In late March, full line-ups for the concerts were confirmed: the events were to be billed as the "Classic East" and "Classic West" festivals and would be held at Citi Field in New York and Dodger Stadium in Los Angeles, respectively. A later announcement by *Billboard* excitedly proclaimed that the Classic East and West festivals would be "the first time in history" that legendary bands Steely Dan, the Doobie Brothers, the Eagles, Fleetwood Mac, Journey, and Earth, Wind & Fire "have ever played together on the same stage in two of America's greatest cities for rock & roll."[14]

After headlining the Classic West festival in mid-July, Fleetwood Mac was the star of *Billboard*'s Classic East festival two weeks later on July 30. Interestingly, as *Billboard* would note in an article published a day after the festival's climax, "The five acts that had preceded them each had been missing a pivotal member — by choice, circumstance or both — but Fleetwood Mac could make the increasingly rare boast of being a classic '70s act with their most successful lineup."[15] The reconvening of all five members of Fleetwood Mac was exciting, but also created some uncertainty; though Buckingham and McVie had just released their duet album, was there still a chance that the band might be able to record a proper "reunion" album with Nicks?

Fascinatingly, *Billboard* would also note in its recap of the night's events that, in reassembling the entire "*Rumours 5*" line-up, the band had been "the safest bet of the weekend. But," *Billboard* also noted, "Fleetwood Mac has so long seemed to thrive on combustibility that without any built-in member drama, it was worth wondering if they might actually come off too safe."[16] Inevitably and unfortunately, *Billboard*'s Classic East recap would ultimately foreshadow what was to come.

A few months later, Fleetwood Mac reconvened again for a special performance at the 2018 MusiCares benefit at Radio City Music Hall in New York. Fleetwood Mac wasn't just a musical guest that night, however—they were also honored as MusiCares' 2018 "Person of the Year." The night featured tribute performances to the band by the Zac Brown Band, Lorde, Miley Cyrus, and others. Ultimately, Bill Clinton presented the band with their award before they engaged in passionate performances of "The Chain,"[17] "Little Lies," "Tusk," and "Go Your Own Way," among others.[18]

That night, the band's performances and speeches went off without a hitch, and Buckingham even noted that what the group was feeling "more than ever in our career [was] love."[19] Therefore, the news that would break only three months later left fans and those close to the band utterly shocked: in April 2018, it was announced that Lindsey Buckingham had been fired from Fleetwood Mac.

In the resulting aftermath, Mick Fleetwood, speaking on behalf of the band, would refuse to label Buckingham's departure as a "firing."[20] Meanwhile, Buckingham himself would announce that it had actually been Stevie Nicks who'd forced him out of Fleetwood Mac, claiming that, in the aftermath of the MusiCares banquet, she'd adamantly declared that she "never wanted to be on the same stage as him again." Nicks would rebuke Buckingham's claim years later, explaining that his "version of events" was "factually inaccurate." Nicks would also state that:

> I did not have him fired, I did not ask
> for him to be fired, I did not demand he
> be fired. Frankly, I fired myself. I
> proactively removed myself from the

band and a situation I considered to be toxic to my well-being. I was done. If the band went on without me, so be it. I have championed independence my whole life, and I believe every human being should have the absolute freedom to set their boundaries of what they can and cannot work with.[21]

Amid the media frenzy that followed Buckingham's departure were claims that the band had also ousted Buckingham after rejecting his request to delay touring with Fleetwood Mac by three months so that he could instead focus on releasing and promoting a new solo album, which he was tentatively calling *Blue Light*.[22]

Regardless of how his firing truly came to be, however, the news came as a shock not just to fans of the band but also to Buckingham himself, who suddenly, after dedicating the better part of the last 40 years of his life to Fleetwood Mac, now found himself ousted from the very band he'd helped to shape into such a massive success.

With the band's 2018 tour dates already booked by the time of Buckingham's firing,[23] Fleetwood Mac again sought out two replacements for Buckingham. This time, they turned to Crowded House's Neil Finn and Mike Campbell of Tom Petty and the Heartbreakers to help fill the void created by Buckingham's firing. As if trying to rub salt in the wound, Fleetwood Mac continued dutifully onward, selling out concerts and seats aplenty on their An Evening with Fleetwood Mac tour, which featured former Crowded House frontman Finn on lead vocals on tracks like Buckingham's "Go Your Own Way."

Buckingham's firing would, of course, continue to sting months after his departure was initially announced; for weeks he would express regret and sorrow over his bandmates' decisions (including making direct reference to Christine McVie's supposed complicity in his firing).[24] Further, he and Nicks would engage in a lengthy war of words (expressed through their publicists and press releases) that included below-the-belt comments about Nicks's personal and love life: "she's lonely. She's alone," Buckingham remarked in an interview with the *L.A. Times*. "She has the people who work for her, and I'm sure she has friends, but, you know."[25]

Finally, and perhaps most dramatically, Buckingham would also sue his former band for "fiduciary duty, breach of oral contract and intentional interference with prospective economic advantage"—a lawsuit that Buckingham and the band would eventually settle in December of 2018.[26]

Buckingham's former bandmates wouldn't be the only ones to thrive in the messy aftermath of his firing and the consistent, often slanderous "he said, she said," that followed, however.

After all, the man behind some of the band's biggest hits was used to going his own way by now.

—————— **AUGUST 27, 2022** ——————

Lindsey Buckingham joins American rock band The Killers on stage at the Banc of California Stadium in Los Angeles. Against the glow of blood-red stage lights and a fiery orange backdrop, Buckingham plays guitar on "Caution," from the band's 2020 album *Imploding the Mirage*. Then, to their fans' delight, the band performs a cover of *Rumours'* "Go Your Own Way" alongside the former Fleetwood Mac frontman. Finally, Buckingham and the band are joined by former Smiths guitarist Johnny Marr to perform The

Killers' 2004 mega-hit "Mr. Brightside," wrapping up the show's encore in dramatic fashion.

Buckingham's surprise guest appearance tonight isn't the world-renowned guitarist's first foray into the world of rock and roll since being fired from Fleetwood Mac four years earlier. Instead, the performance is just another recent notch in Buckingham's belt; since his departure, Buckingham's been on a tear, lending his voice and guitar work to several song features, including to "Darling" from American artist Halsey's 2021 studio album *If I Can't Have Love, I Want Power*.[1] Not only that, but Buckingham's also recently come off a US tour meant to support the release of his own 2021 album, *Lindsey Buckingham*.

While he's seen his share of successes, Buckingham's also struggled. Since his firing he's suffered a heart attack, temporarily lost his voice, and participated in several marriage counseling sessions over the phone with his wife of 21 years, Kristen Messner. However, as *Rolling Stone* put it in late September of 2021, Lindsey Buckingham "just won't stop."[2] Now, even more than four years after his departure from Fleetwood Mac, he's still passionate about embracing his creativity and making music. (He also has "a lot of optimism" that he and Messner can work things out.)[3]

After Lindsey Buckingham was fired from Fleetwood Mac, his son Will exclaimed, "God, they ruined your life!"

Buckingham responded with a smile: "Not even close."[4]

On October 5, 2018, six months after his departure from Fleetwood Mac, Buckingham released *Solo Anthology: The Best of Lindsey Buckingham*, a compilation album made up of selected solo works from Buckingham's six solo albums, from 1981's *Law and Order* to 2011's *Seeds We Sow.*

The album, released digitally and as a 3 CD set and 6 LP vinyl deluxe collection,[5] would peak at #53 on the US *Billboard* 200 Chart and at #78 on the UK Albums Chart. In addition to his biggest hits, like *Go Insane*'s title track and "Holiday Road" from the *National Lampoon's Vacation* soundtrack, the anthology also includes two new songs that "split the difference between Buckingham's folky, finger-picking skill and the muted rhythm guitar of his more popular LPs": "Ride This Road" and "Hunger."[6]

The anthology was generally well-received by critics, including *American Songwriter*'s Hal Horowitz, who wrote in 2018 that the collection immediately makes it clear that Buckingham is "one of the most talented artists to front a major act."[7]

Perhaps predictably, in addition to works from his solo albums, Buckingham's *Solo Anthology* also includes live recordings of tracks like "Bleed to Love Her," "Never Going Back Again," and "Big Love" from Buckingham's *Songs from the*

Small Machine and *One Man Show* albums—meaning that though the collection is well-and-truly a compilation of Lindsey Buckingham's greatest hits, the shadow of Fleetwood Mac still looms relatively large over the former frontman's sensational *Solo Anthology*.

The tension between Buckingham and his old band would soon begin to fade, however (albeit only slightly). Shortly after his firing, and after months of hearing nothing from his old bandmates,[8] Buckingham managed to somewhat rekindle his friendship with Mick Fleetwood, who had recently wrapped up his band's An Evening with Fleetwood Mac tour in mid-November 2019. The two reconnected following the death of original Fleetwood Mac frontman Peter Green in 2020, when Fleetwood decided to reach out to Buckingham via text message.[9] Following their reconciliation, Fleetwood declared, "I know for a fact that I intend to make music and play again with Lindsey… I would love that. It doesn't have to be in Fleetwood Mac." However, Fleetwood did acknowledge his desire for the band to host an "official" farewell tour, saying:

> I'm very aware that we've never played
> that card. I think the vision for me, and
> I think it would be hugely appropriate,
> is that we actually say "this is goodbye"
> and go out and actually do that. That
> has always been my vision and I'm

flatly confident that we can do that. We owe it to the fans.[10]

After Fleetwood's statement was released, Buckingham acknowledged that the drummer "probably didn't want to see him go in the first place," and claimed that, like Fleetwood, he would still hold out hope for some sort of reunion.[11]

While Buckingham and Fleetwood were optimistic about a reunion all the way up until early 2021, others in the band weren't as eager to reunite. Aside from rebuking Buckingham's account of his firing, Stevie Nicks was keeping mostly quiet about the whole affair (if you have nothing nice to say, say nothing at all?) while Christine McVie told the BBC that her ex-husband John was "feeling a bit frail" and didn't "have the heart for it any more."[12]

Buckingham had, of course, recently been in a similarly precarious and debilitating situation; in late 2019, just before reconciling with Mick Fleetwood, Buckingham suffered a heart attack and was forced to undergo an emergency triple-bypass surgery.[13] During the procedure, a surgical instrument nicked Buckingham's vocal cords[14]—a big deal for anyone, let alone for a man who had long made a living using his voice. Luckily, however, the damage was only temporary, and Buckingham's voice experienced only a slight drop in register.[15]

A few months later, back on his feet and with his future with Fleetwood Mac as hazy as ever, Buckingham continued to press on with his solo and other collaborative work, contributing guitar work to albums by The Killers, Brandy Clark,[16] and Halsey. Amidst his numerous collaborations, Buckingham also released an album of his own: a 10-track, self-titled effort that was perhaps more than just an album. Rather, it represented Buckingham's prevailing against seemingly insurmountable odds—his sudden firing from Fleetwood Mac, a near-death experience, his wife filing for divorce, and a move into a house where his only company was his housekeeper and three dogs.[17]

Although *Lindsey Buckingham* was ultimately released on September 17, 2021, Buckingham had begun and almost completed the album nearly four years earlier.[18] Regardless, the album is still a triumph, not to mention that—as if the release of an entire album during this hectic time in Buckingham's life wasn't impressive enough—the guitarist also announced a solo tour in support of the album shortly after its release.[19] Beginning in Milwaukee, Wisconsin on September 1 and concluding in Boulder, Colorado in mid-December, Buckingham's solo tour would make 30 stops in total—an impressive feat for the man who thought only two years earlier that he might never sing again.

As Buckingham intended, the album itself succeeds in listening like a pop album. The first three tracks, "Scream," "I Don't Mind," and "On the Wrong Side," were all released as singles between June and September 2021. The album's opening track, "Scream," immediately creates a poppy, springy atmosphere with an intro reminiscent of Australian indie pop group Sheppard's "Geronimo" that quickly launches into Buckingham's peppy vocals. All this goes to say, of course, that "Scream" makes for an excellent introduction to Buckingham's artful 2021 solo effort.

"I Don't Mind" and "On the Wrong Side" contain similarly airy instrumentals and tender, often hazy vocals, making *Lindsey Buckingham* listen a lot like select albums by Iron and Wine, Fleet Foxes, and Andrew Bird, albeit with slightly harder rocking choruses. The inspiration for the latter of these two tracks, "On the Wrong Side," is perhaps a bit obvious, given its title. This track, which Buckingham performed live on *Late Night with Stephen Colbert* the day prior to his album's release,[20] was written about Buckingham's tumultuous relationship with Fleetwood Mac and, as such, takes on an attitude not unlike 1977's "Go Your Own Way."[21]

Interestingly, 2021's "On the Wrong Side" isn't the first song by Buckingham released under this moniker. Nearly 30 years before the release of his seventh solo album, Buckingham contributed a song with an identical title to the star-studded soundtrack for the 1994 film *With Honors*. The song—which features tender, echoing vocal work—is accompanied on the soundtrack by songs written and performed by other big-name artists like Madonna, Duran Duran, and Kristen Hersh.

"On the Wrong Side's" predecessor, "I Don't Mind"—like many of the songs from Buckingham's prior solo efforts *Seeds We Sow* and *Gift of Screws*—was inspired by Buckingham's relationship with wife Kristen Messner. This time around, however, Buckingham draws inspiration from his marriage's recent hardships as he sings about the challenges of long-term relationships and the need to accept others' flaws and be willing to continually work on the issues that inevitably arise in such enduring partnerships.[22]

Just like "I Don't Mind," track #9 on the album, "Santa Rosa," clearly references Buckingham's developing marital struggles. In it, Buckingham sings directly to his wife Kristen Messner, who left Buckingham in L.A. and moved to Northern California when the couple filed for divorce in June of 2021. As such, the argument could be made that "Santa Rosa" represents a several-decades-in-the-making follow-up to 1977's "Never Going Back Again" as Buckingham sings: "Out on that west side road / We built our home with heart and soul / Oh no, I can't let go again."[23]

Ultimately, despite the noticeably more mournful tone of Buckingham's 2021 solo effort as compared to 2008's *Gift of Screws* and 2011's

Seeds We Sow, special thanks for the album are still credited to Kristen, Will, Leelee, and Stella Buckingham, among others.

The verses to "On the Wrong Side" are similar in style and structure to 2017's "Love is Here to Stay's," which is unsurprising given that several demos for *Lindsey Buckingham* were recorded almost immediately after production for *Lindsey Buckingham/Christine McVie* was declared a wrap in mid-2017. "On the Wrong Side" isn't the only track that borrows a few tips and tricks from Buckingham's previous work, however; track #4 on the album, "Swan Song," was built around a demo entitled "Mind's Eye" that Buckingham had recorded years before beginning work on his 2021 solo album.[24]

Interestingly, "Mind's Eye" was originally written by Canadian singer-songwriter Jordan Zadorozny and American musician Brad Laner, two artists Buckingham had produced tracks for in the early 2000s—one of these being, of course, "Mind's Eye." A few months after his solo effort was released in September, Buckingham would give songwriting credits to Zadorozny and Laner for "Swan Song" after noticing the similarities between his recording and the chorus of "Mind's Eye." Zadorozny would ultimately describe the mistake as a "happy accident" and remark that he was grateful for Buckingham's "rediscovery" and gorgeous reworking of the song.[25]

Ultimately, this "gorgeous reworking" includes lyrics similar to some that Buckingham originally penned a few years earlier. While 2017's "On with the Show" took obvious aim at former lover and bandmate Stevie Nicks's unwillingness to participate in recording sessions for what was supposed to be Fleetwood Mac's final studio effort, 2021's "Swan Song" attacks Nicks's supposed role in Buckingham's 2018 firing from the band—and thus, her apparent sabotage of the band's planned "swan song" tour. As such, throughout "Swan Song," Buckingham wonders whether it's right for Nicks to "keep him waiting" in the "shadow of our swan song."

Like "Swan Song," track #8 on the album, "Power Down," began as a series of drum loops and was a result of Buckingham wanting to do something "a little more techno" on the album: "the drum loops were just a great starting point and pretty much led to everything else," Buckingham would explain. "It was a way of having a little slap across the face just when you thought the album might be a little too pretty." In addition to "Swan Song" and "Power Down" being hugely popular among critics upon their debut, the two songs are Buckingham's favorites on the album.[26]

Finally, other standouts from *Lindsey Buckingham* include "Blind Love," "Blue Light," and album-closer "Dancing." The former is a track that critic Greil Marcus described not as horrendous, but instead as "a doo-wop ballad that sounds like something [Buckingham] and his high school friends made up while cruising up and down the San Francisco Peninsula instead of doing homework."[27] Meanwhile, "Blue Light" is a mournful, reflective tune about heartbreak and "losing our sight," but "never, never, never giving in" to "the house of blue light." Similarly, Buckingham's "Dancing" is a melancholy ballad with lyrics partially inspired by Stevie Nicks and partially by the idea that "on some level, we're all waiting for the circle to come around again, and what we're doing while we wait is basically dancing the dance of life," Buckingham would explain.[28]

Overall, the album was well-received and praised by fans and critics. In particular, critics tended to note their enjoyment of the upbeat instrumentals and youthful vocals that dominate *Lindsey Buckingham*'s entire just over 36-minute runtime. Ultimately, the album would prove to be both a critical *and* commercial success, managing to peak at #13 on *Billboard*'s US Top Album Sales chart, #37 on the US Top Rock Albums Chart, and at #25 on the UK Albums Chart. *Lindsey Buckingham* was most successful on the Scottish Albums Chart, however, managing to peak at #6 before the end of 2021.

Even though the album contains several knockouts and is one of Buckingham's best solo albums of all time, critics that would praise Buckingham's stellar songwriting skills and ability to "get younger verse by verse"[29] would also be the same to bring up Buckingham's recent reconciliation with Mick Fleetwood and suggest that perhaps the success and strength of 2021's *Lindsey Buckingham* would be enough for his old band to invite him to rejoin the wildly successful albeit unendingly toxic and tumultuous Fleetwood Mac fold.[30]

I DON'T MIND
EPILOGUE

Fleetwood Mac is engaged in a dazzling banjo-based rendition of Christine McVie's "Say You Love Me," a track that, by tonight, is nearly 25 years old. Though the band isn't playing some giant, sold-out arena or event center, there's no shortage of adoring fans in the house tonight. The crowd, not seated in hundreds of rows of stadium seats but instead in groups of five to six at well-dressed round tables, drinks champagne instead of over-priced concession stand beer. It is a special occasion, after all, as tonight, more than 30 years after making their debut, Fleetwood Mac is finally being inducted into the Rock & Roll Hall of Fame.

Though they're being inducted alongside superstars and supergroups like Santana, Eagles, and the Mamas and the Papas, Fleetwood Mac is far from a slouch by comparison. After all, in the last three decades, the band has released more than 15 albums, nine of which have managed to chart within the top 40 on the US *Billboard* Hot 200 by 1998, including the 1977 smash-hit *Rumours*—which by tonight has already cemented itself as one of the best-selling albums of all time. Though other members of the band being inducted tonight—including former Mac guitarists Peter Green, Jeremy Spencer, and Danny Kirwan—each had a hand in shaping Fleetwood Mac into the formidable rock and roll icon it is today, it's the band's current lineup that's been the one making the biggest waves since the early 1970s.

Christine McVie's saccharine vocals make for a dreamy "Say You Love Me," while Stevie Nicks's backing vocals give the track an underlying, haunting sound that's been helping to make Fleetwood Mac's greatest hits more than just shimmering FM radio fodder since early 1975. While the band's two leading ladies command the stage, the eccentric Mick Fleetwood hammers away at his drumkit, eyes wide as ever. As for the Mac's other namesake John McVie, he's doing his thing: playing bass while, in a rare occurrence, adding his vocals to the track as well. Finally, Lindsey Buckingham, plucking away at yet another instrument he's come to master in his time with Fleetwood Mac, looks over the crowd—one that has assembled to bear witness to what is essentially his creation: one of the greatest rock and roll bands of all time.

Turn on the radio or take the time to flip through the stacks of used CDs at your local thrift store. Google "rock and roll music," even. Better yet, visit any public place that plays popular music from the last 50 years or so as the soundtrack to your Saturday afternoon grocery-shopping, clothes-buying, or indie record store-scouting experience, and you'll find that no matter where you go, there's an ever-enduring presence that since the late 1960s has been a mainstay in the world of pop culture and popular music: a former blues band turned rock and roll atom bomb called Fleetwood Mac.

Though you're likely to hear much of their work broadcast on your local radio's "variety" or "classic rock" stations, Fleetwood Mac is much more than just your grandad's favorite band of the 1970s. In fact, Fleetwood Mac has a well-established fanbase made up of supporters both young and old: a fanbase also comprised of several big-name supporters including Florence Welch of Florence + the Machine, Harry Styles of One Direction fame, and the late Dolores O'Riordan of the Cranberries, who've each recorded covers of some of the Mac's greatest hits either in concert or for inclusion on albums of their own.

Though much of Fleetwood Mac's popularity stems from their work in the late seventies and eighties, from an era when gas was 50 cents a gallon and singers were their own songwriters, there's a reason why the band has been able to maintain their status as rock and roll royalty even more than 50 years after making their debut as a London-based blues band. Though many consider Fleetwood Mac's magnum opus *Rumours* or 1987's *Tango in the Night* as the main reasons why the band has managed to build such an enduring legacy, Fleetwood Mac's longevity can actually largely be credited to one man: Lindsey Buckingham.

A cool Southern California kid who just happened to make it into the band with a little bit of luck and a whole lot of talent, Buckingham began his career with Fleetwood Mac as the band's lead guitarist, though he quickly became much more than that. The chief architect behind 1975's *Fleetwood Mac*, 1977's *Rumours* as well as any of the albums for which the band is best known, Buckingham, by the late-1980s, had become not only the band's lead guitarist and vocalist, but lead producer and mastermind as well, engineering some of Fleetwood Mac's greatest hits, including 1977's "Go Your Own Way," 1979's "Tusk" and 1987's "Big Love," among others.

Though in collaboration with music industry legends Stevie Nicks, Mick Fleetwood, and John and Christine McVie, Buckingham was responsible for a vast majority of Fleetwood Mac's success, he was also the cause of substantial drama: a chaos that has followed the band from the very beginning. His bitter breakup with Stevie Nicks and his obsessive-compulsive tendencies, coupled with the band's over-excessive drug use—a trademark of 1970s rock and roll bands—meant that some of the band's best material would be born out of screaming matches and physical altercations instigated by none other than Buckingham himself.

Somehow, despite his and his bandmates' problematic behaviors, the formula has always worked. Beginning with 1975's *Fleetwood Mac*—a sort of "rebirth" for the former British blues band—Buckingham has managed to bring out the best in his bandmates to create masterpieces, whether by reworking unfinished material or by pushing his bandmates to their breaking points.

Though his solo work on albums like 1981's *Law and Order* and 1984's *Go Insane* is just as impressive as his work with Fleetwood Mac, Buckingham has never been able to emulate the same level of success on his own that he has with the band that originally thrust him into the throes of rock and roll legendry. Likewise, on the opposite end of the spectrum, history hardly remembers 1990's *Behind the Mask* or 1995's

Time, the only two albums that Fleetwood Mac has released without Buckingham since he joined the band back in 1975.

History, recording-breaking sales numbers, and millions of fans don't lie: there's just something about combining the two forces that makes for an inevitable success story.

Whether it's the sheer force of luck that brought the band together for the creation of *Fleetwood Mac*, the tensions that helped to create *Rumours,* or perhaps Buckingham's obsessiveness and unwillingness to follow a formula that led to the creation of 1979's *Tusk*, combining Buckingham with the force of Fleetwood Mac is always a recipe for commercial success, albeit at the expense of interpersonal turmoil:

This is something that was never lost on Fleetwood Mac's record label Warner Bros., who on two separate occasions in a span of 15 years coerced Buckingham into taking his solo work and using it to spearhead the creation of a new Fleetwood Mac album. On both occasions, the end results—1987's *Tango in the Night* and 2003's *Say You Will*—became hits, in no small part thanks to tracks like Buckingham's "Big Love" and "Peacekeeper."

The full "*Rumours 5*" line-up would never reconvene for a farewell tour or to record any sort of official reunion album. There are several reasons why: for one, Buckingham and Nicks's volatile relationship would persist into late 2022. Not only did Buckingham continue to make disparaging comments about Nicks's personal and love life months after his firing, but the release of the song "Dancing" from his 2021 solo album also cemented the reality that the toxicity between the two former lovers would never be fully resolved.

Meanwhile, as rumors were swirling about John McVie's health and supposed unwillingness to rejoin the band, Buckingham cancelled part of his 2022 European solo tour, citing his own "ongoing health issues"[1]—dealing another blow to Fleetwood Mac fans desperate to see the band get back together one last time.

A few months after McVie and Buckingham's health scares came to light, however, Fleetwood Mac released their "Alternate Collection" on November 25, 2022 for Record Store Day's yearly "Black Friday" event. Available in a 6 CD or 8 LP format, the "Alternate Collection" features "alternate" recordings and outtakes from the band's *Fleetwood Mac, Rumours, Tusk, Live, Mirage,* and *Tango in the Night* sessions. While the release of the band's "Alternate Collection" showed the continued contemporary resurgence of vinyl's popularity among music lovers, the collection's release and widespread popularity also demonstrated the timelessness of Fleetwood Mac.[2] This release, despite the load of bad news that had preceded it, reignited many long-time fans' hopes that maybe a reunion could happen after all.

The worst was yet to come, however: while Buckingham and Nicks were still feuding, it was announced on December 30, 2022 that Fleetwood Mac's songbird, Christine McVie, had passed away at age 79. McVie passed away peacefully, surrounded by her family, after a battle with a "brief illness."[3]

Christine McVie, born Christine Perfect in 1943, was Fleetwood Mac's anchor, having spent more than 30 years of her life with the band. Responsible for some of their biggest hits and known for being one of the Mac's more levelheaded members, McVie's influence on the world of rock and roll and in shaping Fleetwood Mac into the powerhouse it has become cannot be understated. Appropriately, heartfelt tributes to McVie poured in from fans and her bandmates in the immediate wake of her passing.

On the day of McVie's death, Stevie Nicks, on Instagram, posted a handwritten note dedicated to her "best friend in the whole world," which included lyrics to Haim's "Hallelujah," which Nicks claimed she wished she could've sung to McVie before her passing[4]:

> I had a best friend but she has come to pass / One I wish I could see now / You always remind me that memories will last / These arms reach out / You were

there to protect me like a shield / Long hair, running with me through the field / Everywhere, you've been with me all along.[5]

Likewise, soon after her passing, the band issued a statement on Twitter paying tribute to the "truly one-of-a-kind, special and talented beyond measure" McVie[6] while former bandmates Mick Fleetwood and Lindsey Buckingham would also release statements, with the latter, like Nicks, penning a handwritten letter that he posted to his official Instagram. In his letter, Buckingham mourned the loss of McVie, who he labeled "a musical comrade, a friend, a soul mate, a sister."[7]

While some members of the band extensively teased and held out hope for a reunion, the "*Rumours 5*" were never able to put their differences aside. McVie's death both signaled the death of a wonderful singer, songwriter, and soul, but also the end of the most prolific and beloved iteration of Fleetwood Mac. Perhaps there was an important lesson to learn in the aftermath of McVie's tragic passing. As Buckingham sang in 2021: "Sunset I laugh, sun rise I cry / At midnight I'm in-between and wondering why / Time, oh time, where do you go? / Time, oh good good time, where did you go?"[8]

Following McVie's untimely passing and the release of Fleetwood Mac's hefty "Alternate

Collection," which showcased hours of the band and Buckingham's most commercially popular work, Buckingham reflected on a tumultuous 2022, writing on Instagram that:

> The year's polarity of positives and negatives has only strengthened my resolve to remain in the moment and to continue to move forward. Happily, my health has returned, and I've begun work on a new album. Thanks so much to everyone for your support. I'm looking forward to 2023 and beyond![9]

Buckingham's comment effectively summarized not only 2022, but also the history of Fleetwood Mac and his relationship with the band that helped to launch his career as a superstar musician, producer, and solo artist.

Just as Buckingham sang in 2021—"Where there's joy, there must be sorrow / Never far apart"[10]—the polarity of "positives and negatives" that dominated the history of Fleetwood Mac from the late 1960s and well into the 21st century is undeniable. However, the reality that the band will always remain synonymous with the phrase "rock and roll" and that Buckingham is one of the greatest guitarists, singers, songwriters, and producers in the history of rock and roll is as well.

Whether or not the remaining members of Fleetwood Mac ever reconvene for a final "reunion" album, tour, or any other sort of formal send-off,[11] one other thing is certain: people don't (and likely will never) talk about Lindsey Buckingham, Christine McVie, or any other member of the band's involvement with Fleetwood Mac "in the past tense." Their work with Fleetwood Mac may be "chronologically in the past, but it's living now," as Buckingham declared in 2021.[12] As such, while the band's most celebrated line-up was never able to "appropriately" bid fans farewell, Fleetwood Mac and the band's music is (and was always) deathless, despite the toxicity that caused the band to separate and splinter time after time.

Now, two decades into the 21st century, this sentiment is truer than ever, and perhaps it's clearer than ever too that the dysfunctional quintet was never meant to have a true or in any way perfect "happy" ending. Regardless, as Buckingham pushes on with a new solo album and Nicks embarks on a brief 2023 tour alongside Billy Joel,[13] their work—the albums that occupy space on the shelves of record collections all over the world and the tracks that continue to dominate FM airwaves to this day—manages to keep up the spirit of McVie's 1977 hit "Don't Stop" and continues to demonstrate that the magic the continually fragmented five-piece made together is truly timeless.

As time continues to pass and the band's music and story pass from generation to generation, however, it is increasingly important to continually commemorate and *never forget* how the band was able to create such magic and develop such an enduring legacy in the first place.

It all began in 1974 when a struggling British blues band—already sensational in its own right—decided to gamble on two no-name artists from Southern California. Since then, they continue to prove that thunder *does* only happen when it's raining after all...

N O T E S   B Y
CHAPTER

BEFORE THE BEGINNING

1. Mick Fleetwood and Anthony Bozza, *Play On: Now, Then & Fleetwood Mac* (New York: Little, Brown and Company, 2014), 80.
2. John McVie left John Mayall & the Bluesbreakers and joined Fleetwood Mac a few weeks after the band was initially founded because, unlike Green and Fleetwood, McVie wasn't willing to risk giving up a steady income to form a new band. See https://www.mtv.com/news/7dt6wk/ john-mcvie
3. Throughout the late 1960s, the band was often marketed as "Peter Green's Fleetwood Mac." This infuriated Green, who had always intended Fleetwood and McVie to be the band's sole namesakes. See https://www.grunge.com/184217/the-tragic-real-life-story-of-

fleetwood-mac/

4. American rock band Santana covered Green's "Black Magic Woman" for inclusion on their 1970 studio album *Abraxas*. Their cover of the song, which was released as a single from the album in November 1970, would manage to peak at #4 on the US *Billboard* Hot 100 two months later. Green performed the song alongside Santana at the band's Rock and Roll Hall of Fame induction ceremony in 1998. See Sean Egan, *Fleetwood Mac on Fleetwood Mac: Interviews and Encounters* (Chicago: Chicago Review Press, 2016), 336.

5. Barry Gifford, "Peter Green's Fleetwood Mac," *Rolling Stone*, August 10, 1968, https://www.rollingstone.com/music/music-album-reviews/peter-greens-fleetwood-mac-248342/

6. Scott Hopkins, "The Class of 1970: Fleetwood Mac's 'Kiln House'," *MUSICFESTNEWS*, September 17, 2020, https://musicfestnews.com/2020/09/the-class-of-1970-fleetwood-macs-kiln-house/

7. Jean Mendoza and Leslie Veliz, "Christine McVie's Short Marriage to John McVie Explained," *Grunge*, December 1, 2022, https://www.grunge.com/1122468/christine-mcvies-short-marriage-to-john-mcvie-explained/

8. "Rattlesnake Shake" was written by guitarist Peter Green as "an ode to masturbation." In 2014, Mick Fleetwood wrote that, "I'm named in [the song], as a guy who does the rattlesnake shake to jerk away my sadness whenever I don't have a chick. That was an appropriate immortalisation of my younger self." See Fleetwood and Bozza, *Play On*, 105-106.

9. As of 2023, Spencer is still a member of the "Children of God" commune, now called "The Family International." The organization has long been the subject of allegations of radicalism and child abuse. See https://rockcelebrities.net/when-two-fleetwood-mac-members-went-missing-and-secretly-joined-a-cult/

10. Kirwan was kicked out of the band following an intoxicated backstage brawl between himself and Welch in 1972. Welch left the band shortly after, citing difficulties in his marriage and creative burnout as the reasons for his departure. Welch died by suicide at the age of 65 in 2012. Six years later, in 2018, Kirwan died in his sleep. He was 68 years old. See Fleetwood and Bozza, *Play On*, 139-141.
11. Fleetwood and Bozza, *Play On*, 128-131.

SHOW-BIZ BLUES

1. Fred Schruers, "Back on the Chain Gang," *Rolling Stone*, October 30, 1997, https://www.rollingstone.com /music/music-news/fleetwood-mac-back-on-the-chain-gang-243176/
2. "Gregory F. Buckingham," *Olympics*, accessed November 27, 2022, https://olympics.com/en/athletes/ gregory-f-buckingham
3. A member of the Menlo Country Club in Woodside, California, Morris Buckingham initially encouraged all three of his sons to swim competitively. See http://www .fleetwoodmac.net/fwm/index.php?option=com_content &task=view&id=66&Itemid=80
4. Buckingham once recalled that his brother's record collection grew so large throughout his childhood that "it was like having the story of rock and roll unfurled in front of me." See http://www.fleetwoodmac.net/fwm/ index.php?option=com_content&task=view&id=66&It emid=80
5. Russell Hall, "Lindsey Buckingham Talks Guitars, Fleetwood Mac Reunion Tour," *Gibson Magazine*, February 4, 2009, https://www.fleetwoodmacnews.com /2009/02/lindsey-buckingham-talks-guitars.html
6. Ibid.
7. Grace Turney, "Stevie Nicks Said She Would Have Left Fleetwood Mac to Join This Band," *Cheat Sheet*, October 7, 2022, https://www.cheatsheet.com/

entertainment/stevie-nicks-said-left-fleetwood-mac-join-band.html/

8. Stephen Davis, *Gold Dust Woman: The Biography of Stevie Nicks* (New York: St. Martin's Press, 2017), 17.

9. Ibid., 15.

10. Other members of Fritz included founding members Jody Moreing and Calvin (Cal) Roper (Moreing's cousin), who later left the band in 1967. By the time Fritz disbanded in 1971, the band was comprised of guitarist Brian Kane, drummer Bob Aguirre, keyboardist Javier Pacheco, and, of course, Nicks (vocals) and Buckingham (bass). See Davis, *Gold Dust Woman*, 17.

11. Brian Hiatt, "Stevie Nicks: A Rock Goddess Looks Back," *Rolling Stone*, January 15, 2015, https://www.rollingstone.com/music/music-news/stevie-nicks-a-rock-goddess-looks-back-179984/

12. Mick Fleetwood and Anthony Bozza, *Play On: Now, Then & Fleetwood Mac* (New York: Little, Brown and Company, 2014), 162.

13. Keith Alan Olsen, as well as producing *Buckingham Nicks,* also received production credits for over 100 other complete albums, including Pat Benatar's *Crimes of Passion*, Ozzie Osbourne's *No Rest for the Wicked*, and, of course, Fleetwood Mac's 1975 self-titled album, which was released two years after *Buckingham Nicks*. Olsen died in March 2020 at age 74. See https://www.allmusic.com/artist/keith-olsen-mn0000767102/credits

14. "The Early Years II 1966-1975," *In Her Own Words*, accessed November 29, 2022, http://www.inherownwords.com/earlyyrs2.htm

15. Cath Carroll, *Never Break the Chain: Fleetwood Mac and the Making of Rumours* (Chicago: Chicago Review Press, 2004), 134.

16. Ibid.

17. Ken Caillat and Steve Stiefel, *Making Rumours: The Inside Story of the Classic Fleetwood Mac Album* (New York: Wiley & Sons, 2012), 79.

18. Former Fritz members Kane, Aguirre, and Pacheco eventually reunited with Buckingham and Nicks in 2004 at a Fleetwood Mac concert at the Concord Pavilion in California. Pacheco wrote of the experience: "A lot of suppressed love came to the surface. It was as if time and circumstance had not come between us." See https://web.archive.org/web/20120105171454/http://www.fleetwoodmac.net/penguin/fritz.htm/

19. Hiatt, "Looks Back."

20. Ibid.

21. Track number seven on the album, "Django," is a cover of the introduction to an original jazz standard written in 1954 by John Lewis, an American jazz pianist and musical director for the Modern Jazz Quartet. See Gary Giddins, *Visions of Jazz: The First Century* (Oxford: Oxford University Press, 2000), 384.

22. Despite initial (albeit scarce) praise of the song upon the album's debut, contemporary critics, including *AllMusic*'s John Duffy for example, have since criticized the "misogyny" of Buckingham's "Lola" as "a real eye-roller." See https://www.allmusic.com/album/buckingham-nicks-mw0000849583#

23. As of 2023, *Buckingham Nicks* has never been reissued on CD or in any digital format. Around the time 1997's *The Dance* was released, Buckingham floated the idea of a re-release of the album, though nothing ever came of this. However, copies of the original pressing on vinyl are still widely available online—you might also be lucky enough to find a copy in your local record store!

24. Noel Murray, "Stevie Nicks and Lindsey Buckingham made a fine pop record pre-Fleetwood Mac," *AV Club*, September 29, 2015, https://www.avclub.com/stevie-nicks-and-lindsey-buckingham-made-a-fine-pop-rec-1798284894

25. Kevin O'Hare, "The Republican interview: Stevie Nicks," *Mass Live*, April 5, 2009, https://www

.masslive.com/entertainment/2009/04/the_republican_in terview_stevi.html

26. Simon Morrison, *Mirror in the Sky: The Life and Music of Stevie Nicks* (Berkeley: University of California Press, 2022), 38.

27. Caillat and Stiefel, *Making Rumours*, 4.

EYES OF THE WORLD

1. Mick Fleetwood and Anthony Bozza, *Play On: Now, Then & Fleetwood Mac* (New York: Little, Brown and Company, 2014), 164, 169.

2. Ibid., 171.

3. "Keith Olsen Obituary." *The Times*. (March 17, 2020). Accessed via: https://fleetwoodmac-uk.com/wp/keith-olsen-obituary-the-times-uk/

4. In a 2017 interview with *CBS*, Mick Fleetwood explained that founding member Peter Green named the band after Fleetwood and bassist John McVie because Green, who always felt that he would one day leave Fleetwood Mac, "wanted Mick and John to have a band" after he was gone. See https://www.cbsnews .com/news/fleetwood-mac-mick-fleetwood-on-bands-origin-new-book/

5. Bob Doerschuk, "Christine McVie," *Contemporary Keyboard*, October 1980, accessed via: https://web .archive.org/web/20150710065842/http://bla.fleetwood mac.net/index.php?page=index_v2&id=11&c=2

6. Carol Ann Harris, *Storms: My Life with Lindsey Buckingham and Fleetwood Mac* (Chicago: Chicago Review Press, 2009), 198.

7. Doerschuk, "McVie."

8. Christine McVie's first endeavor into the music industry came when she joined a band, along with friends Stan Webb and Andy Silvester, called "Sounds of Blue." Shortly after Sounds of Blue broke up, McVie joined Webb and Silvester in a new blues band they were forming called Chicken Shack in 1967. She contributed to two of Chicken Shack's albums before leaving the

band in 1969. See Steve Clarke, *Fleetwood Mac* (Belleville: Proteus Books, 1984), 48.

9. Russell Hall, "Lindsey Buckingham Talks Guitars, Fleetwood Mac Reunion Tour," *Gibson Magazine*, February 4, 2009, https://www.fleetwoodmacnews .com/2009/02/lindsey-buckingham-talks-guitars.html

10. "Blue Letter" was the only song on Fleetwood Mac's "White Album" written by someone outside the band. The track had instead been written by Richard and Michael Curtis, brothers who befriended Buckingham and Nicks before the duo joined Fleetwood Mac. The four also demoed the song "Seven League Boots," which would later be reworked by Crosby, Stills & Nash and released in 1982 as the smash hit "Southern Cross." See http://www.angellesmusic.com/jennifer curtis/RichardCurtis.html

11. Nigel Williamson, "Fleetwood Mac: 'Everyone was pretty weirded out' – the story of Rumours," *Uncut*, January 29, 2013, https://www.uncut.co.uk/features/ fleetwood-mac-everybody-was-pretty-weirded-out-the- story-of-rumours-26395/

12. Bud Scoppa, "Fleetwood Mac," *Rolling Stone*, September 25, 1975, https://www.rollingstone.com/ music/music-album-reviews/fleetwood-mac-98110/

13. "Warm Ways" was only released in the UK as the lead single from *Fleetwood Mac*. Another McVie track, "Over My Head," was chosen by Reprise as the album's first single in the United States. See Martin C. Strong, *The Great Rock Discography* (Edinburgh, UK: Canongate, 2003).

14. Stephen Davis, *Gold Dust Woman: The Biography of Stevie Nicks* (New York: St. Martin's Press, 2017), 77.

15. Ibid., 17.

16. To be certified "platinum" by the Recording Industry Association of America (RIAA), albums must sell at least one million units and may only be available for certification 30 days after the album's initial release. The award was introduced in 1976, one year after the

release of *Fleetwood Mac.* Later, in 1999, the RIAA instituted the "diamond" award for albums and singles that manage to sell at least ten million units. See https://www.riaa.com/goldandplatinum60/#vinyl-era

17. *Classic Albums – Fleetwood Mac: Rumours,* directed by David Heffeman (1997; London, UK: Eagle Rock Entertainment, 2005), DVD.

18. Davis, *Gold Dust Woman,* 82.

19. Also referred to as "the Colonel" and as "J.C.", Fleetwood Mac's road manager and tour director John Courage is well-known for his legendary introductions of the band during the band's *Rumours* and *Tusk* eras: "Ladies and gentlemen: Would you please give a warm welcome to… Fleetwood Mac!" In addition to being heard live by millions of fans throughout the late 1970s, this line can be heard at the opening of the band's 1980 album *Live.* Courage was fired at the conclusion of the band's *Tusk* tour and passed away in 2016. See https://www.nodepression.com/goodbye-j-c-fleetwood-mac-loses-one-of-its-own/

20. The "falling out" between Fleetwood and Olsen and Olsen's ultimate firing were caused by disputes over royalty payments and Olsen's imposition of a ban on drugs in his recording studio. For the band's subsequent album *Rumours,* Olsen was replaced as producer by his assistant engineer Richard Dashut. See https://fleetwood mac-uk.com/wp/uk.com/wp/keith-olsen-obituary-the-times-uk/

21. Rikky Rooksby, *Fleetwood Mac: The Complete Guide to Their Music.* (London: Omnibus Press, 2005), 60.

22. Under Olsen, *Fleetwood Mac* was recorded in only six weeks and on a strict budget. The band's subsequent album would take several months to record and was at the time of its release rumored to be the costliest album ever produced. See https://fleetwoodmac-uk.com/wp/uk.com/wp/keith-olsen-obituary-the-times-uk/

23. Donald Brackett, *Fleetwood Mac: 40 Years of Creative Chaos* (Westport: Praeger, 2007), 126.

24. Heffeman, *Classic Albums*.

25. An advance order of 800,000 copies of *Rumours* would prove to, at the time, be the largest in Warner Bros.' history. See Donald Brackett, *Fleetwood Mac: 40 Years of Creative Chaos* (Westport: Praeger, 2007), 125.

26. Davis, *Gold Dust Woman*, 86.

GO INSANE

1. Ken Caillat and Steve Stiefel, *Making Rumours: The Inside Story of the Classic Fleetwood Mac Album* (New York: Wiley & Sons, 2012), 83.

2. Ibid., 83-84.

3. Jessica Hopper, *The First Collection of Criticism by a Living Female Rock Critic: Revised and Expanded Edition*, (New York: MCD Books, 2021), 117.

4. Caillat and Stiefel, *Making Rumours*, 130

5. Will Lavin, "Lindsey Buckingham says he never got 'closure' with Stevie Nicks," *NME*, May 8, 2021, https://www.nme.com/news/music/lindsey-buckingham-says-he-never-got-closure-with-stevie-nicks-2936237

6. Caillat and Stiefel, *Making Rumours*, 130

7. Joe Taysom, "The Fleetwood Mac number one Stevie Nicks wrote 'in ten minutes'," *Far Out Magazine*, July 31, 2022, https://faroutmagazine.co.uk/fleetwood-mac-number-one-stevie-nicks-wrote-in-10-minutes/

8. In addition to the release of several cover versions of the song, Nicks also contributed vocals to a mid-2000s remake of the song by DJ duo Deep Dish. The song was included on their 2005 album *George Is On*. A remixed version of the remake also appears on Nicks's 2007 compilation album *Crystal Visions: The Very Best of the Stevie Nicks*. See https://www.rollingstone.com/music/music-news/stevie-nicks-joins-deep-dish-104186/

9. John Swenson, "Rumours," *Rolling Stone*, April 21, 1977, https://www.rollingstone.com/music/music-album-reviews/rumours-189491/

10. Caillat and Stiefel, *Making Rumours*, 231.

11. Daryl Easlea, "Fleetwood Mac Rumours Review," *BBC Music*, December 14, 2007, https://www.bbc.co.uk/ music/reviews/r563/

12. Carol Ann Harris, *Storms: My Life with Lindsey Buckingham and Fleetwood Mac* (Chicago: Chicago Review Press, 2009), xiii.

13. McVie's three-year relationship with Grant ended after the release of *Rumours*. After their breakup, McVie began dating Beach Boy Dennis Wilson while Curry tried to "distract himself with just about every female in the band family… drowning his sorrows with yet another typical cure for an inner-circle crisis: sex with women who were close enough to be your sisters." See Harris, *Storms*, 215, 200.

14. Caillat and Stiefel, *Making Rumours*, 58.

15. Ibid., 61.

16. Nigel Williamson, "Fleetwood Mac: 'Everyone was pretty weirded out' – the story of Rumours," *Uncut*, January 29, 2013, https://www.uncut.co.uk/features/ fleetwood-mac-everybody-was-pretty-weirded-out-the- story-of-rumours-26395/

17. See next chapter, "Behind the Mask."

18. Caillat and Stiefel, *Making Rumours*, 131.

19. In a 2016 interview, McVie described to *The Guardian*'s Peter Robinson how "Songbird" came to be, remarking that "I woke up in the middle of the night, and the song just came into my head. I got out of bed, played it on the little piano I have in my room, and sang it with no tape recorder. I sang it from beginning to end: everything… it was a very spiritual thing." See https://www.theguardian.com/music/2016/oct/06/ christine-mcvie-on-fleetwood-mac-without-one-of-us- were-incomplete

20. Caillat and Stiefel, *Making Rumours*, 133.

21. Despite drawing inspiration from her bitter divorce from husband John McVie while writing songs like "You Make Loving Fun," "Don't Stop," and "Songbird," McVie explained in 2004 that she's

"definitely not a pessimist"—something that is unmistakably evident when comparing her contributions to *Rumours* to those of Buckingham or even Nicks. See Bob Brunning, *The Fleetwood Mac Story: Rumours and Lies* (London: Omnibus Press, 2004).
22. Harris, *Storms*, 8.
23. Caillat and Stiefel, *Making Rumours*, 105.
24. Ibid., 141.
25. Williamson, "Weirded Out."
26. *Classic Albums – Fleetwood Mac: Rumours*, directed by David Heffeman (1997; London, UK: Eagle Rock Entertainment, 2005), DVD.

BEHIND THE MASK

1. Donald Brackett, *Fleetwood Mac: 40 Years of Creative Chaos* (Westport: Praeger, 2007), 125.
2. Nigel Williamson, "Fleetwood Mac: 'Everyone was pretty weirded out' – the story of Rumours," *Uncut*, January 29, 2013, https://www.uncut.co.uk/features/fleetwood-mac-everybody-was-pretty-weirded-out-the-story-of-rumours-26395/
3. Regarding her post-*Rumours* spending spree, McVie would later remark that: "it was totally over the top, I didn't need a Rolls Royce—I ended up getting rid of it and getting something smaller—but it was just the fact that I could." See https://www.bbc.co.uk/programmes/b09jby2m
4. Cath Carroll, *Never Break the Chain: Fleetwood Mac and the Making of Rumours* (Chicago: Chicago Review Press, 2004), 134.
5. Sean Egan, *Fleetwood Mac on Fleetwood Mac: Interviews and Encounters* (Chicago: Chicago Review Press, 2016), 218.
6. In 2015, it was announced that the UK's free-to-air coverage of Formula 1 would be broadcast by Channel 4 beginning in 2016, rather than the BBC, which had held the rights to broadcast the sport since 2009.

Channel 4 quickly announced that it would retain "The Chain" as the opening theme for its coverage of Formula 1 racing in 2016. See https://www.motorsport .com/f1/news/channel-4-to-keep-the-chain-as-f1-theme-song-673047/673047/

7. Ken Caillat and Steve Stiefel, *Making Rumours: The Inside Story of the Classic Fleetwood Mac Album* (New York: Wiley & Sons, 2012), 108.

8. Ibid., 101.

9. *Classic Albums – Fleetwood Mac: Rumours*, directed by David Heffeman (1997; London, UK: Eagle Rock Entertainment, 2005), DVD.

10. Brittany Spanos, "'Silver Springs': Inside Fleetwood Mac's Great Lost Breakup Anthem," *Rolling Stone*, August 17, 2017, https://www.rollingstone.com/ feature/silver-springs-inside-fleetwood-macs-great-lost-breakup-anthem-201303/

11. Ibid.

12. Heffeman, *Classic Albums*.

13. Despite her initial frustrations, Nick later explained that she was glad that "I Don't Want to Know" was the song chosen to replace "Silver Springs" on *Rumours* since she ultimately liked the recording as well as the harmonies she and Buckingham shared on the song. See Heffeman, *Classic Albums*.

14. Carol Ann Harris, *Storms: My Life with Lindsey Buckingham and Fleetwood Mac* (Chicago: Chicago Review Press, 2009), xiii.

15. Mick Fleetwood and Anthony Bozza, *Play On: Now, Then & Fleetwood Mac* (New York: Little, Brown and Company, 2014), 201.

16. Joe Bosso, "Mick Fleetwood: my 11 greatest recordings of all time," *Music Radar*, July 27, 2012, https://www .musicradar.com/news/drums/mick-fleetwood-my-11-greatest-recordings-of-all-time-554519

17. Caillat and Stiefel, *Making Rumours*, 76.

18. Brian Hiatt, "Stevie Nicks: A Rock Goddess Looks Back," *Rolling Stone*, January 15, 2015, https://www

.rollingstone.com/music/music-news/stevie-nicks-a-rock-goddess-looks-back-179984/

19. Carroll, *Break the Chain*, 140.

20. *Lifehouse* was initially conceived as a science-fiction rock opera by Who guitarist Pete Townshend in early 1970. The album was "set in the not-too-distant future, maybe 1990… at a point in history where everyone on earth wore special 'pod-like' Lifesuits connected by wires to a central worldwide 'grid', which 'fed' them entertainment… though not rock music, which was banned." The idea was deemed nonsensical by other members of the band and the album was ultimately scrapped, though some of the planned material for *Lifehouse* was included on the band's 1971 album *Who's Next*. See https://www.loudersound.com/features/how-the-lifehouse-album-was-almost-the-death-of-the-who

21. Jordan Runtagh, "Fleetwood Mac's 'Rumours': 10 Things You Didn't Know," *Rolling Stone*, February 3, 2017, https://www.rollingstone.com/feature/fleetwood-macs-rumours-10-things-you-didnt-know-121876/

22. Williamson, "Weirded Out."

23. Harris, *Storms*, 116.

24. Buckingham was furious when he realized he wouldn't be featured on the cover of *Rumours*. Years after the album's release, photographer Herbert (aka "Herbie") Worthington told *Rumours* co-producer Ken Caillat: "Lindsey has never forgiven me for not being on the *Rumours* cover… [he] came up to me and said, 'I wish I could have been on my own cover.'" See Caillat and Stiefel, *Making Rumours*, 333.

CAN'T GO BACK

1. Daisann McLane, "Fleetwood Mac: They Dared to be Different," *Rolling Stone*, February 7, 1980, https://www.rollingstone.com/music/music-news/fleetwood-mac-they-dared-to-be-different-243618/

2. Bob Stanley, "How to lose 3 million fans in one easy step," *The Guardian*, March 6, 2008, https://www.theguardian.com/music/2008/mar/07/popandrock1

3. Zoë Howe, *Stevie Nicks: Visions, Dreams & Rumours* (London: Omnibus Press, 2015), 128.

4. Cameron Crowe, "The True Life Confessions of Fleetwood Mac," *Rolling Stone,* March 24, 1977, https://www.rollingstone.com/feature/the-true-life-confessions-of-fleetwood-mac-120867/

5. Pink Floyd's *Animals* peaked at #2 on the UK Albums Chart, #3 on the US *Billboard* 200, and #1 in Germany, Italy, and Spain. Queen's *A Day at the Races* meanwhile peaked at #1 on the UK Albums Chart and at #5 on the US *Billboard* 200. As of 2023, *Animals* has been certified 4x platinum in the US while *A Day at the Races* has been certified platinum by the RIAA in the United States. See the Record Industry Association of America's website.

6. Ken Caillat and Hernan Rojas, *Get Tusked: The Inside Story of Fleetwood Mac's Most Anticipated Album* (London: Backbeat Books, 2021), 14.

7. Nicks has explained in interviews that the song "Sara" was written about her friend and eventual wife of Mick Fleetwood, Sara Recor. However, Nicks's ex-boyfriend and Eagle Don Henley has also said that the song was named after an unborn baby he had planned to have with Nicks in the late 1970s. See https://www.billboard.com/music/music-news/stevie-nicks-interview-on-don-henley-fleetwood-mac-24-karat-gold-album-6266329/

8. Buckingham's habit for recording the entirety of a track's (albeit usually sparse) instrumentation would be even more evident upon the release of his debut solo album *Law and Order* in 1981, on which Buckingham alone played the guitar, bass, keyboards, percussion, drums, and provided vocals for nearly every track. See https://web.archive.org/web/20090423070547/http://www.rollingstone.com:80/artists/lindseybuckingham/albums/album/216825/review/5943221/law_and_order

9. In a 1980 interview with Christine McVie conducted by *Contemporary Keyboard*'s Bob Doerschuk, McVie explained that Buckingham's "What Makes You Think You're the One" is "especially tough to play… You have to keep crashing away at chords through the whole thing. By the time it's finished my wrists are like spaghetti. I really have to hammer the acoustic piano on some of his songs." See https://web.archive.org/web/20150710065842/http://bla.fleetwoodmac.net/index.php?page=index_v2&id=11&c=2

10. Ken Caillat and Hernan Rojas, *Get Tusked: The Inside Story of Fleetwood Mac's Most Anticipated Album* (London: Backbeat Books, 2021), 22.

11. Howe, *Dreams & Rumours*, 128.

12. Creation of The Beach Boys' abandoned album *Smile* began immediately after the release of 1966's *Pet Sounds*. In 2011, *The Smile Sessions* was released as a compilation of snippets and songs from the original recording sessions for *Smile*. Though the compilation won universal acclaim, *Smile* is still considered to be one of the most legendary unreleased albums of all time. See Domenic Priore, *Smile: The Story of Brian Wilson's Lost Masterpiece* (New York: Sanctuary Books, 2005).

13. Christopher R. Weingarten, et al., "Fleetwood Mac's 50 Greatest Songs," *Rolling Stone*, May 2, 2022, https://www.rollingstone.com/music/music-lists/fleetwood-macs-50-greatest-songs-192324/

14. See https://societyofrock.com/fleetwood-macs-79-angel-performance-will-make-you-smile-all-day/

15. Ryan Reed, "Fleetwood Mac's 'Tusk': 10 Things You Didn't Know," *Rolling Stone*, October 11, 2019, https://www.rollingstone.com/feature/fleetwood-mac-tusk-things-you-didnt-know-896796/

16. Weingarten, et al., "Greatest Songs."

17. Sam Kemp, "The secret Beatles link in Fleetwood Mac's classic song, 'Beautiful Child'," *Far Out Magazine*,

August 28, 2021, https://faroutmagazine.co.uk/the-beatles-link-fleetwood-mac-classic-song/

18. Weingarten, et al., "Greatest Songs."

19. Joe Bosso, "Mick Fleetwood: my 11 greatest recordings of all time," Music Radar, July 27, 2012, https://www.musicradar.com/news/drums/mick-fleetwood-my-11-greatest-recordings-of-all-time-554519

20. Mick Fleetwood and Anthony Bozza, *Play On: Now, Then & Fleetwood Mac* (New York: Little, Brown and Company, 2014), 238.

21. Nicks's "Fireflies," which was recorded at Santa Monica Civic Auditorium in California, was the only single from the band's *Live* album to chart in the US, reaching #60 on the US *Billboard* Hot 100 following its release. See https://www.billboard.com/artist/fleetwood-mac/chart-history/hsi/

22. Mick Fleetwood and Stephen Davis, *Fleetwood: My Life and Adventures in Fleetwood Mac* (New York: William Morrow & Company, 1990), 219-220.

23. Rikky Rooksby, *Fleetwood Mac: The Complete Guide to Their Music.* (London: Omnibus Press, 2005), 115.

24. Howe, *Dreams & Rumours*, 153.

25. Mike Evans, *Fleetwood Mac: The Definitive History* (New York: Sterling, 2011), 165.

26. Since *Tusk*'s initial rocky release, music review outlets like *Louder Sound, Pitchfork, Rolling Stone*, and *Ultimate Classic Rock have* retrospectively praised the album's experimental nature and seemingly "unfinished" sound. See https://www.loudersound.com/features/why-fleetwood-mac-s-tusk-is-better-than-rumours

STRAIGHT BACK

1. "September Song" was a piece originally introduced in 1938 on Broadway by Walter Huston, long before the track was used in the 1950 film, *September Affair*, for which it is best known. See Tim Lisle, *Lives of the Great Songs* (London: Penguin, 1994), 54.

2. Carol Ann Harris, *Storms: My Life with Lindsey Buckingham and Fleetwood Mac* (Chicago: Chicago Review Press, 2009), 326.

3. Richard Bienstock, "Christine McVie on Fleetwood Mac's 'Peculiar' 'Mirage' Sessions, New LP," *Rolling Stone*, September 26, 2016, https://www.rollingstone .com/music/music-features/christine-mcvie-on-fleetwood-macs-peculiar-mirage-sessions-new-lp-122885/

4. Richard Bienstock, "Mick Fleetwood on Fleetwood Mac's 'Overlooked' Smash 'Mirage'," *Rolling Stone,* September 20, 2016, https://www.rollingstone.com/music/music-features/mick-fleetwood-on-fleetwood-macs-overlooked-smash-mirage-101818/

5. McVie's "Only Over You" was credited "With thanks to Dennis Wilson for inspiration." Wilson and McVie's relationship had ended just before production on *Mirage* began. Wilson would pass away only a year later in December 1983. See Jon Stebbins, *Dennis Wilson: The Real Beach Boy* (Toronto: ECW Press, 2012), 212.

6. Behind the Music, "Stevie Nicks," *VH1* video, 44:05, November 1, 1998. https://archive.org/details/vh1 behindthemusicnovember11998stevienicksconvertvideo online.com

7. Bienstock, "Smash."

8. Craig Marks and Rob Tannenbaum, *I Want My MTV: The Uncensored Story of the Music Video Revolution* (New York: Dutton, 2011), 100.

9. Bienstock, "Smash."

10. James "Jimmy" Iovine is the co-founder of Interscope records. In addition to producing *Bella Donna* for Stevie Nicks, Iovine is also known for his work with Tom Petty and the Heartbreakers, U2, Dire Straits, The Pretenders, Tupac Shakur, and for having co-produced the film *8 Mile* in 2002. See https://www.allmusic.com/ artist/jimmy-iovine-mn0000353668/biography

11. A friend of McVie's, Robbie Patton is an English singer/songwriter who toured with Fleetwood Mac during their 1979 *Tusk* tour. See https://www .allmusic.com/artist/robbie-patton-mn0000284707 /biography

12. Simon Price, "Stevie Nicks: 'Love is fleeting for me… in my life as a traveling woman'," *The Independent*, June 26, 2011, https://www.independent.co.uk/arts-entertainment/music/features/stevie-nicks-love-is-fleeting-for-me-in-my-life-as-a-travelling-woman-2302744.html

13. Bienstock, "New LP."

14. While "Hold Me" and "Gypsy"—the first two singles from *Mirage*—were largely unsuccessful in the UK, Buckingham's "Oh Diane," a track that "verges on doo-wop" and shows "how far back Fleetwood Mac looked in their quest for simpler times," managed to peak at #9 on the UK Singles Chart in early 1983. See https://www.loudersound.com/features/fleetwood-macs-mirage-the-making-of

15. In a 2008 Q&A hosted by Magnet Magazine, Buckingham explained that *Mirage* "kind of represents a treading-water period for me. What happened in the wake of *Tusk* not selling 16 million albums or whatever, this dictum came down from the whole band that we weren't going to engage in that kind of experimentalism anymore." See https://magnet magazine.com/2008/09/07/qa-with-lindsey-buckingham/

16. McVie's "Got a Hold on Me" was released as the first single from her 1984 self-titled album and managed to reach #10 on the US *Billboard* Hot 100 chart. The song remains McVie's only US top 10 solo hit. See Joel Whitburn, *The Billboard Book of Top 40 Hits*, 8th ed. (New York: Billboard Books, 2004), 416.

17. Harris, *Storms*, 342.

DON'T LOOK DOWN

1. Shortly after contributing two songs to the *Vacation* soundtrack, Buckingham was asked to record the title song for the 1984 film *Ghostbusters*. This time, Buckingham denied the request, telling *Vacation* director and *Ghostbusters* star Harold Ramis, "Nah, you know, I did this really well once. It's not something I want to get into as a repetitive part of my identity." See https://www.stereogum.com/2025688/lindsey-buckingham-interview-fleetwood-mac/interviews/

2. Michael Goldberg, "Lindsey Buckingham, Lonely Guy," *Rolling Stone*, October 25, 1984, https://www.rollingstone.com/music/music-news/lindsey-buckingham-lonely-guy-2-186895/

3. Carol Ann Harris, *Storms: My Life with Lindsey Buckingham and Fleetwood Mac* (Chicago: Chicago Review Press, 2009), viii.

4. Ibid., 254.

5. Mick Fleetwood and Anthony Bozza, *Play On: Now, Then & Fleetwood Mac* (New York: Little, Brown and Company, 2014), 254.

6. Harris, *Storms*, 91.

7. Goldberg, "Lonely Guy."

8. Ibid.

9. Ibid.

10. William Ruhlmann, "Go Insane Review," *AllMusic*, accessed December 11, 2022, https://www.allmusic.com/album/go-insane-mw0000649934

11. "Slow Dancing" was released as *Go Insane*'s second single in October 1984. While the album's eponymous first single managed to become Buckingham's second top 40 solo hit in the US, "Slow Dancing" failed to crack the US top 40.

12. I chose "Playing in the Rain" as the title for this book because I felt that Buckingham's "Play in the Rain" (particularly the song's quiet, methodic buildup to a chaotic chorus) mirrored well the cyclical relationship with Fleetwood Mac that Buckingham has maintained throughout his musical career.

13. Goldberg, "Lonely Guy."

14. Fleetwood and Bozza, *Play On*, 268.

15. Cath Carroll, *Never Break the Chain: Fleetwood Mac and the Making of Rumours* (Chicago: Chicago Review Press, 2004), 213.

16. The soundtrack for *A Fine Mess* also features contributions from the Temptations, Los Lobos, and Smokey Robinson, among others. The film itself received mostly negative reviews and, as of 2023, boasts a 4.7/10 rating on IMDb. See https://www.imdb .com/title/tt0091051/

17. Said Buckingham in 1984: "I've heard rumors that if I was not ready to do an album in the next three or four months, or at least talk about it, they were going to seek out somebody else… I can't say that doesn't more or less coincide with the kind of psychology I've seen go on in the group at certain times. If something needs to get done, they'll get it done one way or another. And if Lindsey doesn't want to play ball, then fuck him. They'll fire him and get somebody else. That's the way the band works." See https://www.rollingstone.com/ music/music-news/lindsey-buckingham-lonely-guy-2- 186895/

18. Stephen Davis, *Gold Dust Woman: The Biography of Stevie Nicks* (New York: St. Martin's Press, 2017), 214.

19. Ibid.

20. Rob Tannenbaum, "Stevie Nicks Admits Past Pregnancy with Don Henley and More About Her Wild History," *Billboard*, September 26, 2014, https://www .billboard.com/music/music-news/stevie-nicks- interview-on-don-henley-fleetwood-mac-24-karat-gold- album-6266329/

21. Buckingham would eventually, of course, release a third solo album, *Out of the Cradle*, in 1992. See "Fireflies" chapter.

BREAKING THE CHAIN

1. Stephen Davis, *Gold Dust Woman: The Biography of Stevie Nicks* (New York: St. Martin's Press, 2017), 214.
2. Nick DeRiso, "Fleetwood Mac hit big with *Tango in the Night*, then imploded: 'It was difficult for everybody'," *Something Else!* April 14, 2015, https://somethingelsereviews.com/2015/04/14/fleetwood-mac-tango-in-the-night/
3. Klonopin, generic name clonazepam, is a benzodiazepine primarily used to treat panic disorder in adults and specific seizure disorders in adults in children. Misuse of the drug can cause overdose, death, or, in Nicks's case, addiction. See https://www.drugs.com/klonopin.html
4. Brad Nelson, "Tango in the Night," *Pitchfork*, March 11, 2017, https://pitchfork.com/reviews/albums/22976-tango-in-the-night-deluxe-edition/
5. Michael Goldberg, "Lindsey Buckingham, Lonely Guy," *Rolling Stone*, October 25, 1984, https://www.rollingstone.com/music/music-news/lindsey-buckingham-lonely-guy-2-186895/
6. The distinctive male and female "ooh-ah's" featured in Buckingham's "Big Love" were both recorded by Buckingham. The female vocals, which are sometimes attributed to Stevie Nicks, were achieved by Buckingham playing with the speed of his vocals. See https://ultimateclassicrock.com/fleetwood-mac-lindsey-buckingham-big-love/
7. Annie Zaleski, "'He could be brash; he could be harsh. He was very motivated': The real story behind Fleetwood Mac's 'Tango in the Night'," *Salon*, April 2, 2017, https://www.salon.com/2017/04/02/he-could-be-brash-he-could-be-harsh-he-was-very-motivated-the-real-story-behind-fleetwood-macs-tango-in-the-night/
8. Ibid.
9. Christopher R. Weingarten, et al., "Fleetwood Mac's 50 Greatest Songs," *Rolling Stone*, May 2, 2022, https://www.rollingstone.com/music/music-lists/fleetwood-macs-50-greatest-songs-192324/

10. Ibid.
11. Stewart's *Cat Dancer* failed to chart on the US *Billboard* 200. In addition to "Seven Wonders," Stewart co-wrote three tracks included on Nicks's 1983 solo album *The Wild Heart*: "If Anyone Falls," "Nightbird," and "Nothing Ever Changes." See https://www.allmusic.com/artist/sandy-stewart-mn0000293510/credits
12. Davis, *Gold Dust Woman*, 214.
13. Paramore has performed their cover of Fleetwood Mac's "Everywhere" in concert numerous times. The cover has been well-received by critics and fans of both Paramore and Fleetwood Mac. See https://www .billboard.com/lists/best-fleetwood-mac-covers/ paramore-everywhere/
14. In 2021, Irish singer and former member of One Direction Niall Horan and English singer Anne-Marie released a cover of "Everywhere" for BBC's Children in Need appeal. Said McVie of the cover, "I'm thrilled with this new version of Everywhere and to be part of this year's Children in Need campaign." See https:// www.udiscovermusic.com/news/niall-horan-anne-marie-everywhere-bbc-children-in-need/
15. Andy Gill, "Album: Phil Spector, The Philles Album Collection (Sony Legacy)," *Independent*, December 28, 2011, https://www.independent.co.uk/arts-entertainment/music/reviews/album-phil-spector-the-philles-album-collection-sony-legacy-6282163.html
16. Wrote Alex Henderson in a review of *Tango in the Night*: "Without question, 'Family Man' and 'Caroline' are among the best songs ever written by Buckingham, who consistently brings out the best in his colleagues on this superb album." See https://www.allmusic.com/ album/tango-in-the-night-mw0000189877
17. These "lost" tracks were also included on the "alternate" *Tango in the Night* released on Record Store Day 2018 and later in the band's "Alternate Collection" released for RSD Black Friday in late 2022.

See https://www.fleetwoodmacnews.com/2022/09/rsd-2022-fleetwood-mac-alternate.html

18. "Juliet," with a total runtime of just under five minutes, was released in early 1989 as track #10 on Nicks's *The Other Side of the Mirror*. The song was not released as a single but was included on Nicks's setlist at select shows during her eponymous album tour. See https://stevienicks.info/stevie-nicks-tours/1989-the-other-side-of-the-mirror-tour/

WAIT FOR YOU

1. Directed by Wayne Isham, the band's *Tango in the Night* video feature was recorded over two nights at the Cow Palace in San Francisco and was originally released in 1988 on VHS and laserdisc and later on DVD in 1998 and 2003. A product description for the 2003 DVD release written by Sam Graham remarks that the recording "is a mostly lackluster affair, lacking Buckingham's fire and eccentric stage presence. Mainstays Mick Fleetwood and John McVie soldier on, as ever, with Stevie Nicks and Christine McVie still on hand as well… But when a vest equipped with drum and percussion sounds is the highlight of the show (during Fleetwood's solo spot), you know you're not exactly witnessing history in the making." See http://www.fleetwoodmac-uk.com/albums/tango/titn-dvd-infopage.htm

2. In 2022, Burnette explained that he didn't hesitate "at all" when Mick Fleetwood asked him to join the band in 1987. "How can you?" Burnette remarked, "It was Fleetwood Mac." See https://www.rollingstone.com/music/music-features/billy-burnette-fleetwood-mac-lindsey-christine-stevie-1234639670/

3. Buckingham's "Family Man" peaked at #54 on the UK Singles Chart and at #90 on the US *Billboard* Hot 100. See https://www.billboard.com/artist/fleetwood-mac/chart-history/hsi/

4. Eduardo Quintela de Mendonça, also known as Eddy Quintela, passed away on October 17, 2020. In addition to co-writing the smash hit "Little Lies," Quintela also co-wrote "As Long as You Follow" (from *Greatest Hits*), "Skies the Limit" and "Save Me" (from *Behind the Mask*), "Nights in Estoril" (from *Time*), and "Temporary One" (from *The Dance*) with McVie (among several other tracks). Though McVie and Quintela divorced in 2003, the two also co-wrote the song "Easy Come, Easy Go," which was included on McVie's 2004 solo album, *In the Meantime*. See https://www.fleetwoodmacnews.com/2020/10/eddy -quintela-second-husband-to.html

5. Zoë Howe, *Stevie Nicks: Visions, Dreams & Rumours* (London: Omnibus Press, 2015), 253-254.

6. Brian Hiatt, "Stevie Nicks: A Rock Goddess Looks Back," *Rolling Stone*, January 15, 2015, https://www .rollingstone.com/music/music-news/stevie-nicks-a-rock- goddess-looks-back-179984/

7. "Isn't It Midnight" managed to peak at #60 on the UK Singles Chart in June of 1988. See https://www .officialcharts.com/artist/28702/fleetwood-mac/

8. Mark Beaumont, "Christine McVie, 1943-2022: an eternal songbird," *NME*, December 1, 2022, https:// www.nme.com/features/music-features/christine-mcvie- 1943-2022-an-eternal-songbird-3358828

9. Like aforementioned tracks "Down Endless Street" or "Juliet," "You and I, Part I" would also find a home on the band's 2018 "alternate" *Tango in the Night* release and on their 2022 "Alternate Collection." See https:// www.fleetwoodmacnews.com/2022/09/rsd-2022- fleetwood-mac-alternate.html

10. *Rumours* managed to spend 19 *consecutive* weeks atop the *Billboard* 200 chart (from July 23, 1977 to November 26, 1977). See https://www.billboard.com/ lists/albums-no-1-billboard-200-most-consecutive- weeks/fleetwood-mac-rumours/

11. Howe, *Dreams & Rumours*, 311.

12. Mick Fleetwood and Anthony Bozza, *Play On: Now, Then & Fleetwood Mac* (New York: Little, Brown and Company, 2014), 268.
13. Carol Ann Harris wrote that in the early 1980s, "Mick set out on an embarrassing fiasco of a tour with his new band, Mick Fleetwood's Zoo, to support an unsuccessful follow-up solo album to his first effort, *The Visitor*. Traveling by bus and playing to audiences in almost empty clubs, they met with dismal failure." This follow-up to *The Visitor*, 1983's *I'm Not Me*, is the only album credited to Mick Fleetwood's Zoo. See Harris, *Storms*, 344.
14. Burnette's *Soldier of Love* earned him a nomination for Best New Country Artist in 1987. See https://www .rollingstone.com/music/music-features/billy-burnette- fleetwood-mac-lindsey-christine-stevie-1234639670/
15. Buckingham's third solo album was named after the Walt Whitman poem, "Out of the Cradle Endlessly Rocking." See https://www.rollingstone.com/music/ music-news/lindsey-buckingham-post-mac-attack- 191712/
16. Stephen Davis, *Gold Dust Woman: The Biography of Stevie Nicks* (New York: St. Martin's Press, 2017), 227.
17. McVie's "As Long as You Follow" managed to peak at #43 on the US *Billboard* Hot 100, while Nicks's "No Questions Asked"—the other new recording featured on 1988's *Greatest Hits*—failed to make the *Billboard* Hot 100. See https://www.billboard.com/artist/ fleetwood-mac/chart-history/hsi/

FIREFLIES

1. Brittany Spanos, "'Silver Springs': Inside Fleetwood Mac's Great Lost Breakup Anthem," *Rolling Stone*, August 17, 2017, https://www.rollingstone.com/ feature/silver-springs-inside-fleetwood-macs-great-lost- breakup-anthem-201303/

2. Andy Greene, "Billy Burnette on His Brief, 'Magical' Stint in Fleetwood Mac: 'No Regrets'," *Rolling Stone,* December 6, 2022, https://www.rollingstone.com/music/music-features/billy-burnette-fleetwood-mac-lindsey-christine-stevie-1234639670/

3. Ibid.

4. Greg Ladanyi was an engineer and producer who also worked with Warren Zevon, Toto, the Jacksons, and Linda Ronstadt. Earlier in his life, Ladanyi worked as a manager and bartender at the iconic Whisky A Go Go, the "center of the LA music universe in the 1960s." Ladanyi passed away in 2009. See https://www.soundonsound.com/people/greg-ladanyi

5. "Save Me," from the 1990 album *Behind the Mask,* managed to peak at #33 on the US *Billboard* Hot 100 and at #53 on the UK Singles Chart. Meanwhile, subsequent singles "Skies the Limit" and "Love is Dangerous" failed to chart on the US Hot 100 or in the UK. See https://www.billboard.com/artist/fleetwood-mac/chart-history/hsi/

6. On *Out of the Cradle,* Larry Klein plays bass on tracks 3, 4, 8, and 12. Klein is also a songwriter and music producer who has worked primarily with jazz artists like Herbie Hancock and Dianne Reeves, as well as artists like Bob Dylan, Peter Gabriel, and, of course, Lindsey Buckingham. See https://www.larrykleinmusic.com/bio/

7. Mitchell Froom is best known for having produced Crowded House's first three albums and has received production credits on more than 60 albums. He also released a solo album in 1998 and another in 2005. He has been an official member of Crowded House since 2019. See https://www.allmusic.com/artist/mitchell-froom-mn0000484163/biography

8. Terry Gross, "Remembering Buell Neidlinger, A Genre-Hopping Bassist, Composer and Teacher," *NPR,* March 27, 2018, https://www.npr.org/2018/03/27/

597278380/remembering-buell-neidlinger-a-genre-hopping-bassist-composer-and-music-teacher

9. Scott Lapatine, "Lindsey Buckingham Reveals Stories Behind His Solo Songs And Whether He'll Ever Rejoin Fleetwood Mac," *Stereogum*, December 10, 2018, https://www.stereogum.com/2025688/lindsey-buckingham-interview-fleetwood-mac/interviews/

10. Lindsey Buckingham, "Street of Dreams," Reprise, track #10 on *Out of the Cradle*, June 16, 1992, CD.

11. Lapatine, "Solo Songs."

12. Lindsey Buckingham, "Wrong," Reprise, track #3 on *Out of the Cradle*, June 16, 1992, CD.

13. Paul Elliott, "Drug abuse, violence, and the making of Fleetwood Mac's Tango in the Night," *Louder Sound*, October 5, 2021, https://www.loudersound.com/features/drug-abuse-violence-and-the-making-of-fleetwood-macs-tango-in-the-night

14. Lapatine, "Solo Songs."

15. Devon Ivie, "Lindsey Buckingham on the Most Fulfilling and Dysfunctional Music of His Career," *Vulture*, November 24, 2021, https://www.vulture.com/article/interview-lindsey-buckingham-on-fleetwood-mac-stevie-nicks.html

16. Greil Marcus, "Ringo Starr, 'Sentimental Journey' (5/14/70)," *Greil Marcus*, September 12, 2014, https://greilmarcus.net/2014/09/12/ringo-starr-sentimental-journey-51470/

17. Christopher Connelly, "Christine McVie Keeps A Level Head After Two Decades in the Fastlane," *Rolling Stone*, July 7, 1984, https://www.rollingstone.com/music/music-news/christine-mcvie-keeps-a-level-head-after-two-decades-in-the-fastlane-189459/

18. Ivie, "Fulfilling and Dysfunctional."

19. David Chiu, "Lindsey Buckingham Looks for Life After Fleetwood Mac," *Newsweek*, September 15, 2021, https://www.newsweek.com/2021/09/24/lindsey-buckingham-looks-life-after-fleetwood-mac-1629086.html

20. 8 of the 16 tracks included on *Out of the Cradle* appear on Buckingham's 2018 *Solo Anthology*, a collection touted as his "first-ever career-spanning hits package"; a testament to the strength of the recordings included on Buckingham's third solo effort. See https://www.stereogum.com/2025688/lindsey-buckingham-interview-fleetwood-mac/interviews/

21. History.com editors, "Fleetwood Mac reunites to play 'Don't Stop' at Bill Clinton's first inaugural ball," *History*, April 1, 2010, https://www.history.com/this-day-in-history/fleetwood-mac-reunite-to-play-dont-stop-at-bill-clintons-first-inaugural-gala

22. Andy Greene, "Flashback: Fleetwood Mac Reunite for Bill Clinton's Inauguration," *Rolling Stone*, January 22, 2013, https://www.rollingstone.com/music/music-news/flashback-fleetwood-mac-reunite-for-bill-clintons-inauguration-84419/

23. Andy Greene, "Flashback: Fleetwood Mac Reunite in 1997," *Rolling Stone*, January 14, 2014, https://www.rollingstone.com/music/music-news/flashback-fleetwood-mac-reunite-in-1997-83471/

24. "I Do" failed to chart in the US or the UK, though the song did peak at #62 on the Canada Top Singles Chart and an edit of the song was featured on the band's 2018's greatest hits collection, *50 Years: Don't Stop.* See https://www.allmusic.com/album/50-years-dont-stop-mw0003214000

25. Despite the unpopularity of *Time*, Fleetwood Mac often performed track #12 from the album, "All Over Again," as part of their setlist's encore while on their 2018 *An Evening with Fleetwood Mac* tour. See https://consequence.net/2018/10/live-review-fleetwood-mac-chicago-united-center/

26. McVie did not even intend to participate in the production of *Time*, having already retired from live performances years earlier. However, Warner Bros. insisted she participate. See Mick Fleetwood and Anthony Bozza. *Play On: Now, Then & Fleetwood*

Mac (New York: Little, Brown and Company, 2014), 276.

27. Bekka & Billy's only album, simply titled *Bekka & Billy*, spawned two singles: "Patient Heart" and "Better Days." The album failed to chart in the US or UK, though it achieved mild success in Canada. See https://www.allmusic.com/album/bekka-billy-mw0000019508

28. Bekka & Billy signed with the now-defunct record label Almo Sounds in 1997 prior to their split. See https://web.archive.org/web/20170124223621/http://www.fleetwoodmac.net/penguin/billy.htm

OVER AND OVER

1. Nicks's *Street Angel* peaked at #45 on the US *Billboard* 200 Chart and was certified Gold by the RIAA in 1997. See https://www.riaa.com/gold-platinum/?tab_active=default-award&se=street+angel#search_section

2. Nick DeRiso, "Stevie Nicks, 'Twisted' from *24 Karat Gold* (2014): One Track Mind," *Something Else!* September 28, 2014, https://somethingelsereviews.com/2014/09/28/stevie-nicks-twisted-24-karat-gold/

3. Roger Catlin, "FLEETWOOD MAC, NICKS GET LANDSLIDE APPROVAL," *The Hartford Courant*, September 17, 1997, https://www.courant.com/news/connecticut/hc-xpm-1997-09-18-9709180222-story.html

4. While the band's 1980 *Live* album was a compilation of recordings collected over a period of several weeks, *The Dance* was recorded in a single night. See https://web.archive.org/web/20190601222513/http://www.fleetwoodmac.net/penguin/qa/kencaillat_qa1.htm

5. Fleetwood Mac, "Temporary One," Reprise, track #6 on *The Dance*, August 19, 1997, CD.

6. Scott Lapatine, "Lindsey Buckingham Reveals Stories Behind His Solo Songs And Whether He'll Ever Rejoin Fleetwood Mac," *Stereogum*, December 10, 2018, https://www.stereogum.com/2025688/lindsey-buckingham-interview-fleetwood-mac/interviews/

7. The US 2002 and UK 2009 editions of *The Very Best of Fleetwood Mac* also featured a live recording of 1975's "I'm So Afraid" taken from *The Dance.*

8. The band also performed this banjo-based rendition of "Say You Love Me" (again featuring John McVie performing backup vocals) a year later at their Rock and Roll Hall of Fame induction ceremony. See https://www.rollingstone.com/music/music-news/see-fleetwood-mac-stevie-nicks-enter-rock-and-roll-hall-of-fame-1998-735212/

9. Chad Childers, "When Fleetwood Mac Reunited for the 'The Dance',￼" *Ultimate Classic Rock*, August 19, 2015, https://ultimateclassicrock.com/fleetwood-macs-reunion-album-the-dance-turns-15/

10. A studio recording of Nicks's "Sweet Girl" would later appear on her 1998 album *Enchanted*, a greatest hits collection spanning Nicks's solo career from 1981 to 1994.

11. Paul Elliott, "Drug abuse, violence, and the making of Fleetwood Mac's Tango in the Night," *Louder Sound*, October 5, 2021, https://www.loudersound.com/features/drug-abuse-violence-and-the-making-of-fleetwood-macs-tango-in-the-night

12. The cover photo for *The Dance* was taken by David LaChapelle and features Mick Fleetwood recreating his pose from *Rumours'* album cover and Lindsey Buckingham brandishing the cane featured on the cover of the band's 1975 "White Album." See https://ultimateclassicrock.com/fleetwood-macs-reunion-album-the-dance-turns-15/

13. Fleetwood Mac was inducted into the Rock and Roll Hall of Fame alongside Eagles, the Mamas and the Papas, Lloyd Price, Santana, Allen Toussaint, Jelly Roll Morton, and Gene Vincent. See https://www.rockhall.com/inductees/classes/1998

14. While McVie eventually rejoined the band for a world tour in 2014—16 years after her departure—1997's *The Dance* would prove to be the final Fleetwood Mac

album to feature McVie, aside from a few guest appearances on 2003's *Say You Will*.

15. Andy Greene, "Q&A: Christine McVie Can't Wait for Fleetwood Mac World Tour," *Rolling Stone*, March 27, 2014, https://www.rollingstone.com/music/music-news/qa-christine-mcvie-cant-wait-for-fleetwood-mac-world-tour-183753/

16. Ibid.

17. Andy Greene, "Q&A: Stevie Nicks and Lindsey Buckingham Reveal Lingering Tensions in Fleetwood Mac," *Rolling Stone*, December 5, 2012, https://www.rollingstone.com/music/music-news/qa-stevie-nicks-and-lindsey-buckingham-reveal-lingering-tensions-in-fleetwood-mac-233617/

18. Fred Schruers, "Back on the Chain Gang," *Rolling Stone*, October 30, 1997, https://www.rollingstone.com/music/music-news/fleetwood-mac-back-on-the-chain-gang-243176/

19. Ibid.

20. "Lifelines," *Billboard*, August 15, 1998, 47, https://books.google.com/books?id=EwoEAAAAMBAJ&pg=PA47#v=onepage&q&f=false

21. Christine Rendon, "Go Their Own Way! Fleetwood Mac's Lindsey Buckingham splits with wife of 21 YEARS Kristen Messner… after she files to dissolve their marriage," *Daily Mail*, June 8, 2021, https://www.dailymail.co.uk/tvshowbiz/article-9665721/Fleetwood-Macs-Lindsey-Buckingham-splits-wife-21-YEARS-Kristen-Messner.html

22. Will Harris, "A Chat with Lindsey Buckingham," *Bullz Eye*, November 6, 2008, http://www.bullz-eye.com/music/interviews/2008/lindsey_buckingham.htm

DESTINY RULES

1. "Illume," *In Her Own Words*, accessed December 17, 2022, http://www.inherownwords.com/illume.htm

2. Mark Leibovich, "Edward R. Murrow, Welcome To the Full-Spin Zone," *The Washington Post*, March 27, 2005, https://www.washingtonpost.com/wp-dyn/articles/A3980-2005Mar26.html

3. James McNair, "Return of the Mac," *Independent Review*, April 18, 2003, accessed via: https://stevienicks.info/2003/04/return-of-the-mac/

4. Joel Selvin, "Buckingham gets back into 'that thing' of Fleetwood Mac," *SFGATE*, April 15, 2003, https://www.sfgate.com/entertainment/article/Buckingham-gets-back-into-that-thing-of-2622236.php

5. *Say You Will*'s "Miranda," "Steal Your Heart Away," "Red Rover," "Come," "Murrow," "Bleed to Love Her," and "Say Goodbye," were all tracks originally meant for inclusion on *Gift of Screws*. High-quality recordings of these songs were available for MP3 download in October 2001 via bootlegged copies of Buckingham's then-unfinished project.

6. Zoë Howe, *Stevie Nicks: Visions, Dreams & Rumours* (London: Omnibus Press, 2015), 354.

7. Dylan Jones, "Was Fleetwood Mac's Tusk the greatest self-sabotage in rock and roll history?" *GQ*, August 9, 2020, https://www.gq-magazine.co.uk/culture/article/fleetwood-mac-tusk

8. The title for Buckingham's fifth solo album was taken from a line featured in an Emily Dickinson poem entitled, "Essential Oils are wrung." The poem's first stanza reads: "Essential Oils are rung / The Attar from the Rose / Be not expressed by Suns alone / It is the gift of Screws." These lyrics are also repeated in the album's title track. See https://www.nodepression.com/album-reviews/finding-a-place-for-lindsey-buckingham/

9. *Fleetwood Mac: Destiny Rules*, directed by Kyle Einhorn and Matt Baumann (2004; US: Candlewood Films, 2012), DVD.

10. Ibid.

11. Blair Jackson, "Stevie – Fleetwood Mac's siren soars with her first solo album, *Bella Donna*," *BAM*

Magazine, September 11, 1981, accessed via: http://rockalittle.com/bam9-11-81.htm

12. Fleetwood Mac, "Everybody Finds Out," Reprise, track #15 on *Say You Will*, April 15, 2003, CD.

13. In an interview conducted by Rolling Stone shortly before her passing, Christine McVie confirmed that Fleetwood Mac had essentially "split up" again following their 2018 An Evening with Fleetwood Mac tour. This statement, coupled with her passing in December 2022, all but cement *Say You Will* as the final studio album that will ever be released by Fleetwood Mac. See https://www.rollingstone.com/music/music-features/christine-mcvie-fleetwood-mac-tribute-greatest-songs-1234639376/

14. See *Pollstar*'s 2003 "Year End Top 20 Worldwide Tours" chart. https://www.pollstar.com/charts/pdf/24/top-tours-research

15. Will Harris, "A Chat with Lindsey Buckingham," *Bullz Eye*, November 6, 2008, http://www.bullz-eye.com/music/interviews/2008/lindsey_buckingham.htm

16. Buckingham has previously acknowledged the almost drastic shift in tones between *Under the Skin* and *Gift of Screws*, explaining in 2008 that: "It was always my intention to have [*Gift of Screws*] be up a step or two, at the very least, from what *Under the Skin* was." See https://www.masslive.com/entertainment/2008/10/lindsey_buckingham_on_fleetwoo.html

17. Released in September 2006, the sole single from Buckingham's *Under the Skin*, "Show You How," failed to chart in the US and UK.

18. Scott Lapatine, "Lindsey Buckingham Reveals Stories Behind His Solo Songs And Whether He'll Ever Rejoin Fleetwood Mac," *Stereogum*, December 10, 2018, https://www.stereogum.com/2025688/lindsey-buckingham-interview-fleetwood-mac/interviews/

19. See *Pollstar*'s 2013 "Year End Top 20 Worldwide Tours" chart. https://www.pollstar.com/charts/pdf/24/top-tours-research

STARS ARE CRAZY

1. Edna Gundersen, "Christine McVie rejoins Fleetwood Mac," *USA Today*, March 27, 2014, https://www .usatoday.com/story/life/music/2014/03/27/christine-mcvie-rejoins-fleetwood-mac-for-tour-new-music/ 6841509/
2. Ibid.
3. Dave Swanson, "Fleetwood Mac Might Have a Double Album on their Hands," *Ultimate Classic Rock,* May 8, 2014, https://ultimateclassicrock.com/fleetwood-mac-double-album/
4. Lindsey Buckingham, "Love Runs Deeper," Reprise, track #5 on *Gift of Screws*, September 15, 2008, CD.
5. Maureen Lee Lenker, "Lindsey Buckingham breaks down 10 of his best guitar riffs," *Entertainment Weekly*, September 14, 2021, https://ew.com/music/ lindsey-buckingham-fleetwood-mac-stories-behind-the-songs/
6. Scott Lapatine, "Lindsey Buckingham Reveals Stories Behind His Solo Songs And Whether He'll Ever Rejoin Fleetwood Mac," *Stereogum*, December 10, 2018, https://www.stereogum.com/2025688/lindsey-buckingham-interview-fleetwood-mac/interviews/
7. Ibid.
8. Ibid.
9. Ray Kelly, "Lindsey Buckingham on Fleetwood Mac, solo work and Sheryl Crow," *Mass Live*, October 12, 2008, https://www.masslive.com/entertainment/2008/ 10/lindsey_buckingham_on_fleetwoo.html
10. John McVie played bass on "Wait for You" as well as on *Gift of Screws'* title track.
11. Michael Bonner, "Lindsey Buckingham – Gift of Screws," *Uncut,* September 8, 2008, https://www .uncut.co.uk/reviews/lindsey-buckingham-gift-of-screws-7321/
12. Mick Fleetwood played the drums and percussion on "The Right Place to Fade" as well as on "Wait for

You." He also played drums on *Gift of Screws'* title track.

13. Bonner, "Gift of Screws."
14. Lindsey Buckingham, "The Right Place to Fade," Reprise, track #7 on *Gift of Screws*, September 15, 2008, CD.
15. Despite the overall commercial success of *Seeds We Sow*, the album's lead single and title track failed to chart in the US and the UK.
16. While the Rolling Stones' December 1967 LP *Their Satanic Majesties Request* is often considered to be the band's first foray into the world of psychedelia, critics have argued that January 1967's *Between the Buttons*, with its nontraditional instrumentation and erratic sound play, marks the actual "start" of the Stones' psychedelic era. See https://ultimateclassicrock.com/rolling-stones-between-the-buttons/
17. Lapatine, "Solo Songs."
18. The full title of Buckingham's 2011 live album is *Songs from the Small Machine: Live in L.A. at Saban Theatre in Beverly Hills, CA / 2011.*
19. Andrew Leahey, "Song Premiere: Lindsey Buckingham, 'Trouble (Live)'," *American Songwriter*, accessed December 19, 2022, https://americansongwriter.com/song-premiere-lindsey-buckingham-trouble-live/
20. Andy Greene, "Lindsey Buckingham Talks Fleetwood Mac Tour, New EP," *Rolling Stone*, May 7, 2013, https://www.rollingstone.com/music/music-news/lindsey-buckingham-talks-fleetwood-mac-tour-new-ep-92203/
21. Margaret Eby, "Christine McVie reunites with Fleetwood Mac," *New York Daily News*, January 14, 2014, https:// www.nydailynews.com/entertainment/tv-movies/christine-mcvie-reunites-fleetwood-mac-article-1.1579348
22. Gael Fashingbauer Cooper, "Christine McVie is rejoining Fleetwood Mac," *Today*, March 27, 2014,

https://www.today.com/entertainment/christine-mcvie-rejoining-fleetwood-mac-2D79442915

23. Ibid.

24. Ibid.

25. Tim Jonze, "Fleetwood Mac: new album and tour will be our swansong," *The Guardian*, January 2, 2015, https:// www.theguardian.com/music/2015/jan/02/lindsey-buckingham-says-fleetwood-mac-to-enter-last-act

26. Andy Greene, "Q&A: Christine McVie Can't Wait for Fleetwood Mac World Tour," *Rolling Stone*, March 27, 2014, https://www.rollingstone.com/music/music-news/qa-christine-mcvie-cant-wait-for-fleetwood-mac-world-tour-183753/

ON WITH THE SHOW

1. Amy Kaufman, "Fleetwood Mac fired Lindsey Buckingham. So why won't he let them go?" *Los Angeles Times,* September 8, 2021, https://www.latimes.com/entertainment-arts/music/story/2021-09-08/lindsey-buckingham-fleetwood-mac-stevie-nicks

2. Karl Quinn, "So, Fleetwood Mac didn't 'fire' Lindsey Buckingham. They divorced him," *The Sydney Morning Herald*, April 26, 2018, https://www.smh.com.au/entertainment/music/so-fleetwood-mac-didn-t-fire-lindsey-buckingham-they-divorced-him-20180426-p4zbq6.html

3. Kaufman, "fired Lindsey Buckingham."

4. Alex Young, "Lindsey Buckingham settles lawsuit against Fleetwood Mac," *Yahoo! Finance*, December 8, 2018, https://finance.yahoo.com/news/lindsey-buckingham-settles-lawsuit-against-010612049.html

5. Sean T. Collins, "*Lindsey Buckingham/Christine McVie*," *Pitchfork*, June 12, 2017, https://pitchfork.com/reviews/albums/23221-lindsey-buckingham-christine-mcvie/

6. *Lindsey Buckingham/Christine McVie* performed better than any of Buckingham or McVie's solo works. The

album peaked at #17 on the US *Billboard* 200 and at #5 in the UK. The album was certified silver in the UK for selling over 60,000 copies. See https://www.bpi.co.uk/award/14644-4532-2

7. Brittany Spanos, "Hear Buckingham McVie's Bubbly New Song 'Feel About You'," *Rolling Stone*, April 27, 2017, https://www.rollingstone.com/music/music-news/hear-buckingham-mcvies-bubbly-new-song-feel-about-you-192677/

8. Kevin O'Donnell, "Fleetwood Mac's Christine McVie and Lindsey Buckingham debut galloping new song," *Yahoo! Finance*, May 11, 2017, https://finance.yahoo.com/news/fleetwood-mac-apos-christine-mcvie-130038911.html

9. Like other singles released from Buckingham and McVie's duet album, "In My World" failed to chart on either the US *Billboard* Hot 100 or in the UK Top 100 charts but received substantial airplay in the UK.

10. Michael Gallucci, "Lindsey Buckingham and Christine McVie, 'Lindsey Buckingham/Christine McVie': Album Review," *Ultimate Classic Rock*, June 6, 2017, https://ultimateclassicrock.com/lindsey-buckingham-christine-mcvie-album-review/

11. In addition to "Too Far Gone," "Red Sun" and "Feel About You" (both featuring McVie on lead vocals) were also Buckingham McVie co-writes.

12. Lindsey Buckingham/Christine McVie, "On with the Show," Atlantic, track #9 on *Lindsey Buckingham /Christine McVie*, June 9, 2017, CD.

13. Best Classic Bands Staff, "It's On! Eagles, Fleetwood Mac to Headline Classic East and West," *Best Classic Bands*, April 17, 2017, https://bestclassicbands.com/classic-east-eagles-fleetwood-mac-3-29-17/

14. Ibid.

15. Andrew Unterberger, "Fleetwood Mac Reigns Supreme at Day Two of Classic East Festival," *Billboard*, July 31, 2017, https://www.billboard.com/music/concerts/

fleetwood-mac-day-two-classic-east-festival-recap-
7882114/

16. Ibid.

17. This performance of "The Chain" also featured former
One Direction member and solo star Harry Styles: a
devout fan of Fleetwood Mac and of Stevie Nicks. See
source cited below.

18. Melinda Newman, "Fleetwood Mac Honored by
Lorde, Miley Cyrus, Harry Styles & More at 2018
MusiCares Person of the Year Gala," *Billboard*,
January 27, 2018, https://www.billboard.com/music/
music-news/stevie-nicks-fleetwood-mac-grammy-
awards-musicares-person-of-the-year-tom-petty-
8096584/

19. Ibid.

20. Mick Fleetwood initially insisted on labeling
Buckingham's departure a "divorce." See https://www
.smh.com.au/entertainment/music/so-fleetwood-mac-
didn-t-fire-lindsey-buckingham-they-divorced-him-
20180426-p4zbq6.html

21. Stephen Rodrick, "Lindsey Buckingham Won't Stop,"
Rolling Stone, September 9, 2021, https://www
.rollingstone.com/music/music-features/lindsey-
buckingham-fleetwood-mac-stevie-nicks-new-album-
1221755/

22. Kaufman, "fired Lindsey Buckingham."

23. Ibid.

24. Ibid.

25. Ibid.

26. Young, "Settles Lawsuit."

SWAN SONG

1. Halsey and Buckingham performed "Darling" live on
Saturday Night Live on October 9, 2021. See https://
www.rollingstone.com/music/music-news/halsey-
lindsey-buckingham-snl-1239755/

2. Stephen Rodrick, "Lindsey Buckingham Won't Stop,"
Rolling Stone, September 9, 2021, https://www

.rollingstone.com/music/music-features/lindsey-buckingham-fleetwood-mac-stevie-nicks-new-album-1221755/

3. Ibid.

4. Ibid.

5. In February 2019, Buckingham's official Instagram account announced a giveaway offering fans a chance to win a copy of Buckingham's *Solo Anthology* on vinyl and a set of autographed test pressings. I entered this contest but did not win. See https://www.instagram.com/p/BtXFNMYhMk2/

6. Rob Arcand, "Hear Two New Songs From Lindsey Buckingham's Solo Anthology," *Spin*, October 5, 2018, https://www.spin.com/2018/10/lindsey-buckingham-solo-anthology-ride-this-road-hunger/#content

7. Hal Horowitz, "Lindsey Buckingham: *Solo Anthology – The Best of Lindsey Buckingham*," *American Songwriter*, accessed December 20, 2022, https://americansongwriter.com/lindsey-buckingham-solo-anthology-best-lindsey-buckingham/

8. Debra Filcman, "Read Lindsey Buckingham's Emotional Email to Fleetwood Mac," *Ultimate Classic Rock*, October 13, 2018, https://ultimateclassicrock.com/lindsey-buckingham-email-fleetwood-mac/

9. Daniel Kohn, "Mick Fleetwood and Lindsey Buckingham Reconcile, Open to Another Fleetwood Mac Reunion Tour," *Spin*, March 1, 2021, https://www.spin.com/2021/03/mick-fleetwood-lindsey-buckingham-reunion/

10. Andy Greene, "Mick Fleetwood Open to Reunion with Lindsey Buckingham, Imagines Fleetwood Mac Farewell Tour," *Rolling Stone*, March 1, 2021, https://www.rollingstone.com/music/music-news/mick-fleetwood-reunion-with-lindsey-buckingham-imagines-fleetwood-mac-farewell-tour-1134758/

11. Amy Kaufman, "Fleetwood Mac fired Lindsey Buckingham. So why won't he let them go?" *Los Angeles Times*, September 8, 2021, https://www

.latimes.com/entertainment-arts/music/story/2021-09-08/lindsey-buckingham-fleetwood-mac-stevie-nicks

12. Andy Greene, "Christine McVie Clarifies 'Misperception' That Fleetwood Mac Is 'Done'," *Rolling Stone*, February 17, 2021, https://www.rollingstone.com/music/music-news/christine-mcvie-fleetwood-mac-comments-1129059/

13. Lindsay Zoladz, "Lindsey Buckingham Has Survived It All," *The New York Times*, September 8, 2021, https://www.nytimes.com/2021/09/08/arts/music/lindsey-buckingham.html

14. Rodrick, "Won't Stop."

15. Ibid.

16. Buckingham is featured on the deluxe edition of American country music singer Brandy Clark's 2020 studio album *Your Life is a Record*. Buckingham plays guitar on an alternate version of Clark's "The Past is the Past." See https://www.cmt.com/news/g1adkb/brandy-clark-to-release-deluxe-album-march-5

17. Rodrick, "Won't Stop."

18. Buckingham decided to shelve his self-titled solo effort and instead release his solo anthology in 2018. *Lindsey Buckingham* would then be delayed in 2019 because of Buckingham's heart attack and again in 2020 by the COVID-19 pandemic. See https://www.premierguitar.com/artists/guitarists/lindsey-buckingham

19. Matthew Strauss, "Lindsey Buckingham Announces U.S. Tour and First Solo Album in 10 Years," *Pitchfork*, June 8, 2021, https://pitchfork.com/news/lindsey-buckingham-announces-us-tour-and-first-solo-album-in-10-years/

20. Jon Blistein, "Lindsey Buckingham Brings Ripping Guitar Solos to Late-Night With 'On the Wrong Side'," *Rolling Stone*, September 17, 2021, https://www.rollingstone.com/music/music-news/lindsey-buckingham-on-the-wrong-side-colbert-1228169/

21. Will Lavin, "Lindsey Buckingham shares Fleetwood Mac-inspired new song 'On the Wrong Side'," *NME*, July 23, 2021, https://www.nme.com/news/music/lindsey-buckingham-shares-fleetwood-mac-inspired-new-song-on-the-wrong-side-3001679

22. Claire Shaffer, "Lindsey Buckingham Announces First Solo Album in a Decade," *Rolling Stone*, June 8, 2021, https://www.rollingstone.com/music/music-news/lindsey-buckingham-solo-album-i-dont-mind-1180312/

23. Lindsey Buckingham, "Santa Rosa," Reprise, track #9 on *Lindsey Buckingham*, September 17, 2021, CD.

24. Pamela Chelin, "Meet The Songwriters Behind The Best Song on Lindsey Buckingham's New Album," *Spin*, November 23, 2021, https://www.spin.com/2021/11/jordon-zadorozny-brad-laner-lindsey-buckingham-swan-song/

25. Ibid.

26. David Chiu, "Lindsey Buckingham Looks for Life After Fleetwood Mac," *Newsweek*, September 15, 2021, https://www.newsweek.com/2021/09/24/lindsey-buckingham-looks-life-after-fleetwood-mac-1629086.html

27. Greil Marcus, "Real Life Rock Top 10: November 2021," *Los Angeles Review of Books*, November 26, 2021, https:// www.lareviewofbooks.org/article/real-life-rock-top-10-november-2021/

28. Chiu, "Looks for Life."

29. Marcus, "Rock Top 10."

30. Rhys Buchanan, "Lindsey Buckingham – 'Lindsey Buckingham' review: Fleetwood Mac visionary's stellar return," *NME*, September 15, 2021, https://www.nme .com/reviews/album/lindsey-buckingham-new-soll-album-review-3046525

I DON'T MIND / EPILOGUE

1. Martin Kielty, "Lindsey Buckingham Working on a New Album," *Ultimate Classic Rock*, December 31,

2022, https://ultimateclassicrock.com/lindsey-buckingham-new-album-2023/

2. Further indicative of vinyl's 21st-century surge in popularity and the longevity of Fleetwood Mac is that the band's smash hit *Rumours* was the fifth best-selling vinyl album of 2022. See https://www.billboard.com/pro/vinyl-album-sales-rise-growth-slowing/

3. Benjamin Lee, "Fleetwood Mac's Christine McVie dies at age 79," *The Guardian*, November 30, 2022, https://www.theguardian.com/music/2022/nov/30/fleetwood-macs-christine-mcvie-dies-at-age-79

4. Daniel Kreps, "Stevie Nicks Shares Heartfelt Note to 'Best Friend' Christine McVie: 'See You on the Other Side, My Love'," *Rolling Stone*, November 30, 2022, https://www.rollingstone.com/music/music-news/stevie-nicks-christine-mcvie-best-friend-fleetwood-mac-tribute-1234639085/

5. Haim, "Hallelujah," Polydor, track #15 on *Women in Music Pt. III*, June 26, 2020, CD.

6. Lee, "Christine McVie dies."

7. Tomás Mier, "Lindsey Buckingham Remembers 'Soul Mate' Christine McVie in Handwritten Letter," *Rolling Stone*, December 1, 2022, https://www.rollingstone.com/music/music-news/lindsey-buckingham-christine-mvcie-fleetwood-mac-1234640008/

8. Track #6 on Buckingham's 2021 self-titled solo album, "Time," is a cover of the Pozo-Seco Singers' original hit single. See https://www.rollingstone.com/music/music-news/lindsey-buckingham-solo-album-i-dont-mind-1180312/

9. Kielty, "New Album."

10. Lindsey Buckingham, "I Don't Mind," Reprise, track #2 on *Lindsey Buckingham*, September 17, 2021, CD.

11. In February 2023, Mick Fleetwood explained to reporters at the 65th Grammy Awards that Fleetwood Mac was "done" following the death of Christine McVie in late 2022: "I think right now, I truly think the line in the sand has been drawn with the loss of Chris,"

Fleetwood admitted. That same night, Fleetwood, Sheryl Crow, and Bonnie Raitt performed McVie's "Songbird" during the show's "In Memoriam" segment in honor of the late Fleetwood Mac veteran. See https://news.yahoo.com/done-mick-fleetwood-says-fleetwood-150807111.html

12. Amy Kaufman, "Fleetwood Mac fired Lindsey Buckingham. So why won't he let them go?" *Los Angeles Times,* September 8, 2021, https://www.latimes.com/entertainment-arts/music/story/2021-09-08/lindsey-buckingham-fleetwood-mac-stevie-nicks

13. Nicks and Joel announced their 2023 Two Icons, One Night tour in late 2022. The planned tour was initially set to make stops in Arlington, Texas, Nashville, Tennessee, and at the US Bank Stadium in Minneapolis, Minnesota in early November 2023, among others. See https://www.billboard.com/music/music-news/billy-joel-stevie-nicks-coheadline-2023-concerts-1235165641/

SELECTED BIBLIOGRAPHY

Arcand, Rob. "Hear Two New Songs From Lindsey Buckingham's Solo Anthology." *Spin*. October 5, 2018. https://www.spin.com/2018/10/lindsey-buckingham-solo-anthology-ride-this-road-hunger/#content

Beaumont, Mark. "Christine McVie, 1943-2022: an eternal songbird." *NME*. December 1, 2022. https://www.nme.com/features/music-features/christine-mcvie-1943-2022-an-eternal-songbird-3358828

Behind the Music. "Stevie Nicks." *VH1* video. 44:05, November 1, 1998, https://archive.org/details/vh1behindthemusicnovember11998stevienicks convertvideoonline.com

Best Classic Bands Staff. "It's On! Eagles, Fleetwood Mac to Headline Classic East and West." *Best Classic Bands*. April 7, 2017. https://bestclassicbands.com/classic-east-eagles-fleetwood-mac-3-29-17/

Bienstock, Richard. "Christine McVie on Fleetwood Mac's 'Peculiar' 'Mirage' Sessions, New LP." *Rolling Stone.* September 26, 2016. https://www.rollingstone.com/music/music-features/christine-mcvie-on-fleetwood-macs-peculiar-mirage-sessions-new-lp-122885/

Bienstock, Richard. "Mick Fleetwood on Fleetwood Mac's 'Overlooked' Smash 'Mirage'." *Rolling Stone.* September 20, 2016. https://www.rollingstone.com/music/music-features/mick-fleetwood-on-fleetwood-macs-overlooked-smash-mirage-101818/

Blistein, Jon. "Lindsey Buckingham Brings Ripping Guitar Solos to Late-Night With 'On the Wrong Side'." *Rolling Stone.* September 17, 2021. https://www.rollingstone.com/music/music-news/lindsey-buckingham-on-the-wrong-side-colbert-1228169/

Bonner, Michael. "Lindsey Buckingham – Gift of Screws." *Uncut.* September 8, 2008. https://www.uncut.co.uk/reviews/lindsey-buckingham-gift-of-screws-7321/

Bosso, Joe. "Mick Fleetwood: my 11 greatest recordings of all time." *Music Radar.* July 27, 2012. https://www.musicradar.com/news/drums/mick-fleetwood-my-11-greatest-recordings-of-all-time-554519

Brackett, Donald. *Fleetwood Mac: 40 Years of Creative Chaos.* Westport: Praeger, 2007.

Buchanan, Rhys. "Lindsey Buckingham – 'Lindsey Buckingham' review: Fleetwood Mac visionary's stellar return." *NME.* September 15, 2021. https://www.nme.com/reviews/album/lindsey-buckingham-new-soll-album-review-3046525

Buckingham, Lindsey. "I Don't Mind" [from *Lindsey Buckingham*]. 2021. Reprise, CD.

Buckingham, Lindsey. "Love Runs Deeper" [from *Out of the Cradle*]. 2008. Reprise, CD.

Buckingham, Lindsey. "Santa Rosa" [from *Lindsey Buckingham*}. 2021. Reprise, CD.

Buckingham, Lindsey. "Street of Dreams" [from *Out of the Cradle*]. 1992. Reprise, CD.

Buckingham, Lindsey. "The Right Place to Fade" [from *Gift of Screws*]. 2008. Reprise, CD.

Buckingham, Lindsey. "Wrong" [from *Out of the Cradle*]. 1992. Reprise, CD.

Caillat, Ken and Hernan Rojas. *Get Tusked: The Inside Story of Fleetwood Mac's Most Anticipated Album.* London: Backbeat Books, 2021.

Caillat, Ken and Steve Stiefel. *Making Rumours: The Inside Story of the Classic Fleetwood Mac Album.* New York: Wiley & Sons, 2012.

Carroll, Cath. *Never Break the Chain: Fleetwood Mac and the Making of Rumours.* Chicago: Chicago Review Press, 2004.

Catlin, Roger. "FLEETWOOD MAC, NICKS GET LANDSLIDE APPROVAL." *The Hartford Courant.* September 17, 1997. https://www.courant.com/news/connecticut/hc-xpm-1997-09-18-9709180222-story.html

Chelin, Pamela. "Meet The Songwriters Behind The Best Song on Lindsey Buckingham's New Album." *Spin.* November 23, 2021. https://www.spin.com/2021/11/jordon-zadorozny-brad-laner-lindsey-buckingham-swan-song/

Childers, Chad. "When Fleetwood Mac Reunited for the 'The Dance'." *Ultimate Classic Rock.* August 19, 2015. https://ultimateclassicrock.com/fleetwood-macs-reunion-album-the-dance-turns-15/

Chiu, David. "Lindsey Buckingham Looks for Life After Fleetwood Mac." *Newsweek.* September 15, 2021. https://www.newsweek.com/2021/09/24/lindsey-buckingham-looks-life-after-fleetwood-mac-1629086.html

Collins, Sean T. "*Lindsey Buckingham/Christine McVie.*" *Pitchfork.* June 12, 2017. https://pitchfork.com/reviews/albums/23221-lindsey-buckingham-christine-mcvie/

Connelly, Christopher. "Christine McVie Keeps A Level Head After Two Decades in the Fastlane." *Rolling Stone.* July 7, 1984. https://www.rollingstone.com/

music/music-news/christine-mcvie-keeps-a-level-head-after-two-decades-in-the-fastlane-189459/

Cooper, Gael Fashingbauer. "Christine McVie is rejoining Fleetwood Mac." *Today.* March 27, 2014. https://www.today.com/entertainment/christine-mcvie-rejoining-fleetwood-mac-2D79442915

Crowe, Cameron. "The True Life Confessions of Fleetwood Mac." *Rolling Stone.* March 24, 1977. https://www.rollingstone.com/feature/the-true-life-confessions-of-fleetwood-mac-120867/

Davis, Stephen. *Gold Dust Woman: The Biography of Stevie Nicks.* New York: St. Martin's Press, 2017.

DeRiso, Nick. "Fleetwood Mac hit big with *Tango in the Night,* then imploded: 'It was difficult for everybody'." *Something Else!* April 14, 2015. https://somethingelsereviews.com/2015/04/14/fleetwood-mac-tango-in-the-night/

DeRiso, Nick. "Stevie Nicks, 'Twisted' from *24 Karat Gold* (2014): One Track Mind." *Something Else!* September 28, 2014. https://somethingelsereviews.com/2014/09/28/stevie-nicks-twisted-24-karat-gold/

Doerschuk, Bob. "Christine McVie." *Contemporary Keyboard.* October 1980. Accessed via: https://web.archive.org/web/20150710065842/http://bla.fleetwoodmac.net/index.php?page=index_v2&id=11&c=2

Easlea, Daryl. "Fleetwood Mac Rumours Review." *BBC Music.* December 14, 2007, https://www.bbc.co.uk/music/reviews/r563/

Eby, Margaret. "Christine McVie reunite with Fleetwood Mac." *New York Daily News.* January 14, 2014. https://www.nydailynews.com/entertainment/tv-movies/christine-mcvie-reunites-fleetwood-mac-article-1.1579348

Egan, Sean. *Fleetwood Mac on Fleetwood Mac: Interviews and Encounters.* Chicago: Chicago Review Press, 2016.

Elliott, Paul. "Drug abuse, violence, and the making of Fleetwood Mac's Tango in the Night." *Louder Sound.* October 5, 2021. https://www.loudersound.com/

features/drug-abuse-violence-and-the-making-of-
fleetwood-macs-tango-in-the-night

Evans, Mike. *Fleetwood Mac: The Definitive History*. New
York: Sterling, 2011.

Filcman, Debra. "Read Lindsey Buckingham's Emotional
Email to Fleetwood Mac." *Ultimate Classic Rock*.
October 13, 2018. https://ultimateclassicrock.com
/lindsey-buckingham-email-fleetwood-mac/

Fleetwood Mac. "Everybody Finds Out [from *Say You
Will*]. 2003. Reprise, CD.

Fleetwood Mac. "Temporary One" [from *The Dance*].
1997. Reprise, CD.

Fleetwood, Mick and Anthony Bozza. *Play On: Now, Then
& Fleetwood Mac*. New York: Little, Brown and
Company, 2014.

Fleetwood, Mick and Stephen Davis. *Fleetwood: My Life
and Adventures in Fleetwood Mac*. New York: William
Morrow & Company, 1990.

Gallucci, Michael. "Lindsey Buckingham and Christine
McVie, 'Lindsey Buckingham/Christine McVie': Album
Review." *Ultimate Classic Rock*. June 6, 2017. https://
ultimateclassicrock.com/lindsey-buckingham-christine-
mcvie-album-review/

Gifford, Barry. "Peter Green's Fleetwood Mac." *Rolling
Stone*. August 10, 1968. https://www.rollingstone.com
/music/music-album-reviews/peter-greens-fleetwood-
mac-248342/

Gill, Andy. "Album: Phil Spector, The Philles Album
Collection (Sony Legacy)." *Independent*. December 28,
201. https://www.independent.co.uk/arts-
entertainment/music/reviews/album-phil-spector-the-
philles-album-collection-sony-legacy-6282163.html

Goldberg, Michael. "Lindsey Buckingham, Lonely Guy."
Rolling Stone. October 25, 1984. https://www
.rollingstone.com/music/music-news/lindsey-
-buckingham-lonely-guy-2-186895/

Greene, Andy. "Billy Burnette on His Brief, 'Magical' Stint in Fleetwood Mac: 'No Regrets'." *Rolling Stone*. December 6, 2022. https://www.rollingstone.com/music /music-features/billy-burnette-fleetwood-mac-lindsey-christine-stevie-1234639670/

Greene, Andy. "Christine McVie Clarifies 'Misperception' That Fleetwood Mac Is 'Done'." *Rolling Stone*. February 17, 2021. https://www.rollingstone.com/music /music-news/christine-mcvie-fleetwood-mac-comments-1129059/

Greene, Andy. "Flashback: Fleetwood Mac Reunite for Bill Clinton's Inauguration." *Rolling Stone*. January 22, 2013. https://www.rollingstone.com/music/music-news/ flashback-fleetwood-mac-reunite-for-bill-clintons-inauguration-84419/

Greene, Andy. "Flashback: Fleetwood Mac Reunite in 1997." *Rolling Stone*. January 14, 2014. https://www .rollingstone.com/music/music-news/flashback-fleetwood-mac-reunite-in-1997-83471/

Greene, Andy. "Lindsey Buckingham Talks Fleetwood Mac Tour, New EP." *Rolling Stone*. May 7, 2013. https:// www.rollingstone.com/music/music-news/lindsey-buckingham-talks-fleetwood-mac-tour-new-ep-92203/

Greene, Andy. "Mick Fleetwood Open to Reunion with Lindsey Buckingham, Imagines Fleetwood Mac Farewell Tour." *Rolling Stone*. March 1, 2021. https:// www.rollingstone.com/music/music-news/mick-fleetwood-reunion-with-lindsey-buckingham-imagines-fleetwood-mac-farewell-tour-1134758/

Greene, Andy. "Q&A: Christine McVie Can't Wait for Fleetwood Mac World Tour." *Rolling Stone*. March 27, 2014. https://www.rollingstone.com/music/music-news/qa-christine-mcvie-cant-wait-for-fleetwood-mac-world-tour-183753/

Greene, Andy. "Q&A: Stevie Nicks and Lindsey Buckingham Reveal Lingering Tensions in Fleetwood Mac." *Rolling Stone*. December 5, 2012. https:// www.rollingstone.com/music/music-news/qa-stevie-nicks-and-lindsey-buckingham-reveal-lingering-tensions-in-fleetwood-mac-233617/

Gross, Terry. "Remembering Buell Neidlinger, A Genre-Hopping Bassist, Composer and Teacher." *NPR*. March 27, 2018. https://www.npr.org/2018/03/27/597278380/remembering-buell-neidlinger-a-genre-hopping-bassist-composer-and-music-teacher

Gundersen, Edna. "Christine McVie rejoins Fleetwood Mac." *USA Today*. March 27, 2014. https://www.usatoday.com/ story/life/music/2014/03/27/christine-mcvie-rejoins-fleetwood-mac-for-tour-new-music/6841509/

Haim. "Hallelujah" [from *Women in Music Pt. III*]. 2020. Polydor, CD.

Hall, Russell. "Lindsey Buckingham Talks Guitars, Fleetwood Mac Reunion Tour." *Gibson Magazine*. February 4, 2009. https://www.fleetwoodmacnews.com/2009/02/lindsey-buckingham-talks-guitars.html

Harris, Carol Ann. *Storms: My Life with Lindsey Buckingham and Fleetwood Mac*. Chicago: Chicago Review Press, 2009.

Harris, Will. "A Chat with Lindsey Buckingham." *Bullz Eye*. November 6, 2008. http://www.bullz-eye.com/music/interviews/2008/lindsey_buckinghaminterviews.htm

Heffeman, David, dir. *Classic Albums – Fleetwood Mac: Rumours*. 1997. London, UK: Eagle Rock Entertainment, 2005. DVD.

Hiatt, Brian. "Stevie Nicks: A Rock Goddess Looks Back." *Rolling Stone*. January 15, 2015. https://www.rollingstone.com/music/music-news/stevie-nicks-a-rock-goddess-looks-back-179984/

History.com editors. "Fleetwood Mac reunites to play 'Don't Stop' at Bill Clinton's first inaugural ball." *History*. April 1, 2010. https://www.history.com/this-day-in-history/fleetwood-mac-reunite-to-play-dont-stop-at-bill-clintons-first-inaugural-gala

Hopkins, Scott. "The Class of 1970: Fleetwood Mac's 'Kiln House'." *MUSICFESTNEWS*. September 17, 2020. https://musicfestnews.com/2020/09/the-class-of-1970-fleetwood-macs-kiln-house/

Hopper, Jessica. *The First Collection of Criticism by a Living Female Rock Critic: Revised and Expanded Edition*. New York: MCD Books, 2021.

Horowitz, Hal. "Lindsey Buckingham: *Solo Anthology – The Best of Lindsey Buckingham*." *American Songwriter*. Accessed December 20, 2022. https://americansongwriter.com/lindsey-buckingham-solo-anthology-best-lindsey-buckingham/

Howe, Zoë. *Stevie Nicks: Visions, Dreams & Rumours*. London, Omnibus Press, 2015.

In Her Own Words. "The Early Years II 1966-1975." Accessed November 29, 2022. http://www.inherownwords.com/earlyyrs2.htm

In Her Own Words. "Illume." Accessed December 17, 2022. http://www.inherownwords.com/illume.htm

Ivie, Devon. "Lindsey Buckingham on the Most Fulfilling and Dysfunctional Music of His Career." *Vulture*. November 24, 2021. https://www.vulture.com/article/interview-lindsey-buckingham-on-fleetwood-mac-stevie-nicks.html

Jackson, Blair. "Stevie – Fleetwood Mac's siren soars with her first solo album, *Bella Donna*." *BAM Magazine*. September 11, 1981. Accessed via: http://rockalittle.com/bam9-11-81.htm

Jones, Dylan. "Was Fleetwood Mac's Tusk the greatest self-sabotage in rock and roll history?" *GQ*. August 9, 2020. https://www.gq-magazine.co.uk/culture/article/fleetwood-mac-tusk

Jonze, Tim. "Fleetwood Mac: new album and tour will be our swansong." *The Guardian*. January 2, 2015. https://www.theguardian.com/music/2015/jan/02/lindsey-buckingham-says-fleetwood-mac-to-enter-last-act

Kaufman, Amy. "Fleetwood Mac fired Lindsey Buckingham. So why won't he let them go?" *Los*

Angeles Times. September 8, 2021. https://www .latimes.com/ entertainment-arts/music/story/2021-09-08/lindsey-buckingham-fleetwood-mac-stevie-nicks

Kielty, Martin. "Lindsey Buckingham Working on a New Album." *Ultimate Classic Rock.* December 31, 2022. https://ultimateclassicrock.com/lindsey-buckingham-new-album-2023/

Kelly, Ray. "Lindsey Buckingham on Fleetwood Mac, solo work and Sheryl Crow," *Mass Live*, October 12, 2008, https://www.masslive.com/entertainment/2008/10/lindsey_buckingham_on_fleetwoo.html

Kemp, Sam. "The secret Beatles link in Fleetwood Mac's classic song, 'Beautiful Child'." *Far Out Magazine.* August 28, 2021. https://faroutmagazine.co.uk/the-beatles-link-fleetwood-mac-classic-song/

Kohn, Daniel. "Mick Fleetwood and Lindsey Buckingham Reconcile, Open to Another Fleetwood Mac Reunion Tour." *Spin.* March 1, 2021. https://www.spin.com/2021/03/mick-fleetwood-lindsey-buckingham-reunion/

Kreps, Daniel. "Stevie Nicks Shares Heartfelt Note to 'Best Friend' Christine McVie: 'See You on the Other Side, My Love'." *Rolling Stone.* November 30, 2022. https://www.rollingstone.com/music/music-news/stevie-nicks-christine-mcvie-best-friend-fleetwood-mac-tribute-1234639085/

Lapatine, Scott. "Lindsey Buckingham Reveals Stories Behind His Solo Songs and Whether He'll Ever Rejoin Fleetwood Mac." *Stereogum.* December 10, 2018. https://www.stereogum.com/2025688/lindsey-buckingham-interview-fleetwood-mac/interviews/

Lavin, Will. "Lindsey Buckingham says he never got 'closure' with Stevie Nicks." *NME.* May 8, 2021. https://www.nme .com/news/music/lindsey-buckingham-says-he-never-got-closure-with-stevie-nicks-2936237

Lavin, Will. "Lindsey Buckingham shares Fleetwood Mac-inspired new song 'On the Wrong Side'." *NME.* July 23, 2021. https://www.nme.com/news/music/lindsey-

buckingham-shares-fleetwood-mac-inspired-new-song-
on-the-wrong-side-3001679
Leahey, Andrew. "Song Premiere: Lindsey Buckingham,
'Trouble (Live)'." *American Songwriter.* Accessed
December 19, 2022. https://americansongwriter.com
/song-premiere-lindsey-buckingham-trouble-live/
Lee, Benjamin. "Fleetwood Mac's Christine McVie dies at
age 79." *The Guardian.* November 30, 2022. https://
www.theguardian.com/music/2022/nov/30/fleetwood-
macs-christine-mcvie-dies-at-age-79
Leibovich, Mark. "Edward R. Murrow, Welcome To the
Full-Spin Zone." *The Washington Post.* March 27,
2005. https://www.washingtonpost.com/wp-
dyn/articles/A3980-2005Mar26.html
Lenker, Maureen Lee. "Lindsey Buckingham breaks down
10 of his best guitar riffs." *Entertainment Weekly.*
September 14, 2021. https://ew.com/music/lindsey-
buckingham-fleetwood-mac-stories-behind-the-songs/
"Lifelines." *Billboard,* August 15, 1998. https://books
.google.com/books?id=EwoEAAAAMBAJ&pg=PA47#v
=onepage&q&f=false
Lindsey Buckingham/Christine McVie. "On with the Show"
[from *Lindsey Buckingham/Christine McVie*]. 2017.
Atlantic, CD.
Marcus, Greil. "Real Life Rock Top 10: November 2021,"
Los Angeles Review of Books. November 26, 2021.
https:// www.lareviewofbooks.org/article/real-life-rock-
top-10-november-2021/
Marcus, Greil. "Ringo Starr, 'Sentimental Journey'
(5/14/70)." *Greil Marcus.* September 12, 2014. https://
greilmarcus.net/2014/09/12/ringo-starr-sentimental-
journey-51470/
Marks, Craig and Rob Tannenbaum. *I Want My MTV: The
Uncensored Story of the Music Video Revolution.* New
York: Dutton, 2011.
McLane, Daisann. "Fleetwood Mac: They Dared to be
Different." *Rolling Stone.* February 7, 1980. https://

www.rollingstone.com/music/music-news/fleetwood-mac-they-dared-to-be-different-243618/

McNair, James. "Return of the Mac." *Independent Review.* April 18, 2003. Accessed via: https://stevienicks.info/2003/04/return-of-the-mac/

Mendoza, Jean and Leslie Veliz. "Christine McVie's Short Marriage to John McVie Explained." *Grunge.* December 1, 2022. https://www.grunge.com/1122468/christine-mcvies-short-marriage-to-john-mcvie-explained/

Mier, Tomás. "Lindsey Buckingham Remembers 'Soul Mate' Christine McVie in Handwritten Letter." *Rolling Stone.* December 1, 2022. https://www.rollingstone.com/music/music-news/lindsey-buckingham-christine-mvcie-fleetwood-mac-1234640008/

Morrison, Simon. *Mirror in the Sky: The Life and Music of Stevie Nicks.* Berkeley: University of California Press, 2022.

Murray, Noel. "Stevie Nicks and Lindsey Buckingham made a fine pop record pre-Fleetwood Mac." *AV Club.* September 29, 2015. https://www.avclub.com/stevie-nicks-and-lindsey-buckingham-made-a-fine-pop-rec-1798284894.

Nelson, Brad. "Tango in the Night." *Pitchfork.* March 11, 2017. https://pitchfork.com/reviews/albums/22976-tango-in-the-night-deluxe-edition/

Newman, Melinda. "Fleetwood Mac Honored by Lorde, Miley Cyrus, Harry Styles & More at 2018 MusiCares Person of the Year Gala." *Billboard.* January 27, 2018. https://www.billboard.com/music/music-news/stevie-nicks-fleetwood-mac-grammy-awards-musicares-person-of-the-year-tom-petty-8096584/

O'Donnell, Kevin. "Fleetwood Mac's Christine McVie and Lindsey Buckingham debut galloping new song." *Yahoo! Finance.* May 11, 2017. https://finance.yahoo.com/news/fleetwood-mac-apos-christine-mcvie-130038911.html

O'Hare, Kevin. "The Republican interview: Stevie Nicks." *Mass Live.* April 5, 2009. https://www.masslive.com /entertainment/2009/04/the_republican_interview_stevi. html

Olympics. "Gregory F. Buckingham." Accessed November 27, 2022. https://olympics.com/en/athletes/gregory-f-buckingham

Price, Simon. "Stevie Nicks: 'Love is fleeting for me… in my life as a traveling woman'." *The Independent.* June 26, 2011. https://www.independent.co.uk/arts-entertainment/music/features/stevie-nicks-love-is-fleeting-for-me-in-my-life-as-a-travelling-woman-2302744.html

Quinn, Karl. "So, Fleetwood Mac didn't 'fire' Lindsey Buckingham. They divorced him." *The Sydney Morning Herald.* April 26, 2018. https://www.smh .com.au/entertainment/music/so-fleetwood-mac-didn-t-fire-lindsey-buckingham-they-divorced-him-20180426-p4zbq6.html

Reed, Ryan. "Fleetwood Mac's 'Tusk': 10 Things You Didn't Know." *Rolling Stone.* October 11, 2019. https://www.rollingstone.com/feature/fleetwood-mac-tusk-things-you-didnt-know-896796/

Rendon, Christine. "Go Their Own Way! Fleetwood Mac's Lindsey Buckingham splits with wife of 21 YEARS Kristen Messner… after she files to dissolve their marriage." *Daily Mail.* June 8, 2021. https://www. .dailymail.co.uk/tvshowbiz/article-9665721/Fleetwood-Macs-Lindsey-Buckingham-splits-wife-21-YEARS-Kristen-Messner.html

Rodrick, Stephen. "Lindsey Buckingham Won't Stop." *Rolling Stone.* September 9, 2021. https://www .rollingstone.com/music/music-features/lindsey-buckingham-fleetwood-mac-stevie-nicks-new-album-1221755/

Rooksby, Rikky. *Fleetwood Mac: The Complete Guide to Their Music.* London: Omnibus Press, 2005.

Ruhlmann, William. "Go Insane Review." *AllMusic*. Accessed December 11, 2022. https://www.allmusic .com/album/go-insane-mw0000649934

Runtagh, Jordan. "Fleetwood Mac's 'Rumours': 10 Things You Didn't Know." *Rolling Stone*. February 3, 2017. https://www.rollingstone.com/feature/fleetwood-macs-rumours-10-things-you-didnt-know-121876/

Schruers, Fred. "Back on the Chain Gang." *Rolling Stone*. October 30, 1997. https://www.rollingstone.com/music/music-news/fleetwood-mac-back-on-the-chain-gang-243176/

Scoppa, Bud. "Fleetwood Mac." *Rolling Stone*. September 25, 1975. https://www.rollingstone.com/music/music-album-reviews/fleetwood-mac-98110/

Selvin, Joel. "Buckingham gets back into 'that thing' of Fleetwood Mac." *SFGATE*. April 15, 2003. https://www.sfgate.com/entertainment/article/Buckingham-gets-back-into-that-thing-of-2622236.php

Shaffer, Claire. "Lindsey Buckingham Announces First Solo Album in a Decade." *Rolling Stone*. June 8, 2021. https://www.rollingstone.com/music/music-news/lindsey-buckingham-solo-album-i-dont-mind-1180312/

Spanos, Brittany. "Hear Buckingham McVie's Bubbly New Song 'Feel About You'." *Rolling Stone*. April 27, 2017. https://www.rollingstone.com/music/music-news/hear-buckingham-mcvies-bubbly-new-song-feel-about-you-192677/

Spanos, Brittany. "'Silver Springs': Inside Fleetwood Mac's Great Lost Breakup Anthem." *Rolling Stone*. August 17, 2017. https://www.rollingstone.com/feature/silver-springs-inside-fleetwood-macs-great-lost-breakup-anthem-201303/

Stanley, Bob. "How to lose 3 million fans in one easy step." *The Guardian*. March 6, 2008. https://www .theguardian.com/music/2008/mar/07/popandrock1

Strauss, Matthew. "Lindsey Buckingham Announces U.S. Tour and First Solo Album in 10 Years." *Pitchfork*. June 8, 2021. https://pitchfork.com/news/lindsey-buckingham-announces-us-tour-and-first-solo-album-in-10-years/

Swanson, Dave. "Fleetwood Mac Might Have a Double Album on their Hands." *Ultimate Classic Rock.* May 8, 2014. https://ultimateclassicrock.com/fleetwood-mac-double-album/

Swenson, John. "Rumours." *Rolling Stone.* April 21, 1977. https://www.rollingstone.com/music/music-album-reviews/rumours-189491/

Tannenbaum, Rob. "Stevie Nicks Admits Past Pregnancy with Don Henley and More About Her Wild History." *Billboard.* September 26, 2014. https://www.billboard.com/music/music-news/stevie-nicks-interview-on-don-henley-fleetwood-mac-24-karat-gold-album-6266329/

Taysom, Joe. "The Fleetwood Mac number one Stevie Nicks wrote 'in ten minutes'." *Far Out Magazine.* July 31, 2022. https://faroutmagazine.co.uk/fleetwood-mac-number-one-stevie-nicks-wrote-in-10-minutes/

Turney, Grace. "Stevie Nicks Said She Would Have Left Fleetwood Mac to Join This Band." *Cheat Sheet.* October 7, 2022. https://www.cheatsheet.com/entertainment/stevie-nicks-said-left-fleetwood-mac-join-band.html/

Unterberger, Andrew. "Fleetwood Mac Reigns Supreme at Day Two of Classic East Festival." *Billboard.* July 31, 2017. https://www.billboard.com/music/concerts/fleetwood-mac-day-two-classic-east-festival-recap-7882114/

Weingarten, Christopher R., David Browne, Jon Dolan, Corinne Cummings, Keith Harris, Rob Sheffield, and Angie Martoccio. "Fleetwood Mac's 50 Greatest Songs." *Rolling Stone.* May 2, 2022. https://www.rollingstone.com/music/music-lists/fleetwood-macs-50-greatest-songs-192324/

Williamson, Nigel. "Fleetwood Mac: 'Everyone was pretty weirded out' – the story of Rumours." *Uncut.* January 29, 2013. https://www.uncut.co.uk/features/fleetwood-mac-everybody-was-pretty-weirded-out-the-story-of-rumours-26395/

Young, Alex. "Lindsey Buckingham settles lawsuit against Fleetwood Mac." *Yahoo! Finance.* December 8, 2018. https://finance.yahoo.com/news/lindsey-buckingham-settles-lawsuit-against-010612049.html

Zaleski, Annie. "'He could be brash; he could be harsh. He was very motivated': The real story behind Fleetwood Mac's 'Tango in the Night'," *Salon*, April 2, 2017, https://www.salon.com/2017/04/02/he-could-be-brash-he-could-be-harsh-he-was-very-motivated-the-real-story-behind-fleetwood-macs-tango-in-the-night/

Zoladz, Lindsay. "Lindsey Buckingham Has Survived It All." *The New York Times.* September 8, 2021. https://www.nytimes.com/2021/09/08/arts/music/lindsey-buckingham.html

INDEX
A-Z

Tyler Martin Sehnal is an author living in Las Cruces, New Mexico with his wife, Anna, and their pets Kibby, Heidi, and Bongo. He holds a B.A. and an M.A. in English and multicultural literature and is a Ph.D. candidate at New Mexico State University. In addition to *Playing in the Rain: Lindsey Buckingham & Fleetwood Mac*, Sehnal has also published work in the *Iowa Journal of Cultural Studies* and *New Literaria*. His hobbies include spending time with his wife, reading, writing, and proving anyone who ever thought that Stevie Nicks was "the only good songwriter in Fleetwood Mac" wrong.

www.ingramcontent.com/pod-product-compliance
Lightning Source LLC
Chambersburg PA
CBHW071552030726
47593CB00001BA/124